UNDERSTANDING RELIGIOUS EXPERIENCES

UNDERSTANDING RELIGIOUS EXPERIENCES

What the Bible Says about Spirituality

J. Harold Ellens

Psychology, Religion, and Spirituality

Westport, Connecticut
London

Library of Congress Cataloging-in-Publication Data

Ellens, J. Harold, 1932–
  Understanding religious experiences : what the Bible says about spirituality / J. Harold Ellens.
      p. cm. — (Psychology, religion, and spirituality, ISSN 1546–8070)
  Includes bibliographical references and index.
  ISBN 978–0–275–99547–8 (alk. paper)
  1. Spirituality—Biblical teaching. 2. Experience (Religion). I. Title.
  BS680.S7E55 2008
   248.2—dc22   2007029643

British Library Cataloguing in Publication Data is available.

Library of Congress Catalog Card Number: 2007029643
ISBN-13: 978–0–275–99547–8
ISSN: 1546–8070

First published in 2008

Praeger Publishers, 88 Post Road West, Westport, CT 06881
An imprint of Greenwood Publishing Group, Inc.
www.praeger.com

Printed in the United States of America

The paper used in this book complies with the Permanent Paper Standard issued by the National Information Standards Organization (Z39.48–1984).

10 9 8 7 6 5 4 3 2 1

For Brett Alexander Ellens Hutchison
My dear son
As he is turning 10

That he may learn and love
in youth
What I know best and love most
At 75

CONTENTS

SERIES FOREWORD

The interface between psychology, religion, and spirituality has been of great interest to scholars for a century. In the last three decades a broad popular appetite has developed for books that make practical sense out of the research on these three subjects. Freud expressed an essentially negative outlook on this matter and said that he saw the relationship between human psychology and religion to be destructive. Carl Jung, on the other hand, was quite sure that these three aspects of the human spirit, psychology, religion, and spirituality, were constructively linked, could not and should not be separated.

Anton Boisen and Seward Hiltner derived much insight from both Freud and Jung, as well as from Adler and Reik, while pressing the matter forward brilliantly and skillfully. Boisen and Hiltner provided sound and sensible definitions of how the relationship between psychology, religion, and spirituality might best be described. We are indebted to them for that.

This series of general interest books, so wisely urged by Greenwood Press, and particularly by its editors, Suzanne I. Staszak-Silva and Deborah Carvalko, intends to define the terms and explore the interaction of psychology, religion, and spirituality at the operational level of daily human experience. Each volume of the series identifies, analyzes, describes, and evaluates the full range of popular and professional issues. These deal with the psychological factors at play (1) in the way religion takes shape and is expressed, (2) in the way spirituality functions within human persons and shapes both religious formation and expression, and (3) in the ways that spirituality is shaped and expressed by religion. The interest is psycho-spiritual. In terms of the sciences of psychology and theology this series of volumes investigates the *operational dynamics* of religion and spirituality.

The verbs "shape" and "express" in the above paragraph refer to the forces which form and inform religion in persons and communities. They are terms that also refer to the way religious behavior shows up (1) in personal forms of spirituality, (2) in acts of spiritually motivated care for society, and (3) in ritual behaviors such as worship services. In this series of books the psychological and spiritual drivers in persons and communities are described in terms of the way they unconsciously and consciously operate in religious thought and behavior.

These books are written for the general reader, the local library borrower, and the undergraduate university student. They are also of significant interest to the informed professional, particularly in fields corollary to his or her primary interest. These volumes have great value for clinical settings and treatment models, as well.

This series editor has spent an entire professional lifetime focused specifically upon research into the interface of psychology in religion and spirituality. These matters are of the highest urgency in human affairs today when religious motivation seems to be playing an increasing role, constructively and destructively, in the social ethics, national politics, and world affairs. It is imperative that we find out soon what the psychological illnesses are that cause religious persons to launch deadly assaults upon the World Trade Center in New York and murder 3,000 people. What is wrong with a religion that motivates suicide bombers to kill themselves and murder dozens of their neighbors weekly. What is going on in a religion that prompts such unjust national policies as pre-emptive defense. All of these are wreaking havoc upon the social fabric, the democratic processes, the domestic tranquility, the economic stability, and the legitimate right to freedom from fear, in every nation in the world today.

This present volume, *Understanding Religious Experience: What the Bible Says about Spirituality*, is an urgently needed and timely work, the motivation for which is surely endorsed enthusiastically by the entire Christian world today. The international community is searching for strategies that will afford us better and deeper religious self-understanding as individuals and communities. This project addresses the deep psychosocial, psychospiritual, and biological sources of human nature which shape and drive our psychology and spirituality. Careful strategies of empirical, heuristic, and phenomenological research have been employed to give this work a solid scientific foundation and formation. Human spirituality is seldom studied or described at the depth this book offers.

For fifty years such organizations as the Christian Association for Psychological Studies and such Graduate Departments of Psychology as those at Boston University, Fuller Graduate School of Psychology, Rosemead

Graduate School of Psychology, Harvard, George Fox, Princeton, and the like, have been publishing important building blocks of research on issues dealing with religious behavior and psycho-spirituality. In this project the insights generated by such patient and careful research is synthesized and integrated into a holistic psycho-spiritual world view that takes seriously this special aspect of religious tradition called psycho-spirituality. This volume employs an objective and experience based approach to discerning the value of our spiritual quest and whether it has any important relationship to traditional institutional or new and innovative religious practices.

Some of the influences of religion upon persons and society, now and throughout history, have been negative. However, most of the impact of the great religions upon human life and culture has been profoundly healing and of great good. It is urgent, therefore, that we discover and understand better what the psychological and spiritual forces are which empower people of faith and genuine spirituality to give themselves to all the creative and constructive enterprises that, throughout the centuries, have made of human life the humane, ordered, prosperous, and aesthetic experience it can be at its best. Surely the forces for good in both psychology and spirituality far exceed the powers and proclivities toward the evil that we see so prominently perpetrated in the name of religion in our world today.

This series of Greenwood Press volumes is dedicated to the greater understanding of *Psychology, Religion, and Spirituality*, and thus to the profound understanding and empowerment of those psycho-spiritual drivers which can help us (1) transcend the malignancy of our earthly pilgrimage, (2) enhance the humaneness and majesty of the human spirit, and (3) empower the potential for magnificence in human life.

J. Harold Ellens

PREFACE

Today most people in our world are feeling less interested in religion and more interested in spirituality. If you ask what they mean, they will tell you that organized religion tends to turn them off; but, nonetheless, they feel a hunger in the heart that they cannot seem to fill. Friendship does not quite fill it. Sex does not quite fill it. Entertainment does not do it. Their experiences of religion, from childhood up, do not fill it. So they signal their sense of incompleteness or even emptiness by asserting that they do not like organized religion. They do not mean by their assertion that they would rather have disorganized religion; they mean that *institutional* religion, as they have experienced it, does not seem to satisfy their spirits. They keep feeling that there is something more, some better way of experiencing whatever it is for which they are hungry.

If you press them further, or reflect upon it yourself, you come fairly quickly to the sense that there must be more meaning to life than our trivial popular cultural and traditional religious practices are providing. Hollywood movies, Disney's violent videos, seaside holidays, trips to Las Vegas, hunting and fishing, sports on TV, church on Sunday, and playing with the adult toys that fill up so many people's time just do not seem to answer the haunting hollow echoes of the soul.

Much new experimentation is going on as a result. Some of it is a *psychological* search for the meaning that will fill the soul and satisfy the spirit. Much of it is a direct search for meaning on the *spiritual* level itself. Unfortunately most of us do not know the language of spirituality well enough to discern or discuss what we are seeking or missing. Few of us understand our own inner psychological and spiritual selves clearly enough to describe even to ourselves what it is that we mean with our spiritual and psychological quests, our feelings of neediness, and our psychospiritual desires. If we cannot clarify very well what it is for which we hunger and search, we will most likely continue to find it difficult to recognize it, if we ever run into it. This is the book for people who are genuinely intent upon exploring, perhaps even resolving, that quandary.

In this volume we will carefully and sensitively explore the full range of our spiritual natures and all the possible spiritual experiences of which we are capable, describing meaningfully the way our souls and psyches work in our hunger and thirst for meaning. I have tried to provide an enlightening and unconventional way of appreciating the human spiritual quandary and the quest upon which it sets all of us. I have attempted to describe carefully why and how every person desires to savor the flavor of a heartfelt experience of God and of genuine relationship with cherished human persons. This book is about reflecting upon, learning about, and sharing that unusual human opportunity. Spirituality always reaches toward the question about the meaning of God, the meaning of relationship with others, the meaning of intimacy, and the meaning of soul-gratifying insights into truth.

So you will find in this book a description of the meaning of the biblical stories about spiritual experiences; but you will find equally prominent an ample description of the kinds of spiritual experiences that ordinary people of our day are having. You might say that this book is written with the Bible in one hand and today's newspaper in the other. I have described how people like you and me are achieving those spiritual experiences of which humans are capable and the ways in which such folk are filling their lives with meaning. That kind of meaning goes beyond the ordinary horizons of material life on this earth. This volume paints the picture in such a way as to let us in on what authentic spirituality and spiritual experience really is, and why it may or may not necessarily have anything to do with traditional institutionalized religion.

This volume not only discusses spiritual experiences but also sheds an entirely new light on religious conversions, visions, and parapsychological ways of knowing truth. It discusses the importance and meaning of near death experiences, religion, and magical thinking and what prayer really amounts to and what it is worth. Here you will find the definition of piety and whether being pious has anything to do with spirituality or religion. This quest raises the fundamental issue of whether spirituality is mainly a relationship connection with God, with other people, or with both. The book closes with a discussion of whether spirituality has to do with living life before the face of God, somehow in the presence of God, or in constructive connection with the created world of persons, animals, and things. Whichever is primary in spirituality, can religion really be of much help in that?

This is a book in which you can find all you ever wanted to know about your own inner spirituality or traditional religious experience and never quite knew how to ask it.

ACKNOWLEDGMENT

I am particularly grateful to Buena Carlson for reading the entire manuscript with meticulous precision, and to Frank Shiflett who also read it with enthusiasm, proofed the entire document for typos and infelicities, and kept my computer system in top notch condition, making my task as smooth and efficient as possible from the beginning of the idea to the composition of the final word of this book.

CHAPTER 1

INTRODUCTION

Spirituality and religion are related, but they are not the same thing. Moreover, a person may practice a religion and be religious without that being connected to his or her spirituality. Conversely, one may be intensely spiritual without being religious or engaging in religious practices. Humans may hunger for healthier spirituality but for some reason resist any interest in religion or in religions of any kind. This chapter intends to introduce some of the problems and perplexities involved in understanding authentic religious experience: its psychological, spiritual, and biblical dimensions.

Spirituality is that quality of the inner human spirit or psyche that makes us feel a strong interest in understanding the meaning of things in life. So spirituality is a term we use to identify that quest of the human spirit for meaning. It is equally spiritual if the meaning for which we hunger is a longing for a lover or a longing for God, a longing for understanding intellectual interests like philosophy or for understanding how a carburetor worked in a 1937 Ford. All our hunger for comprehending the meaning of things reflects our spiritual natures.

It always seems more centrally spiritual if it is a hunger for relationship: a better understanding of our lover, our friend, our child, or God. It seems especially spiritual if it is a hunger to learn about the nature of God, the transcendent world, or eternity. However, while these are more ethereal kinds of spirituality, they are not kinds of quests for meaning different than trying to understand the complexities of a computer, the mechanics of a tractor, or the way fertilizer produces better corn.

Our spiritual quest is a desire to discern more deeply how all of that is related to us and to the meaning of our unfolding selves. So spirituality is first of all a very personal quest. As we discover others on the same quest and share our questions and insights with them, spirituality also becomes a communal experience. Sometimes this results in mutual enlightenment about the questions and the answers of our human spirituality.

Religion, on the other hand, is made up of the forms and ideas in which we express our ethereal spiritual needs and discernments. Religion is the word we use to describe the practices in which we engage, such as worshipping, individually or together as a community of believers. It also refers to the creeds we recite and the theology we claim to be our understanding of the truth about God and the world. So religion includes the liturgies we sing or say in worship. While spirituality is the inner quest for meaning, religion is the outward behaviors that seem appropriate to express the meanings we create or discover inside ourselves in this quest, and that we want to act out with each other or toward God.

That is why it is often true that the religious behaviors and practices with which we grew up do not satisfy the spiritual hunger in our spirits as we mature. Those behaviors were fashioned by our parents or ancestors because those practices expressed well their sense of the meaning of their own spirituality, in their time and setting. If we have grown up without the same character and quality of spiritual quest as they had, or without the same travail and challenges that shaped their experience, their religious expressions may not speak for our hearts' hungers. Why should we be so surprised about that? The main reason that the religious expression of the American generations of 1900–1940 continued to work meaningfully as the religion of the generations of 1930–1960 is because that mid-century generation had learned very well the theological answers of the prior generation to the spiritual questions both generations felt, and had internalized them as their own.

However, the generations of 1960–1990 did not learn the Bible well, did not study the basic theological questions and formulations, and did not immerse themselves in the spiritual expressions of their forebears. Moreover, this later generation did not live before the eradication of polio and small pox, before penicillin and modern medications, before global internationalism, or during the time of limited resources for education, health, and security. The main travail and challenges to life, liberty, and the pursuit of happiness that shaped the pilgrimage of their parents have not shaped their questions about the meaning of life. Until 1960, life and death, time and eternity, were very close to each other all the time. The line between them was very thin.

Today good medicine, clever surgery, societal stability, personal security for most people, and high levels of comfort and convenience are common, compared to previous eras. The generations since 1960 have not had to deal with the common and pervasive death of their own children, the universal threat of rampant, ordinary diseases, and many immediately threatening disorders for which there is no cure. Consequently, they are largely ignorant of the meaning of the religious formulations of 1900–1960, when life was always on the very edge of death every day in every household. How can the post-1960 generations be aware of the way the religious expressions of the past related to the deep spiritual meaning quest of their parents and grandparents, who lived daily under the pressure of eternity—before the very face of God, as it were?

Moreover, the *culture* of the generations from 1900–1940 was very similar to the culture that subsequently developed for the generations of 1930–1960. However, the culture of the generations shaped during 1960–1990 was very different from that of 1900–1960. The culture of the last half of the twentieth century was more mobile, more anonymous, less family oriented, educated according to different educational theories, more entertainment oriented, more affluent, and, according to Christopher Lasch,[1] increasingly narcissistic.

Recently we have become aware that the watershed of cultural change that took place in the 1960s and 1970s has resulted in a cultural division between the computer literate and illiterate. This has directly to do with the way in which a person acquires and processes information, develops knowledge, discerns the shape of essential questions, and expects the nature of the answers. I notice that my students can acquire an amazing *quantity and quality* of information online but hardly know how to find the encyclopedia or the humanities section, to say nothing about discovering a book on theology or religion, in a good municipal library.

This implies that the means and methods employed today for acquiring information, asking the essential questions, formulating the shape of the meaning quest, and hence keying one's self to the satisfying answers are remarkably different than they used to be. So how could the religious formulations and patterns of their parents and grandparents possibly make any sense to more recent generations or satisfy their meaning quest. If the rising generations do not know what the historic spiritual questions were and how the religious answers of the past satisfied the soul, how can they figure out the relevance of past religious ways of doing things like public worship, private devotional life, formulating meaningful theological claims, and identifying real metaphysical issues? If we lose our grip on the past we are compelled to reinvent the wheel, so to speak. If the last 1,000 years or more of human wrestling with these issues is lost to us today, we have no option but to start over in spiritual primitivity. It is understandable that there are many who end up declaring that traditional institutional religion (organized religion as they call it) is of no interest to them because it is of no central meaning for them. If they do not know in their hearts what our questions are how can they find our answers meaningful?

Now, of course, this disconnection between our own personal journey in the quest for meaning and the journey of our parents or ancestors happens to some extent in every generation. There is no avoiding it. The issues that impose upon our lives in each new generation are different from those of the past. While the basic spiritual questions are always exactly the same, the way in which they arise and present themselves to us differs from generation to generation. The spiritual meanings, challenges, and anxieties of parents before the polio vaccine was invented were different than since the elimination of polio.

I know because I was parenting six young children at the very moment that the vaccine became available. Since I had lost five close high school buddies and a number of relatives to polio in the 1940s, the arrival of the vaccine in time to save my children from the dread disease changed my prayer life, as you can imagine. Such practical cultural things of all sorts impact a generation's spiritual quest and questions. Those changes, then, reshape the religious answers and behaviors that make meaningful spiritual sense. If each young person does not realize that he or she must undertake this spiritual journey of his or her own spirituality all over again, and that he or she cannot just ride on the traditions of the past, in belief or practice, that person is not taking his or her spirituality seriously.

In the end, adopting the creeds or liturgies of the past without making them our own at the deep inner level prevents us from having either genuine spirituality or authentic religion. In the end it is only my own real meanings that can authentically satisfy the hunger in my own soul. How can I possibly be God's authentic person if I am not my own real and true self? It will be interesting to see how things turn out spiritually for the generations who are now saying that traditional institutional religion does nothing for them.

I suspect that in the long run, as they age, (1) each generation of humans will either lose its way spiritually and land in a kind of no man's land of emptiness, despair, and withered spirituality, as seems to have happened in postwar Germany; (2) those people will invent meaningful new ways of expressing their true spiritual quest and incorporate into it much that has been sorted out for them by previous generations; or (3) they will revert to the traditional religious formulations of the past as they age and as they contemplate the eternal world more graphically and urgently.

The *first* case happens if the new generations do not pursue their spiritual quest with enough vigor and so remain largely uninformed about their own inner selves and do not learn anything from the journey others have pursued along this way. There are plenty of things around to entertain them while they pursue their empty lives. The *third* case results from a generation that wearies of trying to reinvent the wheel and so immerses itself in the historic formulations and practices and finds therein something of the meaning that their forebears found there. This is a convenient shortcut in the individual's spiritual journey. However, it runs the risk of being inauthentic if the younger folk merely embrace the form of their tradition without grasping its depth of meaning and the reasons for it being what it is.

The *second* case will develop in those bright and honest folks who have lots of energy, motivation, and vigor for their spiritual quest, inform themselves well on human psychology and spirituality, review honestly and learn the positives and negatives from those traditions of spirituality and religion they are setting aside or moving beyond, and are creative enough to formulate genuine new ways to fashion religious expressions that both feed and fruit their consequent inner spiritual fullness.

There are, of course, major perplexities in our spiritual quest and religious practices that arise from problems we have in discerning exactly what our psychological and spiritual aspects or functions really are. What do we mean by such terms and concepts as psychology and spirituality? Are they different or the same? Both seem to speak of and to the inner self of every person. What does the Bible have to say about all this stuff of the inner world of humans that might conceivably be of some help? These are good and legitimate, indeed urgently necessary, questions. They must be asked! They cannot be avoided! They are complex and perplexing.

So much of the tradition and values of Western culture is derived from the ancient Greeks and from the Bible. Moreover, the Bible itself came up for interpretation largely in terms of Greco-Roman culture in the period 100–500 C.E. As a result, Greek terms shaped biblical meanings and interpretation. Two Greek words lie at the center of the biblical teaching regarding spirituality and religion. Those words are *pneuma,* for the inner human spirit, and *psyche,* for the inner human sense of self. It is from these ancient terms that we get our language for spirituality and psychology. It is possible to discern only a slight difference between psyche and pneuma in biblical usage. That was also true in the general Greek culture in biblical times.

Psyche and pneuma are both used to refer to and name the inner human self or the ego, with the former referring essentially to "the organ" of the inner self and the latter naming the force of vitality in that "organ," so to speak. So we are fairly accurate when we speak of the psychology of a person being the describable inner vital self or ego; and when we use the word spirituality, it is the term for the meaning-oriented vigor and longing experienced by our vital self. In a rough and ready way, one could say that psychology and spirituality are two terms for essentially the same thing. They are two differently colored umbrellas that cover the same domain or territory, the functioning inner self. This is often referred to as the Living Human Document, the dynamically alive person.

The only real reason for having two different umbrellas has to do with the orientation of our discourse. The two terms are interchangeable, in my view, but they get at the inner human self from different perspectives, with different languages or universes of discourse, with differing ways of asking the questions, different formulations of the answers. Spirituality approaches the human inner self mainly from the perspective of the human quest for the meaning of our relationship with others and with God. Psychology approaches the human inner self mainly with a view to understanding the self's relationship with itself, and in terms of that, with the social setting.

Freud thought that human sexuality was the central dynamic or force shaping our psychology, namely, forming the psyche's relationship with itself, and thence with other persons. He thought sexuality produced sickness or health, depending upon how it functioned in any person. He was on to something very important. He taught us to realize that the relational dynamics of the self are of the most crucial nature. Because of some limitations in his own development, he just missed the central point, namely, that human sexuality and spirituality are two sides of the same vital force in the psyche. They are not different forces, which might conceivably be in opposition with each other. They are the same force.

When this psychospiritual or sexual-spiritual force reaches out for meaning through relationship it has two options. It can reach out horizontally or vertically, so to speak. It can reach out horizontally for meaningful relationship with other humans and take the psychophysical (psychosomatic) form of sexuality; or it can reach out for transcendent relationship—for meaningful relationship with God—and then we call it spirituality. When we reach out for meaningful relationship with each other in terms of intellectual, theological, religious, or emotional sharing and mutuality, it is spiritual. Of course, it is also always sexual, in the sense that we are always aware of the gender of the person to whom we are relating. In any case, in whichever direction the psyche reaches in its quest for meaning and fulfillment, if it is a healthy quest it involves the full force of our psychospirituality.

This process of finding meaning and fulfillment is a very personal and individual process, even though it tends to take similar and predictable human courses and patterns in all of us. It is rooted in each person finding the definitive questions for which the psyche hungers spiritually and fashioning answers that really work for that individual person's spirit. That means that routine ritual, in public worship, communal celebrations, or personal devotional life, is never enough and cannot, in and of itself, be authentic. Religious practices, formulae, patterns, or liturgies that exist merely for their own sake, or that we simply rehearse as ritual, do not work for any of us. In the past many people saw the religious institutions and leaders as having supreme authority and hence followed prescribed programs of religiosity because they were thought to be required, not because they afforded deep spiritual meaning. That is mere ritual for ritual's sake, and it is a sick form of spirituality.

If younger generations feel greater freedom to exercise more discernment and seek more authenticity in their personal and communal spirituality, thus finding institutionalized religion as they encounter it to be unsatisfying, that is a mark in their favor. However, if they then are led to abandon the quest for spiritual meaning, no longer seeking to discern the real questions or working hard to find the authentic answers for belief and practice, they cannot be respected nor taken seriously. Then they are just lazy and self-indulgent, coasting along at a very superficial level of life. They will live and die empty—T. S. Elliot's "hollow" souls.

So how can the Bible help? St. Augustine summarized the answer to that question in a poetic and profound way in the fifth century after Christ. After living half his life in an uproariously sensuous, promiscuous, and profligate way, he was converted to the Christian faith and practice. He made the shift because his former life, with all its desperate chase after fulfillment through sensuality, proved empty and meaningless. When he balanced his life between his spiritual and psychological quests for real relationship with God and other persons, he realized true spiritual fulfillment and religious authenticity. He exclaimed, "Oh God, you have made us for yourself; and our souls are restless until they rest, dear Lord, in you!"

The Bible has a lot to offer for spiritual authenticity and genuine religion. The chapters in this book are built around the questions of the psyche regarding such spirituality and religious practice, illumined by what the Bible offers on the matter. That is the reason for the title, *Understanding Religious Experience: What the Bible Says about Spirituality*. Since this is the pilgrimage in which we are all engaged, just by our very natures, whether we like it or not, it is important that this volume leads the way to examining the problems and perplexities of understanding authentic religious experience, in all its psychological, spiritual, and biblical dimensions.

CHAPTER 2

The Varieties of Religious Experiences

One of the most famous books ever written on spiritual experience is now a century old, but it is as current as if it were written last week. Everyone in the Western world knows about it, of course. It is William James' *The Varieties of Religious Experience.* This durable work on religious experience and human spirituality was formulated originally as 20 Gifford Lectures to be delivered at the University of Edinburgh in Scotland. The lectures were published in book form in 1902 when James was on the faculty of Harvard University.

James established, at the outset, that it was of the highest importance that his investigation and description of religious experience be as thoroughly empirical as possible, that is, built upon demonstrable facts of human experience. By that he meant that he wished to take with the utmost seriousness the reality of what he and his subjects discerned to be spiritual experiences, and to deduce from them "spiritual judgments only." That is, he intended to discern and describe the nature of the experience and interpret or appreciate the meaning of it in terms of the significance it gave to the spiritual and religious life of the person and the community experiencing it. He indicated, after presenting his research, that his conclusions could not be as "sharp as dogmatic conclusions," implying that the social sciences do not produce the hard data that the mathematical sciences do. Nonetheless, he was confident in the reality and truth of his conclusions since they were based on a broad sample of experience and were replicable in the sense of recurring similarly in numerous persons, circumstances, and occasions.

In a remarkable letter, written to Henry William Rankin on June 16, 1901, between the ninth and tenth of his 20 Gifford lectures, James summarized his foundational idea.[1]

> In these lectures the ground I am taking is this: The mother sea and fountain head of all religions lies in the mystical experiences of the individual, taking the word mystical in a very wide sense. All theologies and all ecclesiasticisms are secondary growths superimposed; and the [mystical] experiences make such flexible combinations with the intellectual prepossessions of their subjects [theologians or philosophers], that one may almost say that they [mystical experiences] have no proper *intellectual* deliverance of their own, but belong to a region deeper, and more vital and practical than that which the intellectual inhabits. For this they are also indestructible by intellectual arguments and criticisms. I attach the mystical or religious consciousness to the possession [existence in us] of an extended subliminal self with a thin partition through which messages make irruption. We are thus made convincingly aware of the presence of a sphere of life larger and more powerful than our usual consciousness, with which the latter [our conscious awareness] is nevertheless continuous. The impressions and impulsions and emotions and excitements which we thence receive help us to live, they found invincible assurances of a world beyond the senses, they melt our hearts and communicate significance and value to everything and make us happy. They do this for the individual who has them, and other individuals follow him. Religion in this way is absolutely indestructible. Philosophy and theology give their conceptual interpretations of this experiential life. The farther margin of the subliminal field being unknown, it can be treated as by Transcendental Idealism, as an Absolute mind with a part of which we coalesce, or by Christian theology, as a distinct deity acting on us. Something not our immediate self, *does* act on our life!

From his work James was able to distill the following judgments.[2] First, the visible world is part of a more spiritual universe from which it draws its chief significance. Second, that union or harmonious relation with that higher universe is our true end purpose in life. Third, prayer or inner communion with the spirit of that higher universe, be that spirit "God" or "law," is a process wherein work is really done, and spiritual energy flows in and produces effects, psychological and material, within the tangible world of real phenomena.

It is important to remind ourselves here of our definition of spirituality, namely the irrepressible inner human quest for meaning. This quest is a function of the *psyche* or *pneuma* and expresses itself in religious behavior. This quest reaches for transcendental meaning and relationship, and for the meaning of relationship with our material world and the persons we encounter within it. James did not make quite the crisp distinction between spirituality and religion that I make, but it is not difficult to discern, at each turn of the road, to which of the two he is referring.

He continued the summary of his findings with the following observations on the psychological characteristics that religion includes. First, it affords a new zest for the human spirit that adds itself, like a gift, to life; and it takes the form either of lyrical enchantment or of appeal to earnestness and heroism. Second, it provides an assurance of safety and a temper of peace, and, in relation to others, a preponderance of loving affections. James collected a vast variety of phenomenological evidence about human religious experience and drew firm heuristic conclusions from that data.

The things regarding spirituality and religion that interested James tended to be those of individual experience, rather than general categories. He was always looking for the experienced reality, not the theoretical concept or unified theory. He acknowledges at the outset that religious fervor and spiritual quest can produce psychological pathology as well as a full sense of well-being. He is interested in what makes the difference and how we can tell the difference. He says candidly, "There is no doubt that as a matter of fact a religious life, exclusively pursued, does tend to make the person exceptional and eccentric" (24).

However, in assessing the history of religious traditions, his important emphasis is upon the fact that persons who simply follow conventional religious rituals of any sort, Buddhist, Christian, Jewish, or Muslim, are simply acting out a religious practice made for them by others. James thinks this cannot possibly do much for a person's spiritual quest. "His religion has been made for him by others, communicated to him by tradition, determined to fixed forms by imitation, and retained by habit" (24). James calls this second-hand religion, and he has no interest in commenting further upon it. The important thing is the original experiences, the pattern-setting processes that produced the religious traditions we encounter in our own day.

James focuses the issue further by declaring, "These experiences we can only find in individuals for whom religion exists not as a dull habit, but as an acute fever…" (24). He suggests that people who are that intense about pursuing their quest for meaning are spiritual geniuses and, as such, are worthy of both commemoration and emulation. They show us the way. Sometimes the nature of their spiritual intimations, insights, vision, perceptions, and experiences seem ethereal or even otherworldly. In any case, authentic human meaning quest generally requires exalted spiritual and emotional sensitivity and intuitive understanding. James observes that such levels of spiritual experience, which fill one with a sense of connection with God or transcendent understanding, accord a certain aura of authority and influence to the experience itself and to the testimony of the person who lives on that plain of spiritual awareness, vision, and insight.

William James challenged those who reduced such authentic height-ened spirituality to mere psychopathology or to the sublimation of sexual forces in our persons and personalities. He insisted that, while certain types of psychotic ideation and behavior are often centered around reli-gious terms, notions, and claims, or other religious material, it is easy to tell the difference between true spirituality and genuine religion, on the one hand, and mental illness, on the other. As Jonathan Edwards had already insisted three centuries before James, in *A Treatise Concerning Religious Affections*,[3] the roots of human spiritual and religious qualities and expressions are much deeper than we can plumb, but true religion is known by its fruitfulness. "Our *practice* is the only sure evidence, even to ourselves, that we are genuinely Christian" (34, emphasis added). Edwards had put it quite similarly in saying, in effect, that the degree to which our spiritual experience and religious behavior produces good concepts, character, and conduct demonstrates the degree to which it is genuinely spiritual and divine.

Thus, by his challenges of those who take a superficial view of the human hunger for meaning and the spiritual quest it engenders, James once again confirms the importance of his insistence upon an *empirical* approach to un-derstanding the varieties of religious experience. It is in the workable quality of the practical results, produced by a person of superior achievement in the spiritual quest for meaning and religious relevance, that we can establish the firm foundation of certainty regarding the genuiness of his or her spiritual vision or understanding.

Of course, it helps a person in the spiritual quest to be somewhat neurotic. As Karen Horney said so well in her book, *The Neurotic Personality of Our Time*, to be neurotic means to have a slightly or seriously larger sense of anxiety about things, about anything, than reality would warrant.[4] I have said for many years that ministers of the gospel need to be mildly neurotic or they cannot ever hear the voice of God's Holy Spirit calling them into ministry. If one does not have a somewhat exaggerated sense of the serious-ness of the problems out there in life, one will never be moved by the urgency needed to sense a call into ministry. This dedication of one's entire life to such self-sacrificial service requires a heightened sense of the need being addressed. In preparing this chapter, I was pleasantly surprised to notice that William James insists that this quality of normal-range neuroticism is necessary, or at least helpful, for anyone's authentic spiritual sensitivity. He insisted that regarding inspiration from God's realm, "it might well be that the neurotic temperament would furnish the chief condition of the requisite receptivity."

He was writing in the context of nineteenth-century "faculty psychol-ogy" in which it was assumed that personalities came in four forms: hysteric, dependent, compulsive, and paranoid.[5] These were not intended as terms identifying types of mental illness but as terms describing how various personalities acquire meaning from experience. Hysteric personalities acquire meaning through the drama of life, dependent personalities through relationality in life, compulsive personalities through careful regulation and orderliness, and paranoid personalities through meticulous use of the precise meaning of words. A neurotic personality, presumably, would have a nice balanced combination of hysteric and dependent features, finding meaning in dramatic and relational experiences. James considered this desirable and constructive, because there is always something solemn, serious, and tender about such authentic spirituality and true religion.

It is most interesting that James continues his thoughtful analysis by observing that the other side of this spiritual reality is the fact that authentic spirituality and genuine religion take away the anxieties of life. Fear is not merely held in abeyance by deep spirituality and heartfelt religion, as it is by mere moral achievement. It is positively expunged. The central thing he found in his examination of religious experience was

> how infinitely passionate a thing religion at its highest flights can be. Like love, like wrath, like hope, ambition, jealousy, like every other instinctive eagerness and impulse, it adds to life an enchantment which is not rationally or logically deducible from anything else. This enchantment, coming as a gift when it does come—a gift of our organism, the physiologists will tell us, a gift of God's grace, the theologians say—is either there or not there for us, and there are persons who can no more become possessed by it than they can fall in love with a given [person] by mere word of command. Religious feeling is thus an absolute addition to the Subject's range of life. It gives him [or her] a new sphere of power. When the outward battle is lost, and the outer world disowns him, it redeems and vivifies an interior world which otherwise would be an empty waste.
>
> If religion is to mean anything definite for us, it seems to me that we ought to take it as meaning this added dimension of emotion, this enthusiastic temper of espousal...It ought to mean nothing short of this new reach of freedom for us, with the struggle over, the keynote of the universe sounding in our ears, and everlasting possession spread before our eyes. This sort of happiness in the absolute and everlasting is what we find nowhere but in religion... "It is the infinite for which we hunger, and we ride gladly on every little wave that promises to bear us towards it." (53–56)

James slips the keystone into the finely wrought arch of his argument with a brief summary. The universe and human existence is what it is. The reality of the unseen cannot be disputed by anyone who is aware enough of his or her own nature to have experienced the psychospiritual hunger and quest for the profound meaning of human life. These are those who have experienced the parapsychological and transcendental intimations that entice us to genuine spirituality and authentic religion. Coping with these realities, these givens, in the long run requires that we settle with some renunciation, sacrifice, and surrender. Ultimately we must renounce our notions of being in control and being able to insure our own comfort and security. We are dying persons in generations of dying persons. Along the way we must sacrifice our narcissism and our private, personal claims on having things the way we want them. We must surrender to the process of life from the cradle to the grave, and to the fact that we cannot make meaning out of that process on our own by mere moral character. Finally, mere morality is a container too incomplete and empty to feed the hunger of our spirits for the infinite.

"For when all is said and done, we are in the end absolutely dependent on the universe" and our only permanent position of repose is to accept that, consciously and deliberately. If we do so merely as a moral necessity, we may do it grudgingly or, at best, without complaint.

> In the religious life, on the contrary, surrender and sacrifice are positively espoused: even unnecessary givings-up are added in order that the happiness may increase. Religion thus makes easy and felicitous what in any case is necessary; and if it be the only agency that can accomplish this result, its vital importance as a human faculty stands vindicated beyond dispute. It becomes an essential organ of our life, performing a function which no other portion of our nature can so successfully fulfill. (56)

In her appreciation of the work of William James, Catherine Madsen observed that James' Gifford Lectures have an immediacy that is like plugging into a "live current of intelligent scrutiny and active compassion." She found that this aspect of the work can readily modify one's thought processes and provide both a guide to religious experience and a "map to the availability of transformation." She seems to have caught James' vision:

> The numinous is so uncanny that in addition to its unexpected approaches it can be created—as a theater artist knows, as the newly observant Jew knows when lighting the Sabbath candles, as the sick soul reaching toward sanity knows whenever a habitual reaction of violence or self-loathing is replaced by a conscious turn toward equanimity and peace. The locus of transformation is wherever we choose to establish it: the sanctuary, the seminar room, the dinner table, the bed. We can invite the numinous and it will appear; even, perhaps especially, in the aftermath of disaster, it knows our voice and will answer. One of the most welcome patterns of the brain is its capacity to arrive—having survived its own history, and thus with a sense of permanence and completion—at

peace, the energy and the moral presence of those whom James called the "twice-born."[6]

The work of Huston Smith was generally considered to be the pre-eminent authoritative source on religion at the end of the twentieth century. His book, *The Illustrated World's Religions, A Guide to Our Wisdom Traditions*, was very well received. It was based upon, as well as updating and attractively illustrating, his early work, *The Religions of Man* (1958) and its later inclusive language edition, *The World's Religions* (1989).[7] In his opening paragraph he focuses his work on "the enduring religions at their best," with the acknowledgement that "their theological and metaphysical truths are...inspired" (13). In this regard, Smith's work is quite congenial to the insights of William James. He had a great appreciation for James' positive approach to religion as experiential, alive, and "an acute fever." Smith declared,

> Religion alive confronts the individual with the most momentous option life can present. It calls the soul to the highest adventure it can undertake, a projected journey across the jungles, peaks, and deserts of the human spirit. The call is to confront reality, to master the self. Those who dare to hear and follow that secret call soon learn the dangers and difficulties of its lonely journey...But they know its deliverances, too. When a lone spirit triumphs in this domain, it becomes more than a ruler. It becomes a world redeemer. Its impact stretches for millennia, blessing the tangled course of history for centuries...for authentic religion is the clearest opening through which the inexhaustible energies of the cosmos pour into human life. (14)

Smith quoted a Katha Upanishad from Hindu poetic tradition, to finely hone his point about the lonely mystical journey:

> The sharp edge of a razor, hard to transverse
> A difficult path is this, the poets declare....(14)

He despaired of finding words and logic to capture spiritual states of consciousness and corner insights about which he wished to speak and which he had observed or experienced himself. In the end he thought only two things were necessary to take religion and its spiritual sources as seriously as they deserved: first, we must remember that religion reflects the hunger of real human beings, driven by our common and irrepressible spiritual quest, and second, we must keep our minds sensitively open to any new insights which that human quest might reveal to us.

At about the time William James was preparing his Gifford Lectures, delivered in 1901–12 in Edinburgh, Sir James George Frazer wrote *The Golden Bough*. Theodor H. Gaster brought out an edited, critiqued, and abridged version of that work in 1959 and observed about it that no other work in the field of anthropology has contributed so much to the mental and artistic climate of our times. Indeed, what Freud did for the individual, Frazer did for civilization as a whole. For as Freud deepened men's insights into the behavior of individuals by uncovering the ruder world of the subconscious, from which so much of it springs, so Frazer enlarged man's understanding of the behavior of societies by laying bare the primitive concepts and modes of thought which underlie and inform so many of their institutions and which persist, as a subliminal element of their culture, in their traditional folk customs.[8]

Frazer attempted to tell the story of human spirituality as he observed it or heard about it being practiced in folk religions and primitive societies. From that he attempted to draw correlations with contemporary practices in the world's great religions. In that process he zeroed in on the irrepressible inner human quest for connection with the ethereal, numinous world of transcendent spirit as the key source for the meaning of life. He wanted to distill out of the worldwide human religious behavior what could be identified as the universal spiritual essence of human nature.

Gaster says that Frazer enabled us to see more clearly, "the rock whence we are hewn," as well as giving us a broad psychological frame of reference within which to interpret the religious and spiritual evidence we are able to find. Frazer, himself, summarized his views by pointing out that what sophisticated world religions and cultures, like the Judaic and Christian Western world, hold as central to the spiritual quest and religious practice is similar to rather than different from primitive people and their spirituality. What we retain as true and useful, we owe to the essential quest of our own primitive forefathers.

While Frazer's work is a classic, much new and more helpful work has been inspired by it during the century that has elapsed since its publication. The three most prominent and generative scholars who carried Frazer's work forward are Mircea Eliade, Ninian Smart, and Joseph Campbell. While Frazer's perspective was essentially secular and anthropological, he opened up and correlated the entire world of myth and ritual in religious thought and practice, spanning the entire time from the misty mythic past of prehistory to the practices of primitive people at the end of the nineteenth century. Eliade and Smart developed the study of the spiritual world reflected in religious ritual while Campbell psychoanalyzed the nature and function of religious mythology and spiritual or theological confessional myths—statements of belief.

Joseph Campbell's work is today the supreme authority on mythology as the psychologically symbolic way in which humans tell the stories of their own personal and communal spiritual journey and pass them along to each other and to subsequent generations. He would agree for the most part with our working definition of myth as a confessional statement, describing the meaning of what we perceive to be truth, which has both an earthly and heavenly meaning. In Christianity, for example, our teaching about the Eucharist, the sacrament of Holy Communion, emphasizes the fact that the earthly elements of broken bread and poured wine have a heavenly meaning. That symbolic story, our confessional myth or belief statement, about the meaning of these simple earthly things is what makes this event sacramental.

That makes the drama of the table or altar into a sacrament: earthly symbols with heavenly meaning. Campbell is especially interested in that kind of teaching—in the "I believe" statements and behaviors that express the story of our spiritual experience. In such stories, the meaning lies beyond the words, in the elaborated explanation of the meaning-signification. That is the mythic nature of the faith statement: the confessional, "I believe," story of the meaning of these spiritual things. When I conduct the sacrament of Holy Communion I often pray that God will turn the earthly elements into heavenly meaning that will nurture the spirituality of the congregation with eternal life. I mean it in terms of Paul's notion of eternal life: life on God's plain of thought, experience, and perception, here and now and forevermore, life in the conscious matrix of God's unconditional, radical, and universal grace.

Campbell opened his book, *The Hero with a Thousand Faces*, by declaring that he wished to "uncover some of the truths disguised for us under the figures of religion and mythology by bringing together a multitude of not-too-difficult examples and letting the ancient meaning become apparent of itself. The old teachers knew what they were saying. Once we have learned to read again their symbolic language, it requires no more than the talent of an anthologist to let their teaching be heard. But first we must learn the grammar of the symbols" (vii).[9]

By looking into the psychospiritual nature of the universal human quest, Campbell demonstrates not only the specific, definite shape of this human adventure, but also its direct relevance to our lives today. He argues that understanding the universal nature of this spiritual quest is necessary to the life of any person who wishes a fully realized existence. Myth, according to Campbell, is the projection of the human community's dream upon the personal spiritual quest of each of us. Like *Star Wars*, which Campbell's book is said to have inspired, *The Hero with a Thousand Faces*, together with his other work, *The Masks of God*, is a demonstration of the cumulative human confessional myth that reflects and inspires our continuing spiritual quest. By knowing this universal myth we reconcile ourselves to the unalterable psychospiritual truths of human existence, says Campbell. These include our joys and sorrows, our pains and pleasures, which are the same for all people and always have been.

A myth is, in that sense, a philosophical text, a theological truth, and a psychological narrative, but one in which the truths are revealed symbolically. The heroic journey of life, captured in our religious confessional myths, has all of us as its subject, including our own personal journeys from childhood, and potentially to full self-hood, spiritual fulfillment or wholeness, and religious maturity.

Whenever human beings have looked for something solid on which to found our lives, we have not chosen the facts with which the world abounds, but the confessional myths of immemorial imagination and of our own deepest spiritual recesses. These mythic statements of faith spring from the same psychospiritual source in the human spirit, regardless of the religious mode in which they are acted out, or the faith tradition that prompts them. In the closing lines of her incomparable little book, *Red Land, Black Land*, Barbara Mertz once remarked on this very thing, in pathos that still bring tears to my eyes.[10] Observing upon the ancient Egyptian quest for spiritual clarity, she said that we are the beneficiaries of their search for God, and we will not find their religious modes and style so strange or different from our own if we see beneath them reflections of *our common human terror and our common hope.*

Eliade considered his most important work to be his *Cosmos and History, the Myth of the Eternal Return.*[11] He opened the book with an observation reflecting Frazer's perspective. He wrote, "The chief difference between the man of the archaic and traditional societies and the man of the modern societies with their strong imprint of Judaeo Christianity lies in the fact that the former feels himself [*sic*] indissolubly connected with the Cosmos and the cosmic rhythms, whereas the latter insists that he is connected only with history... But this 'history' of the Cosmos and of human society is a 'sacred history,' preserved and transmitted through myths" (vii–viii). Eliade concludes by acknowledging, therefore, that it is this universal sense of the sacred history that is instructive for our understanding of the nature of humans and human development.

Eliade notes that a rather remarkable set of archetypes, such as the holy city, or the sacred space, the sacred meal, the waters of initiation, the sacred mountain or high place, and the like, appears to be universal in all religions and religious rituals and liturgies. These archetypes take on and express remarkably similar things for all humans, ancient to modern, primitive to sophisticated. The main thing expressed by these earthly phenomena is a metaphoric spiritual connection with the transcendent world. For example, the history of religions is full of the metaphoric description of a temple as the image of the world or the cosmos and its relationship with God. In Christianity, basilicas and cathedrals often represented for the worshippers the heavenly holy city, the celestial Jerusalem. This material form and structure responded to and inspired the spiritual quest for God and the heavenly realm for those who came up to that sacred place for worship.

We can only speak of God and the things of God by analogy or metaphor, of course. That is the reason why Frazer and those who followed him, indeed, anyone who thinks profoundly about spirituality and religion, must resort to metaphor and confessional myth to think and talk about these ethereal matters of the innermost spirit of each of us. Humans are driven to talk about these transcendental things, Eliade contends, because of the terminal nature of life and history. To find meaning in life we must find meaning for death. The human spiritual quest for meaning is inherent and irrepressible, but its content is derived in part from this "terror of history." It is interesting that he emphasizes this point, since the biblical narratives from Genesis to Revelations may also be seen clearly as the persistent and urgent attempt on the part of the ancient Israelites and the early Christians to answer the simple but perpetually mystifying question, "How is God in history?"

Eliade thought that humans have only two alternatives, despair or faith (159). Ultimately, this is obviously true. However, James' entire point was that faith is not merely a reaction to the potential of despair. It is generated in the human spiritual quest because it is such a gratifying and meaning-affording benefit to the person who walks and talks with God. It is the natural fulfillment of the inherent spiritual hunger of the person who lives life in perpetual consciousness of the presence of God in his grace. Sailing one's ship close to the wind, so to speak, brings the gratifications and life-changing intimations that afford hope and joy.

Ninian Smart's most popular and most helpful work is *The Religious Experience of Mankind.*[12] It is particularly notable for two reasons: First, it is a comprehensive survey of all of the mainstream religions from the ancient past down to the present day; and second, he has approached the entire spectrum of religions from the perspective of the spiritual experience that is at the core of each religion. From beginning to end he follows the defining fact that throughout all prehistorical and historical time, religion has been the vital and pervasive characteristic of human life. If we wish to understand that history and that life we must understand the religious dynamics that pervaded it. Today, if we wish to understand other nations' or cultures' ideologies or faith systems, we must understand their religious perspectives and practices. Only in this way, Smart argues, can we grasp the meaning of life.

Smart lives up to his name by immediately explaining that religious rituals and buildings can be seen, but the essence of religion is the spirituality that drives it, and that cannot be seen. Thus, to understand the role of religion we must discern the function and experience of the inner spirituality of persons, operating individually and communally. "So it is not enough for us to survey the course which the religious history of mankind has taken: we must also penetrate into the hearts and minds of those who have been involved in that history" (3).

Taking that approach, Smart observes that

Religion is a doubly rich and complex phenomenon. Not only has it the complexity indicated by this need to hold together its outer and inner aspects, but it also has existed and exists in a variety of forms of faith. There are many religions to be discovered in the world. The study of these is a fascinating and stimulating task, for not only is this variety a testimony to the richness of the religious sense and imagination of mankind, and often—though by no means always—to the nobility of the human spirit, but also it gives rise to some profoundly important questions about the truth of religion. (3)

This confirms all that we have already observed about spirituality and religion in the preceding line of thought of this book. It is clear, as Smart agrees, that it is not helpful to merely speculate about religious truth or the nature of human spirituality. It is crucial to explore these crucial realities by discovering the experiences that real people have spiritually and in their religious practices. Smart's book is an attempt to do this. His report on his finding is not a matter of passing judgment upon the variety of religious experiences, but of describing what they seem to mean for real persons. He has realized from the outset that the important thing is not to decide which religion is true or better, but what the true nature of universal human spirituality really is and how it typically expresses itself.

Since we who are religious people are by nature passionate about the religion we espouse, invested in it so to speak, it is inevitable that we are not objective or dispassionate about it. Believers are devotees. They see their religion from the inside because that is where the drives of their personal spirituality are intensely experienced. In the face of this, it is the case that each great religion is like a growing plant or organism. To understand it we must not only see how each differs from or is like our own. We must also try to understand spiritual life as experienced from the inside of that faith tradition as well as understand the way that faith tradition became what it is, given its unique history.

Christianity, for example, cannot be understood without learning about the circumstances of its birth 2,000 years ago. Jews realized this about their religion at a very early stage, and so they tried to keep a record of both the history of their religious practices and of the spiritual experience that they discerned were driving them. The result is the Hebrew Bible, the Old Testament. Christianity followed this example for its first century and produced the New Testament.

Smart observes that within 30 years after Jesus' crucifixion "the literary tradition which was to form the books of the New Testament was already started.... Virtually within a hundred years of Jesus' crucifixion the works which now comprise the canon of the New Testament (the new covenant which followed on from the old) came into being" (314). Smart saw Jesus' explanation of the reign of God, as love that works and grace that heals, to be a paradigm for all human spirituality. He sees the implication of this perspective to be the essential story of the universal human hunger for the meaning of life and death. Our spiritual quest is always a reach for that fullness or satisfaction of heart and mind that produces a sense of tranquility, being at peace with life on this horizontal plain and life that is linked intimately to the vertical reach of our spirits. That is, being at peace in a life already experienced to be on God's plain of function or existence. This is a *quality* of life currently experienced, but already participating in "the heavenly." Paul consistently calls it eternal life, here and now and for ever. That is a matter of sailing really close to the wind of God's spirit!

The reign of God that Jesus perceived as already present in human experience, as a leaven in a loaf, was very different from the aspirations and modes of thought that the religious leaders around him had fostered for so long a time and that in his day were being nourished with increasing vigor and fervency. While his disciples scarcely understood him, "Part of the reason for the allusive and parabolic nature of his teaching lay in the fact that he was trying to induce in his hearers a new vision, a turning-around of their point of view. He was concerned with shaking people from their old categories, whether they were the sophisticated thought-patterns of the learned or the simple faith of the farmers, prostitutes, and fisher folk among whom he moved" (319).

He wished them to shift from the ossified structures of religious ritual to the dynamic possibilities of getting in touch with their inner spirituality. In the process, he hoped they would get in touch with God as their father, in the sense that was so real for him. Paul followed on this track that Jesus had laid down, so to speak. Paul's entire world of spirituality, following his conversion to Christianity, assumed in a vivid way that the same spirit that had been the driver in Jesus was a present and vital force in all of us who seek to follow his trajectory of spiritual life. Both Jesus and Paul wished us to learn to walk and talk with God, in our search for deeper perceptions of who God is and how he is present to us in our own variety of religious experience.

The Bible presents a rich panoply of data on the varieties of spiritual experience and religious behavior. It is of great interest to look carefully at those narratives in which the Bible presents or implies illumining depictions of the human quest for meaning. They are invariably narratives of the hunger of the human spirit for meaningful relationship with other humans and with the Lord. All the biblical stories of spiritual experience speak in some degree of the longing humans have always had for intellectual, emotional, psychological, and spiritual fulfillment from others; and especially from that infinite, transcendent, wholly other person, God. Most of those biblical reports inform us directly of the nature of genuine spiritual experience and authentic religious practice.

CHAPTER 3

BIBLICAL SPIRITUALITY AS WALKING WITH GOD

Throughout the Bible walking is considered to be an important matter. That term, as employed in the ancient Hebrew language of the Old Testament, is turned into a poetic metaphor or word picture. That word picture is used throughout the Bible to describe profound spiritual experience and wholesome religious behavior. This is the very first concept used by the biblical authors in their attempt to describe the mysterious experience of our spiritual quest. Right from the beginning of those sacred Judeo-Christian scriptures, spirituality is described as walking with God, walking in the spirit, or walking in the wholesome way of God or godliness.

Everybody knows about the story of Noah and the great flood in Genesis chapter 6. Now we know that this story, like so many others in the Bible, is a myth. A myth is a symbolically developed story designed to tell an important truth in which those who hold to that story as truth utterly believe. It is not a mere fairy tale or legend. As we noted in chapter 1, a myth is an "I believe" story or creed for the community that reveres it. Therefore, Noah may or may not have been a real man who lived long ago. That is not the important issue in the story. He may well have been a man who lived in some ancient patriarchal culture of prehistory, around whom this story was built. His real name may have been Noah or something else. He may have actually built an ark and saved his family from a great flood.

Archaeological evidence has recently suggested that in some ancient era the Black Sea was a much smaller sweetwater inland lake, cut off from the Mediterranean Sea, just as the Caspian Sea is today. Its water level was much below that of the Mediterranean Sea, as is the case of the Dead Sea today.

Around that early form of the Black Sea a significant human habitation had been built. At some point, the excavated evidence now suggests, the land barrier at the Dardanelles was eroded by earthquake and a rise in sea levels, resulting from the retreat of the ice ages. Then the Mediterranean Sea flooded into the Black Sea basin, raising the water level of that inland sea so much that it wiped out all of the richly developed civilization that had established itself along the shores. The Bible tells us that,

> Noah was a righteous man, blameless in his generation; Noah walked with God.... Now the earth was corrupt in God's sight, and the earth was filled with violence. And God saw the earth...it was corrupt; for all flesh had corrupted their way upon the earth. And God said to Noah, "I have determined to make an end of all flesh...Make yourself an ark of gopher wood...For behold, I will bring a flood of waters upon the earth...But I will establish my covenant with you; and you shall come into the ark, you, your sons, your wife, and your sons' wives with you. And of every living thing of all flesh, you shall bring two of every sort into the ark, to keep them alive with you; they shall be male and female.... And Noah did all that the Lord had commanded him.... In the six hundredth year of Noah's life, in the second month, on the seventeenth day of the month...all the fountains of the great deep burst forth, and the windows of the heavens were opened. And rain fell upon the earth forty days and forty nights...and the waters increased, and bore up the ark and it rose high above the earth.... And the waters prevailed upon the earth a hundred and fifty days.... In the six hundred and first year, in the first month, the first day of the month, the waters were dried from off the earth. In the second month, on the twenty seventh day of the month, the earth was dry. Then God said to Noah, "Go forth from the ark..." (Gen. 6:9–8:16a—excerpts, RSV)[1]

Whether there really was a great flood is somewhat beside the point for our interest here. This story is an ancient narrative that the Israelites borrowed from earlier Mesopotamian legends. We know this because we now have in writing the original Mesopotamian stories in a number of different editions, and we can date them to long before the Israelites fashioned upon them their framework for their biblical report of the flood. As in the case of this report and most of the rest of the first 11 chapters of the Bible, the ancient Israelites borrowed *many* earlier Canaanite and Mesopotamian legends and turned them into narratives by which they tried to tell the story about their experiences with God. That is how they fashioned the stories of creation, the flood, the tower of Babel and other reports on prehistory. We know that the Israelites used the more-ancient legends as the core of their narratives because the language they used is, in many cases, virtually quoted from those Mesopotamian or Canaanite legends.

Of course, the reason why the Israelites worked so hard at doing this had to do with their spiritual longing to understanding the meaning of

God's actions in their world. They were asking, "How is God in history, particularly in our complicated and perplexing history?" Those old stories seemed to give them a good start in answering such a question, particularly as it related to understanding the creation of the world: where it came from and how it got into the condition they found it in. They wanted to figure out how God could possibly be related to the good and the bad they experienced, and that they even perpetrated, in the world as they knew it. That is, their hunger to feed their spiritual quest was all about their desire to understand their longing for meaningful relationship with each other and with the transcendent source of all things.

What they managed to figure out quite early in their quest was that there are experiences that seem to contribute to wholesome and fruitful relationships with others, and there are ways of acting that destroy relationship. Likewise, they discerned, according to the biblical reports, that there are experiences that put one in touch with God or make life seem like one is in gratifying relationship with God; and there are experiences that seem like alienation from transcendent meaning and the unseen world. Those alienating experiences, they discerned, leave us feeling empty and out of touch with life and ourselves. Sometimes life seems so "tuned up" that it seems like we are walking with God, and some moments in life feel like God is absent and we are as lonely as hell. That much they figured out quite early in their quest for a deep inner sense of the meaningfulness of life.

In the Hebrew's old flood story, that contrast between the heavenly mode of human existence and the hellishness of life is quite evident. The picture painted by the narrative in Genesis 6 depicts a world in which humans seem to be rather hellish, from God's point of view. We are not interested here in whether that was a sound judgment upon humans or whether the disaster of the flood is justified. That story is probably a pathological biblical myth in the way it depicts God as vengeful rather than redemptive. After all, humans did not ask to be created, nor did humans cause whatever potential for flaws exist in us that make wickedness possible; but that is not the issue here for us. The issue for our purposes here is Noah's character.

Noah is a character in a story—and some character he is! Whether he was ever a real person is beside the point; though, as I said earlier, there probably was such a guy. This is a story that distills an important aspect of the biblical author's perception about a crucial fact of spirituality. The author would not have made this fact up out of thin air. He or she must have seen people who had the spiritual experience the story says Noah had. Most likely the author had experienced it himself or herself. The story tells us that Noah walked with God. Most everyone else in his world seemed brazenly insensitive to the presence of God in human life and had attempted to fulfill his or her spiritual hunger by rather exaggerated sensual distractions to sexual experimentation, violence, and materialistic gratifications. That does not sound unfamiliar to us, since that seems like the story of what so many folks still seem to be doing today.

Since sexuality and spirituality are two sides of the same God-given force at the center of every human being, it is easily possible to try to fulfill our sexual needs for communion with other persons by exaggerating our spiritual preoccupations, as did the medieval saints.[2] Likewise it is easy to try to fulfill our spiritual hunger for God by exaggerating our sexual obsession with human relationships. Moreover, this erroneously rechanneling of our spiritual drives need not be sexual, but can just be obsessions with other forms of materialistic efforts to fulfill the meaning-hunger of our spirits. For some people it is merely money, luxury, lots of toys, exotic vacations, or travel, all of which are really good in themselves, but in the end come somewhat short of giving us the soulful of meaning that we crave and are trying to find or acquire.

According to this mythic story, crafted to set forth in word pictures a spiritual reality, Noah's world seemed to be running rather madly down a fruitless track. Noah, on the other hand, walked with God. The fellow was apparently doing something right. There is no indication in the story that he was some kind of perfectionist or moral model or towering spiritual paragon. Only a few verses later in this same story he is drunk, immodest, abusive of his children, and generally a rather well-experienced and thoroughgoing sinner. I do not like this guy very much. Moreover, his behavior resulted in a grossly dysfunctional family. But Noah walked with God, and that meant he was the kind of guy to whom God could intimate insights that infused important meaning into Noah's hungering spirit.

Apparently, as the ancient Israelites saw it, walking with God does not require moral, material, or spiritual perfection. That is, ordinary humans can walk with God. Flawed folks like you and I can walk with God. In the end, because he walked with God and acted upon the spiritual meaning that came from that, Noah became a symbol of God's constructive presence in flawed human lives. In the New Testament, particularly in the four Gospels, Jesus makes frequent references to Noah, holding him up as an example of how God's presence and intimations to people who walk with God improve their quality of meaningful life. In the later epistles (Heb. 11:7, I Pet. 3:20, II Pet. 3:5) Noah is specifically cited as an example of the spiritual benefit of walking with God.

Well of course, all of that makes for an interesting, indeed an intriguing, ancient narrative with deep roots in the spiritual quests of even more ancient pre-Israelite people. They were all trying to figure out God and what it means to experience a meaningful relationship to God. We do not need to take the details of the legend seriously. Like parables, such legends or myths always have one point at the center that the author is trying to establish. If we get preoccupied with or make too much of the peripheral details, or whether the story is history or myth, we miss the point. This story means to say only one thing: It is possible for humans, in our quest for meaning, to experience what should be called walking with God, and that makes a great difference for good in our spirituality, and hence in the shape of our religious behavior.

What we have not yet figured out here is what it means to walk with God and why that helps in our spiritual quest for a heart full of meaning. Perhaps it will be helpful for us to look at other biblical stories. In those first 11 mythic chapters of Genesis there are other stories about walking with God that shed light on the question of what it means and what the experience is like.

Adam missed out on a nice walk with God in paradise, in the cool of the evening (Gen. 3:8). He missed out on walking with God because ignorance, fear, guilt, and shame made him feel alienated from God. That is always true. It is always true for every human being. It always has been. Read that story of the fall again. You see how incredibly fanciful that story in Genesis 3 really is, but at the center is this one spiritual truth. It is always our ignorance (lack of information), fear (lack of trust), guilt (lack of security), and shame (lack of confidence) that distance us from the sense that we are walking with God in our quest for meaning. Adam's story is borrowed from an even more fanciful Mesopotamian fertility story than the Noah story, but the Hebrews turned it into a creedal myth about their God, Yahweh, and his relationship to them in their spiritual quest. Here is the Hebrew version of the story.

> The Lord formed man of dust from the ground and breathed into his nostrils the breath of life; and man became a living being. And the Lord God planted a garden in Eden....The Lord God took the man and put him into the garden of Eden, to till it and keep it. And the Lord commanded the man, saying, "You may freely eat of every tree of the garden; but of the tree of the knowledge of good and evil you shall not eat, for in the day that you eat of it you shall die....And the man and his wife were both naked, and were not ashamed. Now the serpent was more subtle than any other wild creature...He said to the woman, "Did God say, 'You shall not eat of any tree of the garden?'" And the woman said to the serpent, "We may eat of the fruit of the trees of the garden; but God said, 'You shall not eat of the fruit of the tree which is in the midst of the garden, neither shall you touch it, lest you die.'" But the serpent said to the woman, "You will not die, for God knows that when you eat of it your eyes will be opened, and you will be like God, knowing good and evil." So when the woman saw that the tree was good for food, and that it was a delight to the eyes, and that the tree was to be desired to make one wise, she took of its fruit and ate; and she also gave some to her husband, and he ate. Then the eyes of both were opened, and they knew that they were naked...And they heard the sound of the Lord God walking in the garden in the cool of the day, and the man and his wife hid themselves from the presence of the Lord God...But the

Lord God called to the man, and said to him, "Where are you?" And he said, "I heard the sound of thee in the garden, and I was afraid, because I was naked; and I hid myself." He said, "Who told you that you were naked? Have you eaten of the tree of which I commanded you not to eat?" (RSV)

As with Adam and Eve in the mythic story, our inadequate experience with God makes walking with God seem unlikely or uncommon for us. This is the concept that forms the framework of the entire message of the whole Bible. It is reinforced by our real or neurotically imagined fear, guilt, and shame, as it was for Adam and Eve. This realization or notion is the structure of the narrative from Genesis 3 to Revelation 22. In the Genesis story, God came to walk in the garden of Eden and Adam was hiding from God. God called to Adam and asked him why he was hiding. Adam said, "Because I was afraid—because I was naked." That is in interesting contrast with the closing words of Revelation, "I saw a new world descend from God out of heaven, and a great voice said, 'God lives with humans. They shall be God's people. God himself will be with them....Come, everyone who is spiritually thirsty. Drink of the water of life, without cost or condition'" (JHE, trans).[3]

Quite obviously, it is precisely within this framework that the main message of the entire scripture makes spiritual sense and illumines our question about walking with God. Human inadequacy or lack of information, together with fear, guilt, and shame, distance us from a sense of life being a walk with God. They distance us from a sense of living life all the time in the mode of savoring the flavor of our spiritual hunger, connecting us to the ethereal realities that William James demonstrated are alone the source of real wholeness or fulfillment in humans. Human limitations, fear, guilt, and shame do that to us, because we are flawed persons, as Noah was.

Paul declares in Romans 8:38–39 that it is precisely those obstructions that God has removed from the equation of our relationship with God. Anyone who "walks with God" is operating in life out of that realization. Paul declares, "I am convinced that neither life nor death, neither powers from heaven or hell, neither angels nor demons, nor anything in the past, present, or future, and nothing in all God's world or ours, can separate us from the love of God" (JHE trans).

The Bible is full of such declarations about the essence and source of the transcendental truth that provides the spiritual fulfillment for which we all hunger. In Micah 7:18–20 we find the Old Testament passage that undoubtedly influenced Paul in this sense of his walk with God. Micah, a prophet who lived six or seven centuries before Jesus, forcefully asked the key question.

Who is a God like our God. He pardons iniquity. He passes
    over transgression.
He does not hang onto his anger forever. He delights in steadfast love.
He is faithful to us when we are unfaithful to him.

He treads our iniquities under his feet.
He casts all our sins into the depths of the sea.
Moreover he has guaranteed this to us through our ancestors,
From the days of old. (JHE trans)

Adam missed out on a nice walk with God in the garden of paradise in
the cool of the evening; not because God was not there, but because Adam
was hidden behind his fear, guilt, shame, and ignorance of what God is really
like. God was not absent. Adam was. God was not distant, but Adam was "on
the other side of his own world." He was busy fixing the wrong things—
the things that did not count with God, so far as walking with God is concerned. God wanted to walk with Adam (humankind). He tracked him down
to walk with him. He ferreted out the distancing obstruction. God worked
around it.

God made Adam's fear, guilt, and shame irrelevant to the matter of walking with God and, by persisting in walking with us in spite of ourselves,
offers the information that removes the original and persisting ignorance.
As William James noted, what makes spirituality produce human wholeness
is the realization that the universe, unseen reality, ultimate truth, God, can
be trusted to certify us as being acceptable, in spite of ourselves. That is the
one thing we do not inherently believe and we must discover. It is the driving
energy behind our spiritual quest and our religious practices. Paul nails this
down especially well in Ephesians 2:8–9 when he declares, "By grace you
have been saved, through faith; and this is not your own doing, it is the gift
of God—not because of works, lest anyone should boast" that he or she has
earned or crafted life's wholeness (RSV).

There is a story about walking with God that appears quite early in the
Bible and is more enjoyable than that of Noah or Adam. I mean it is more
enjoyable than the ambiguous stories about those two rather flawed figures.
The Bible tells us that Enoch also walked with God. In Genesis 5:18–24
Enoch is twice described as a man who walked with God. It apparently had a
radically life-changing impact on his character and experience. The text does
not tell us exactly what that meant for Enoch or how he did that, but it does
imply that it connected him to God and eternity in a unique way. Moreover,
Enoch became a legendary figure in the imagination of Israelite believers for
centuries, because of his special life of walking with God.

In fact, much study is given to understanding Enoch to this very day. During the 500 years between the end of the Israelite exile in Babylon and the
life of Jesus of Nazareth, a very important collection of books was written
and assembled, which is now called the First Book of Enoch (I Enoch). It
had a life-shaping effect upon Judaism during those years, and it influenced
Jesus' outlook on things, as well as the rise of the Jesus Movement and of
the Christian Church. The book I Enoch tells a story about the legendary

figure, Enoch, walking with God in such a way that he was taken up to the eternal world where he saw the future and was commissioned to carry out the final divine work of purifying the world by bringing down evil kingdoms, empires, and powers and instituting the reign of God on earth.

Enoch is called the Son of Man in I Enoch, a title of great importance in the Judaism of that time. It implied that the power and authority of God was imputed to such a person. It is of great interest that Jesus later identified himself as the Son of Man, with such power and authority. Nonetheless, in the gospel of John, Jesus indicates that he does not intend to exercise that power and authority for judgment, as judge and prosecutor, but rather as savior, for saving the *world* (Jn 3:14–18, 5:27–47, 8:15–16, 12:47); "For God sent not his son into the world to condemn the world but that the world through him should be saved" (Jn 3:17).

Jesus obviously discerned that to walk with God meant to live life out of the constant realization that God had removed all human inadequacy, fear, guilt, and shame from the equation of our relationship with God. That is a divine act of grace. Grace means unconditional acceptance and forgiveness that is so radical that it gets around behind all these obstructions and all our psychospiritual resistance and defenses and declares a universal deliverance from them for everyone for evermore; deliverance from anything that would get in the way of our walking with God.

So Jesus, and apparently Enoch, knew that these defeating spiritual obstructions were wasted energy. They drained off the psychic and spiritual energy that God wants us to use for the growth and healing of our *psyche* and *pneuma* and in the pursuit of our psychospiritual quest for wholeness. To walk with God is to live life in continuing sensitivity to that radical grace of God, giving up our attachment to our fear, guilt, and shame and living free, as those unconditionally embraced by God, as we make our way through this perplexing world. It means that we should unconditionally accept God's unconditional forgiveness and acceptance of us.

There is a lot of talk throughout the Bible, as I hinted earlier, about walking this walk instead of just talking this talk. In Genesis 17:1 God enjoined Abraham, "Walk before me and be whole." Later Abraham told his chief of staff that the "God before whom I walk" would guide him in search of a wife for Isaac, Abraham's son (Gen. 24:40). Twenty-four chapters later Jacob, while blessing all his sons from his deathbed, said to Joseph, "The God before whom my fathers walked, Abraham and Isaac, and who led me all my life long to this day, bless your sons" (48:15–16). The notion of walking with God as a mode of living in the full awareness of the presence of God and of the nature of God's disposition of grace toward us pervades the Bible.

The Gospel of John repeatedly links this idea with walking in the light as opposed to stumbling around in darkness (11:9–10, 12:35). That metaphor is easy to figure out, is it not? It means the same thing to John as walking in the

truth—the truth about God's way of handling us in radical and freeing grace
(I Jn 1:7, III Jn 3–4). This is, of course, already an Old Testament idea, for it
is not only suggested by Micah 7:18–20. It is explicit in Hezekiah's prayerful
plea (Isa. 38:3), "Remember now, O Lord, I implore you, how I have walked
before you in faithfulness (truth) and with a whole (authentic) heart, and have
done what is good in your sight."

Paul speaks of this as walking in a renewed kind of life (Rom. 6:4), as walking by faith in communion with the unseen world to which William James
refers, and not merely walking by sight as we are generally inclined to do
(II Cor. 5:7). Paul calls it a matter of walking in the spirit (Gal. 5:25). For
Paul, walking by sight would be to sense in our inner selves only what we can
understand or comprehend with our rational minds. Walking by faith, however, is for Paul living in a deep sense of trust in the assurances of grace—
knowing that God is a God of unmitigated goodwill to us. Life is a win-win
enterprise for us all, because God is God and grace is grace. Holding that as
the healing experience of life is walking with God.

For Paul, walking in the spirit, walking in love, and walking in the light of
the Lord all seem to be the same thing: walking with God, that is, living life
with a sense of his presence and in the assurance of his grace (Eph. 5).

> Therefore be imitators of God, as beloved children. And walk in love, as
> Christ loved us and gave himself up for us, a fragrant offering and sacrifice
> to God....Let no one deceive you with empty words...Take no part in the
> unfruitful works of darkness, but instead expose them....Look carefully
> then, how you walk, not as unwise men but as wise, making the most of
> the time...be filled with the Spirit, addressing one another in psalms and
> hymns and spiritual songs, singing and making melody to the Lord with
> all your heart, always and for everything giving thanks in the name of our
> Lord Jesus Christ to God the Father.

This must be directly linked to Paul's notion of eternal life. His theology
of eternal life is not just life after death, but life on God's plane of experience starting as soon as we perceive the reality and relevance of God's radical
grace. That way of walking with God starts in the here and now and continues
through all eternity. Death is just a small transitional step across a threshold
into a new but continuous phase of life, as walking with God. Paul had a
dynamic, durable, and dramatic sense of what it means to walk with God.

CHAPTER 4

BIBLICAL SPIRITUALITY AS SEARCHING
FOR GOD

Such figures as Adam, Noah, and Enoch come to us from a very misty mythic past, as their stories unfold in the Bible. They represent long epochs of time and story by which the ancient Israelites tried to paint in the empty spaces in their historic narrative. The borrowed myths with which they filled the first 11 chapters of Genesis were attempts to complete the record from creation on down to the time that they had some historical data of their own. Their story really starts in Genesis 12 with the life of Abraham. He was the most important ancestor in the ancient Israelite story and religion. They thought that their distinctive national story started with him and thereby separated them from the rest of the nations of the world.

Scholars debate vigorously whether Abraham ever existed and whether his story is history or a prehistoric confessional myth. Some are sure that a man named Abraham existed and that his life's story fits the record in the Bible. Others think his story is merely mythic; sort of like that of Adam, Enoch, and Noah. For our purposes here, it makes no difference which is which. The Israelite sense of being a nation, with a special experience of walking with God and enjoying his promises of radical grace, begins psychospiritually, without question, with the story of Abraham.

It is interesting that the Bible does not make a point of representing Abraham as one who walked with God. In fact, the story of Abraham is a very human kind of story, full of iniquity, failure, deceit, and absurd ideas. Twice he told kings whom he was visiting that his wife was his sister, and he got into a lot of trouble for it. He did it because he was afraid the kings would kill him and take Sarah, because she was so beautiful. On another occasion, Abraham was absolutely sure that God told him to kill his son. His son, Isaac, was very special to him; but nonetheless he nearly carried out the dastardly deed before he got his head screwed back on straight—and he only stopped the killing because he thought he heard a voice from heaven stopping him. What a mixed-up guy he could be sometimes. Abraham had a lot of unusual intimations that he believed were from God, and, in the end, many of them really were.

We do not read that *he walked with God* in that consciously intense way described in the case of Enoch and Noah, or of which Paul and John speak so readily. Instead, the Bible emphasizes repeatedly that Abraham lived his whole adult life *searching for God*. Searching for God is also a way of life, seeking to experience a sustained sense of God's presence and of the meaning that comes with knowing the assurances and consolations of God's grace. Life was apparently that kind of a quest for Abraham, a quest to know what God is really like, and to know how to anticipate and discern when and in what way God can be present to a person.

The ancient Israelites remembered their patriarchal ancestors as wandering Aramaeans (Deut. 26:5). Aram was a country in northern Syria. In English translations of the Bible the passage that enshrines this memory usually uses the term Syria instead of Aram. Abraham came from Aram into Canaan. Before he lived in Aram the Bible tells us he came from a place further south in Mesopotamia called Ur of the Chaldeans. That was on the opposite side of the Fertile Crescent from Canaan or Palestine, which we know today as Israel. Ur and Aram were civilized Mesopotamian nations whose religious practices were polytheistic.

The Abraham story gives the distinct impression that Abraham was impatient with those unsatisfying religious traditions and sought something that rang more true to his psychospiritual hunger. Polytheism had little meaning for him apparently. Moreover, the gods of Mesopotamia tended, as did those of the Greeks, to behave with less moral character and decent generosity than did reasonably sensible human beings. It is no surprise that a really thoughtful man like Abraham looked for something better. It is highly likely that there were a number of other things about the cities of Chaldea and Aram that Abraham disliked.

When we consider the nature of Abraham's ultimate spiritual insight and illumination regarding the nature of God, we must draw the conclusion that he also left Ur because the gods of Mesopotamia were gods of threat. The Mesopotamians conceived of the gods as dangerous to humans, and those gods could not be counted on to be agents of goodwill. Abraham seems to have realized that any god who is a threat or is dangerously vengeful is a monster; and no one should worship or walk with such a god. He sought something better.

I imagine that, like Socrates, Abraham must have envisioned that any notion of God that is inferior to a halfway decent human being in moral character, rational judgment, honor, justice, or passionate good will cannot be real. Such a notion of God must be a mistake of human imagination or ideology. Abraham and Socrates were correct in that perspective, of course. Human beings did not ask to be created or to exist. We are all alive without our having had any choice in the matter. We do have some choice as to whether we stay alive, but even in that case there is something in our moral character that abhors self-extermination. Our survival instinct, like that of all other animals, incites us to cherish life, once we have it. But our existence is an arbitrary act of God, not of ourselves. Therefore, it is a reasonable expectation that any God worth his salt should treat us decently.

Moreover, the fact that humans, on our own, are inadequate to the responsibilities of life and the challenges of godliness is inherent to our nature, as God made it. Whether you take the fall story of Genesis literally, it is nonetheless the case that God created humans with the potential for flawed behavior, for mistaken choices—arising from our ignorance, fear, or bad will. Creating us with limited or flawed character is not something we thought up. God did. The real story, of course, is that the fall story is not a literal report, but a symbolic story of the process of the human race moving from infancy in the cradle of Eden, through the individuation of adolescent decision making to mature self-realization and responsible agency. It was not a fall down, but a fall up to maturity for the human race. That is the only sense in which that metaphoric old Mesopotamian fertility story makes any sense in its Hebrew formulation.

That is, the real story about human limitations, intellectually, psychological, socially, morally, and spiritually, is that we are incompletely evolved. The human organism, body, soul, psyche, and spirit, has evolved by means of God's incredibly wonderful evolutionary mode of creating this material world. We have come a long way in our development, but we are far from whole and complete. We are creatures with only human resources, and we are faced with a divine-sized responsibility to manage this material world wisely and search out God successfully. We did not choose this kind of destiny. God decided to fashion things this way. That is why Abraham left the Chaldeans and later Aram and tried to find a place where he could see through these things about God more clearly. He sought God in increasing solitude and living close to nature.

The remarkable thing about his quest, apparently, if we can judge from the end result, is that he found his spiritual insights about these things clarifying increasingly as he wandered along his life pilgrimage, always focusing on his search for the real God. He realized that any God who took the actual human predicament seriously and took responsibility for it within God's self had only two options. God had to be either unconditionally cherishing of flawed humans or God had to accept the fact that God is a reprehensible monster. God has no other choices. The driving force behind Abraham's spiritual search seems to have been, like that of Socrates and Jesus, the pursuit of clarity about that fact.

He seems to have longed for a life closer to nature, closer to the land, closer to the sun by day and the moon and stars by night. In his story he seems regularly to be contemplating, and meditating upon, those heavenly things. Perhaps he had the sense that being closer to creation and the agrarian world of nature would give him a chance to be closer to the creator. I suspect that he also felt that the further he got away from the cities, with their noise and pollution, the further he got away from their foolish notions about monstrous gods. Those messy centers of human habitation probably seemed to him to be corrupting all the things important to him: air, soil, tranquility, mental rationality, religious clarity, and spiritual quest.

I personally do not believe that being closer to nature is being closer to God. Nature is mean, and the first chance it gets it will bite you in sensitive places where you do not want to be bit. I was born on a farm in northern Michigan during the Great Depression. I know about nature firsthand, and I want as little to do with it as possible. I feel much closer to God in the refinements, conveniences, and comforts of a sophisticated modern city, where the division of labor is helpful and the best of human wisdom may be savored. But Abraham did not have exactly the same choices in that regard as I do today. Cities did not represent fresh water, good sewers, sanitary toilets, nice streets, fine restaurants, luxuriant grocery stores, and excellent institutions. In Abraham's day, cities could be a travail to negotiate and survive. You had to work hard to get to live on the northwest corner of the city so that the smoke of everybody's cooking fires and the stench of everybody's outhouses did not drive you out of your mind, as the steady currents of the west winds inevitably blew with each rotation of the planet earth. Try to keep a clear head in your search for God in a place like that: ancient Ur, Babylon, Nineveh, Damascus, or Haran!

In any case, Abraham set out for new horizons, not knowing just where he was going. Already at that early moment in his pilgrimage of life he is said to have had the sense that as he searched for the true and living God, he would be led into his true destiny. He went up from Ur of the Chaldeans to a new location in northwestern Aram (Syria) and stayed there for a while. However, he continued to hear the echoes of his spiritual quest ringing in his head. Increasingly it turned into a conviction that the God he was seeking was teasing him further out in his pilgrimage, so he left most of his family in the city of Haran, in the land of Aram, and with his flocks, herds, and household he became a wandering Aramaean in Canaan, Egypt, and Arabia. All the while he had this growing sense that he was experiencing more and more intensely the presence and assurances of the God whom his soul sought.

One day the full force of it exploded in his head. His persistent search bore fruit. He had an overwhelming intuition that God was revealing God's real divine nature to him. It was his sense that his growing awareness of what a real and worthy sort of God should be like was exactly what the one true and living God really is like. As though God spoke aloud to him, he heard the words, "I am God. I am almighty. Carry on your life pilgrimage with me and be honorable. I promise that you and your descendants will prosper and achieve great things, that I will be your God forever, unconditionally; and the nations of the earth shall be blessed because of you and your descendants" (Gen. 17 and 12). Wow! That was some outcome in a man's steady, sturdy search for a God that made every kind of good sense!

It was that insight of Abraham, that God is a God of unconditional and radical grace, that shaped the mainstream of spiritual insight throughout the rest of the history of the Israelite people and throughout the entire Bible. That insight, about God as the God of grace, is the form of spirituality that blossoms in many of David's Psalms, in the prophecy of Isaiah, in Micah 7:18–20, and in the gospels of Jesus and Paul in the New Testament. It is the cornerstone of who we are in Western Christendom today, even though many folks try to turn Christianity and Judaism back into a kind of pagan conditional grace. Gospel means good news. The message of the New Testament is called the gospel because it is the good news that Abraham perceived regarding God and that Paul saw. Paul understood this word from God, about God. He understood that it is a word, not only about *unconditional and radical* good news, but also about *universal* good news: God's unconditional goodwill, forgiveness, and acceptance for everyone, always, forevermore (Rom. 8).

Abraham is not alone in this kind of spirituality, which may best be called a search for God rather than walking with God. Moses' life was very similar in that he tried hard to figure out what was the right course for his personal life and what was his proper responsibility to his people and to God. When, in trying to figure that out, he ran into nothing but dead-end streets, he left his important government role in the highly civilized country of Egypt and resorted to living in the desert, close to nature, with quiet alien people. There his spiritual hunger led him into surprising insights about God. You could say that his first 80 years were nothing but a kind of desperate search for God, that is, for an understanding of and experience with God that would fill his spirit with meaning and gave him a clear-headed sense of his destiny.

For Moses, it all came together when his constant search led him to a special awareness of God's purposes in his life. He had this strong sense that God meant for him to deliver the Israelites from their oppressed existence under the heavy Egyptian boot. This message was as clear to him finally as if God has said it out loud to him. Perhaps God actually did. Moses saw a strange fire in the desert, and when he went to see what was up, he heard God say, "I am the God of Abraham. The Israelites are Abraham's children.

I have a special interest in them. Go and get them out of Egyptian oppression and take them to Canaan."

Well, that is pretty straightforward. Moses did it and it worked. There were a few glitches along the way, but the signal about biblical ideas of spirituality, epitomized by Moses' experience, is clear. Search for God until God comes to you. Then take that at face value and act on it. You may be a believer who needs to take all the elements of Moses' story literally—the burning bush, the voice of God, the encounter with Pharaoh, the ten plagues, the tablets from Mt. Sinai, and the like—or you may understand all those things as I tend to, as metaphoric descriptions of the meanings and perceptions of God's presence to Moses and the Israelites. It makes little difference what Moses actually experienced, formally. What counts is what he experienced spiritually, that is, what all this meant to him in terms of the fulfillment of his spiritual hunger and the wholeness he felt because of his search for God, and his finding God to be real and full of grace for him.

Moses probably heard God's voice from the burning bush, as Abraham apparently did as he gazed at the moon and stars on a crisp clear desert night in Palestine a thousand years or so earlier. I believe in those kinds of experiences. I could tell you of at least a dozen such experiences in my own life, that is, experiences in which major turning points were caused in my spiritual pilgrimage by events that cannot be accounted for except as paranormal, parapsychological, ethereal, or divine events. I believe that the world is filled with the Holy Spirit of God and that we can encounter and experience that divine spirit readily.

One of my own important spiritual experiences is particularly illustrative of why I am completely open to the special encounter with God described in the story of Abraham in his quest and Moses at the burning bush. I am not a Fundamentalist Evangelical, and I do not believe that the Bible is verbally inspired and inerrant, or some type of magical book, as some of my fellow Christians do. However, I do believe that if we shape our lives as a walk with God or a search for God, we do experience God as gratifyingly as we experience a good meal and a nice glass of wine at a good table. I believe the biblical characters lived in the same kind of spiritual world, in that regard, as we do. That is why I believe that the Bible is full of the word of God, that is, the testimony of those biblical people regarding how they experienced God in their lives. Much of the time they were accurate in their discernment. Sometimes they were very inaccurate and even pathological in what they thought was God's presence to them. It is easy to tell the difference, because those experiences that help and heal human life are surely of God, and those that fail to do so surely are not. To believe that God is telling you to kill your son is obviously crazy. To believe that God so loves the world that he intends to save the whole thing, as John and Paul thought, and not to condemn it is obviously of God (Jn 3:16–17; I Cor.15:22, Rom. 5:15–18).

There was a time in my life when I was going through a particularly trying ordeal. I was supporting my family on a minister's modest salary. I had five children in college, my wife in graduate school, and a sixth child in a private Catholic high school. I was beginning to publish an occasional article and had written a couple of books that did not hit the *New York Times* bestseller list. An elder in my congregation charged that I was preaching and teaching heresy because I thought that God intended to save all human beings into blessed eternal life. The charge of heresy moved up the ecclesiastical ladder and I was condemned on four or five counts by the national Synod.

Now, I am a rather settled and stable guy, psychologically, and not overly neurotic. However, the charge and condemnation of heresy gave me a great deal of distress since it appeared that I would lose my ordination to the Christian ministry Therefore, I would lose my livelihood and would, then, be unable to support my family. My wife and children would need to drop out of their educational pursuits. Of course, I would be dishonored in my family and denomination, and most importantly, I would lose my opportunity to exercise my life-calling in ministry.

Consequently, as you can imagine, I found myself in considerable distress and quite unable to sleep soundly at night. At the height of this crisis, in a night of intense worry and restlessness, I lay awake in my bed, trying to reflect, strategize, and pray. At about midnight I fell into a profoundly deep sleep. Suddenly at 2:00 A.M. I was awakened by a plainly audible voice, which rang through the dark room, saying, "Trust in the Lord and do good." I sat bolt upright in bed, tried to get my bearings, and then realized I had been awakened by what was apparently an audible theophany.

The event did not seem unusual or otherworldly to me at the time. My first thought was that the message sounded like a line from the Bible. As a child I was required to memorize about 250 fairly lengthy scripture passages in order to qualify for graduation from the eighth grade at the Christian school I attended. So I have a wonderful memory bank of biblical quotations that I can recall at will. That has proven to be a treasure trove in my mind, and very useful in my work. However, I was sure the message of that dark night was not a passage I had memorized. Where did it come from? I went downstairs to my study and picked up my *Thompson Chain Reference Bible.* I found that line of scripture in the King James Version of Psalm 37:3. That Psalm is not a particularly interesting Psalm, since it is one of those in which David is rather hostile toward his enemies, so it would not have been selected for Christian memorization; but there in the third verse is the wonderful line: "Trust in the Lord and do good!" How did it get into my head in the middle of the night?

Well, there are a number of things we can say about that. First, my father read the Bible, a chapter at a meal, from cover to cover, repeatedly during my childhood—every time we sat down to eat. Sixteen years of listening to him read the Bible through and through means that I probably heard the whole thing at least 10 times before I went off to college at 16. Psalm 37 would have been repeated in my hearing on every one of those trips through the whole Bible. You could say, therefore, that the voice and the message came that night out of my memory bank, prompted by my intense distress.

Or you could say that God somehow spoke out loud in that room that night. I suppose you could also explain the event as some divine emissary visiting me in my special need. Remember that I mentioned above that this was one of 10 or 12 such illuminations I have experienced during my lifetime—since the age of five. If you knew me, you would think that I am the last guy to be playing around the edges of psychotic ideation. My problems would be on the other end of the psychological continuum. I am more likely to be too rational, empirical, pragmatic, and resistant to anything paranormal. I am a child of the Enlightenment, and by nature a Foundationalist, though I have learned that both of those postures have enormous flaws, and consequently I have had to adjust my perspectives over the years and be more appreciative of the suggestions of postmodernism.

So what kind of a spiritual experience is that sort of audible theophony? I call it a theophony because I experienced it as an audible sound from God. I must tell you that from the minute I heard those words, "Trust in the Lord and do good!" my distress about my life situation, the heresy charges and trial, completely dissipated and never returned. I felt completely free of any further anguish over the matter. The heresy trial had lasted for three years, during which I was never given a chance to intervene or defend myself. I never got to lift a finger on my own behalf. I suppose that was part of what heightened my anguish. However, from the moment of the theophony I gave the whole matter up—and miracle of miracles, over the next 12 months a sequence of events unfolded, quite without my doing anything. Those events led the national synod to conclude that the matter had come before it erroneously. So I was vindicated on a church-polity technicality. All that I feared disappeared by itself, so to speak.

So the data is plain. I was in intense anguish in my spiritual quest for understanding God's leading in my life. In my desperation I heard a voice loud enough to awaken me. Its counsel resolved my travail and set me on a newly illumined course of life and ministry. The way before me was opened and cleared for my work and my quest for transcendent meaning. So what happened?

In my own inner spirit I have a deep sense that what happened to me is very much like what happened to Abraham and Moses. In the intensity of their quests they received illumination and guidance for life and spirit. Whether, in their cases or mine, the message from God was literally a voice from the transcendent world or a spontaneous illumination from our own minds and psyches makes not the slightest bit of difference. In both cases it is the same thing: a word from God. The difference is merely the method and tool God used. It was, in either case, a word from God that changed life in a profoundly constructive way. That is the empirical issue that counts as the truth here.

Was the "miracle" in these cases in the fact that God reached through the normal barriers between our tangible world and God's apparently ethereal world? Or was the "miracle" some accumulated critical mass of unconsciously remembered cognitive information or mysterious psychological process that our human brains, psyches, or spirits produced to illumine us with what seemed like an audible voice? I cannot tell, but it makes no difference. It is the same act of God either way.

The nature of the theophany, the content of the message, and the exquisite timing of the events are the "miracle" that changed our lives: mine, Moses', and Abraham's. Three persons, in intense lifelong pursuit of our irrepressible spiritual quest, experienced God's visitation, and our lives were illumined and constructively changed. Moreover, the process seemed to all of us that it was exactly what we hungered for and that it was from God. There is no doubt about it. It can be accounted for in no other way. God is closer in our daily lives than we usually tend to think.

Of course, Abraham, Moses, and I are not alone or special or unique in this. It is *potentially* the experience of everyone, and it is the *actual* experience of most people who pursue their psychospiritual quest profoundly. Moments of divine illumination are common, not uncommon, and are readily distinguishable from psychopathological ideations in that they produce markedly constructive outcomes in the lives of the persons who experience them.

Many such moments of flowering in the spiritual quest are less dramatic than those I have described above. Joshua is described in the Bible as a spiritually conscious Israelite general officer, who felt strongly that the course of his life was guided by a clearly evident divine providence. He was second in command to Moses as long as Moses lived. Thereafter, Joshua was the man in charge of the Israelite nation. With conscious intentionality he tried to discern the spiritually authentic course for his leadership and life.

This led him, over time, to believe that he could discern the will of God for him. At a time of crisis in the Israelite nation he boldly announced to his fellow Israelites, "Choose today for whom and along what spiritual trajectory you wish to live your lives. As for me and my house, we will serve God" (Josh. 24:15). Such an uncompromising posture over against a national rebellion was possible for him, against all opponents, because he too had had a significant moment of illumination. At the outset of his assumption of command, Joshua had some anxiety about his capacity and responsibility as national leader. In this intense psychospiritual moment his long-standing spiritual pursuit of God's way for and with him paid off. At that time he discerned an intimation from God clarifying things for him. He sensed the divine message, "Be strong and of good courage; do not be afraid or dismayed, for God is with you wherever you go" (Josh. 1:9b). The message was not a surprise, I am sure. He had been living his life under that assumption for a long time. It is just that at this critical moment it became a vivid consciousness to him. That is how God works, responding to our lifelong search for God. That is what happened to me, I think. Moses, Abraham, and I humbly and gratefully acknowledge it.

When one spends his or her life on that search, he or she will experience such illuminations at the moments they are really needed. It is happening all the time and there is an enormous record of empirical evidence and warrantable testimony that this has always happened for persons since human life began. This kind of spirituality, as a lifelong and ultimately fruitful search for God, is both a common biblical phenomenon and a frequent human experience in our own time. Living every day in that kind of spirituality, that is, always crowding consciously as close to the quest for God's presence as one can discern how, is like sailing a sailboat as close to the wind as possible. Sailors will understand my metaphor. You cannot see the wind. Sometimes you cannot even tell exactly from which direction it is blowing. However, you can feel a gentle tugging or a strong force. Usually to make progress in your quest it is important to sail as "close to the wind" as possible. Then you periodically are surprised by the great gains you experience in your journey's progress.

A lot of people spend much of their lives simply "running before the wind." They have no clear sense of where they are really going. They are glad the sailing is no more difficult than it is. They do not know that the wind before which they are running is, nonetheless, the providence of God and the flow of time, of life, and of the spirit. Then something happens in life and they are forced to realize that they are a long way from home, spiritually, psychologically, emotionally, and in their social relationships. Their lives do not feel authentic or meaningful to them. Then they must figure out how to turn around and learn how to sail close to the wind so they can find and return to their true home: their authentic psychospiritual meaningfulness. They need to regain a sense of fullness with the presence of God.

The biblical prophets, Isaiah and Jeremiah, were men with lives like that. Their sense of God's constant presence was so intense that they thought most of their good ideas were inspired by the intimations of God's spirit in their own spirits. There seems to be good reason to take them at their word. They spoke prophetic words, and their words ultimately proved to be authentic, a sign of a true prophet, I suppose. We associate their names with three long sections in the Old Testament: the books of Isaiah, Jeremiah, and

Lamentations. Scholars generally agree that of the 66 chapters in Isaiah's long book, at least 39 came from his hand or at least from his heart.

In one of the watershed sections of his book, Isaiah described a moment of illumination that he thought was a visual theophany (Isa. 6). He saw God in an exalted and majestic scene one Sabbath Day as he was at a rather routine worship service. The liturgy, sermon, and litanies were apparently not particularly interesting. Isaiah does not mention them at all, and he was busy thinking about other things. Nonetheless, he had the sense that God filled the entire worship space. This scared the living daylights out of him and he felt unworthy to stand before God. Then he heard a voice, in the room or in his head, declaring that he was OK as the flawed human that he was, and that God had a mission for him to carry out. He quickly agreed that he would do it. That put his life on its permanently constructive track.

Authentic spirituality often takes that form. When I was five years old I was severely traumatized by helplessly watching as my dearest little five year old girlfriend, Esther Van Houten, burned to death. We lived on a remote farm in northern Michigan in the middle of the Great Depression. Within six months, five other children close to me died of various diseases; two of them were my siblings. A black pall settled over me as I struggled with how God could be in any way related to such disasters. The darkness did not lift until I was seven. Then one bright summer day, as I stepped out of the horse barn into the beautiful sunlight, I had a life-changing sense of the meaning of things. It suddenly seemed to me as clear as the sunlight that what I could do with my life was to spend it trying to help people through the intense suffering I thought I saw everywhere in that primitive farm community of Dutch and German immigrants, who were eking out a meager existence in those economically restricted days.

The only person in the community who seemed to me, at that time, to stand somewhat above the travail of our people, and who had the ability to actually help people somewhat, was the dignified and highly effective pastor. It therefore seemed wholly clear to me that my calling of God was into ministry, to the neediest of humankind. It was a straight line from that moment to my graduation from college and seminary, my years as an army chaplain, the decades of my role as a pastor, theologian, and professor, and my training and work as a psychologist. That line is straight to the writing of this chapter. I have never known any distraction from this lifelong pursuit, all the way to this very moment when I am telling you my story as illustration of how God responds to the spiritual quest of an ordinary human being. I am sure that is how Isaiah felt. I am also sure that his theophany need not have been any more magical than my own, and those that overtake humans all the time: persons who from psychospiritual hunger are searching for the ways of God in their lives.

The same might be said, I suppose, of Samuel, David, Hosea, Amos, and of such early prophets as Micah, from whom we have already heard, above. Samuel was the son of an intensely God-oriented mother. The intensity of her spirituality, prayer, and devotion to worship made her minister think she was drunk or really mentally disturbed. She might have been. She wanted a child so badly that she was desperate in her search for how God was in her life and how God could influence things so she could get pregnant. Her husband was as enthusiastic about the idea as she was. Well, finally, after a life of spiritual quest, it worked. She brought forth Samuel and immediately declared that he was dedicated to ministry.

Well, if that is not enough to make a kid neurotic and confused, her next move surely was. Practically before he could get off to elementary school she brought him to the minister and left him there to be trained in ministry. The minister was old and not a very good teacher, and a really rotten example. His own two kids were hell-raisers. However, Samuel seems to have come along in a rather balanced way and made more sense, early on, than a lot of the adults around him. I think it was because he took his mother's spirituality at face value and undertook the same psychospiritual quest himself. That is, he tried hard to sail his boat close to the wind, and occasionally he was surprised by the progress and spiritual gains he got from doing so.

When he was still quite young he had an experience a little like that of Isaiah. He was awakened out of a sound sleep by a voice calling him. He thought it was the minister who slept in another bedroom. However, when he went to the fellow to answer the call, the minister knew nothing of it. When this call was repeated a number of times in a row that night, instead of getting disturbed by it, the minister discerned that Samuel was having a significant psychospiritual experience—something that would probably definitively shape his life. He suggested to him that it might be God calling him, so Samuel should respond, "Speak, God, I am listening."

So he did that the next time he heard the call, and in response he received the illumination as to what he should do with his life. He became a very influential prophet in the spiritual development of Israelite life and religion, the best thing that had happened to the Israelites for a long time. He lived a long time and set the people on their constructive path as a nation among the nations of the Middle East. He even provided them with a king. This led to the enormously prosperous reigns of Saul, David, and Solomon. You could even say that it led indirectly to the establishment of the Jesus Movement a thousand years later.

Likewise, David, as a shepherd, apparently spent much of his time alone on the hills of Judea watching his father's sheep. He apparently sat there, day after day and night after night, thinking about the heavenly lights and the wonder of this created world. In the process he was led to an intensely spiritual contemplation of God. His spiritual journey is described in

surprising detail in the psalms he wrote. In Psalm 19 he declares poetically, "The heavens speak loudly of the glory of God. The sky demonstrates
clearly God's creative skill. Each day shouts to the next the incredible truth
about God; and each night informs us of remarkable knowledge about God's
thoughts. Though there are no words exchanged in the process, the voice
of creation is loud, and can be heard by anyone listening, throughout the
earth—indeed, even to the ends of the universes" (JHE trans). What a finely
tuned spiritual perception about everyday reality all around us! What a
poetic way of saying it.

In Psalm 32 David got closer to the spiritual bone, so to speak. There
he writes of his worry about being a godly person. He says, "That person is
truly happy who knows God's forgiveness and has no worry about his failures. A person whom God does not hold guilty for anything has an especially
tranquil and meaningful life, especially if he or she is also of genuine and
authentic spirit" (JHE trans). This is followed by autobiographical remarks
about his spiritual quest. David says that when he felt guilty or ashamed and
swallowed it all down inside, it devastated him psychologically and physi-
cally, and eventually it affected his biological health. However, when he gave
it up to God, trusting God's unconditional, radical, and universal grace, he
was cured of bodily distress and spiritual confusion. Well, that is how it is, in
the psychospiritual quest for God and the meaning that comes from sensing
God's presence in our lives.

There was a time when David was less than candid with himself and with
God; that is, he was less than genuine and authentic in his own spirituality.
He stole another man's wife and had the guy murdered to clean up his mess.
He was not in an authentic mode, and he tried to repress his consciousness
of it. That is when another man of spiritual integrity and intensity discerned
an illumination from God. Nathan, a prophet, had the distinct sense that he
had to go to David and call his attention to the dastardly things he had done
and get the mess cleared up. Without some straight talk from God, through
Nathan, apparently, David could not experience forgiveness, direction, relief,
and restoration to a meaningful life in leading the nation. So Nathan went to
David and said, in effect, "There is some rich guy in your kingdom who stole
a poor man's lamb to slaughter for a feast for his friends." David said, "Hang
him." Nathan said, "You are that guy." That is when David wrote Psalm 51, I
think, and perhaps later, Psalm 32.

In Psalm 51 David says this about his confused and anguished spiritual
quest, "God, have mercy. I need your steadfast love. Blot out my failures.
Wash me clean with your forgiveness. Clean my spirit. Restore to me the
joyfulness of my authentic search for you, God. Clean up my mess, as I am
now laying it all on the table before you" (JHE paraphrase). He had heard of
the insight of Abraham, quite obviously, and that is the unconditional grace
he realized characterized the authentic experience of the presence of God.

Hosea, the prophet, is even more remarkable in his realization that discernment of the truth of that divine grace is the centrally authentic thing about the human search for God and walk with God. Hosea thought of it this way. He was passionate about the wretched neediness of humankind, and he realized the tremendous possibilities for good that were available to all who undertook the authentic psychospiritual search. As a result he felt strongly led of God to try to salvage a woman lost in prostitution. So he found one and married her. He tried to surround her with the care and love a good woman should have. However, she repeatedly ran off and reverted to her old ways. Each time he took her back and cherished her in true love and care. Things got infinitely more difficult when she became pregnant with someone else's child. Hosea was really angry and named the child with a Hebrew word that meant *Punishment.* It happened again, however, and a third time. Hosea continued to love, care for, and cherish the woman and her children, but his disgust is evident in the names he gave the children: *No Pity* and *Not Mine.*

Then his real illumination came to him. He knew the insight he received could only be from God. He saw, in his struggle to care for this woman and her children, a metaphor of God's struggle to care for flawed humans. Once that insight hit him, he had an entirely new perspective on things. He realized that those children did not ask for the terrible destiny the names he gave them imposed upon them. So he renamed them with good names. He realized that if it seems sometimes, in some situations, that it should be said of the human race, "You act like children of the devil," that is exactly the moment and place that God says, in effect, "Children of the living God" (Hos 1:10). Now that is quite an amazing spiritual insight. We know it is of God, because it is the only thing that works in human life to change things and set us on a constructive path through the thickets of life's psychospiritual complications and perplexities. Moreover, it is not the kind of idea humans, by nature, create. Such grace is divine!

So where do those kinds of insights and illuminations come from? How does God do that to us and for us? Or are those just conjured up out of our own imagination and good sense? Does it make a difference which is which? Of course not! Either way it is a constructive transcendental illumination that enhances our psychospiritual life enormously.

In my student days the professor at Calvin College who was most highly revered by progressive thinkers, and most intensely discounted by the Fundamentalist Evangelicals, was a brilliant philosopher named Harry Jellema. I visited him decades later, in his advanced old age, and had a long afternoon's conversation about philosophy. In the process of our discussion I observed that he had always been known particularly for his profound and innovative ideas. He acknowledged that and then asked with some mystification, "Where do you think those creative ideas come from? I did not learn them from my teachers or read them in books. They really were largely new and innovative." He paused briefly at that point, and then continued, "Over my lifetime I have increasingly come to the conviction that they are given us from the Holy Spirit." I agree, and my personal experience is that one must sail his or her boat quite close to the wind to hear the divine whisper, that is, to perceive the intimations that really count.

CHAPTER 5

BIBLICAL SPIRITUALITY AS CELEBRATING GOD: WORSHIP

Many of the biblical characters spent considerable amounts of time celebrating God. David surely is the most obvious one. He wrote many songs of praise about God, which we call the Psalms of David. He also commissioned musicians in his court and in the temple to write many more. He seems to have been a very creative musician himself, playing the harp, writing litanies and songs for the Sabbath worship, dancing in worship on a number of occasions just for the psychospiritual fun of it, and generally making a very aesthetic thing out of his spiritual life and quest. He wrote some pretty nasty poems against his enemies, and even a number of laments or complaints against God, but then he had some real things to complain about and be depressed about, as all of us do. However, most of the time he was fairly upbeat in his psychospiritual quest for God.

David saw God present in a lot of places in his life. He was sure he saw the signature of God in creation (Ps. 19), in the way his own body was fashioned in the womb (Ps. 22, 71, 127, 139), in the special characteristics of his psyche and spirituality (Ps. 32, 51), and in the providential way the pattern of life unfolds for humankind (Ps. 33, 34, 37, 136; please refer to the Psalms at the end of this chapter). From the time he was a young shepherd boy, David seems to have been a celebrator of God's nature and presence, as he sought and sensed it in his life. He trusted in God to care providentially for him and for his sheep. Psalm 136 recalls the history of the Israelite people, as David had been taught it, and that celebrative psalm repeats 26 times, "God's steadfast love endures forever." You can practically hear the Israelite choir singing it, and thereafter the congregation shouting in unison, "Praise be to God!"

In Psalm 23 he says quite clearly that he saw his work as a shepherd to be a metaphor of God's care for him. That means that he was a sensitive and thoughtful child, with a creative capacity for symbolic associations of ideas and experience. His meaningful interpretation of life as he lived it arose from his impression that God was present to him in a rather tangible way all the time. "The Lord is my shepherd; I shall not hunger or thirst; he gives me green pastures of nutrition and tranquil places to drink; he refreshes me to the center of my being," he said (JHE trans). So we know he had a deep sense of the goodwill and providential care and guidance that he believed God provided in his life.

Once his sheep were beset by a lion, and he confidently killed the critter. We are not sure how he did that. He probably did not catch it in his bare hands and tear it apart as Samson is said to have done (Judg. 14:5–6).[1] We know David was good with a slingshot, so he probably knocked the lion out with a slung stone and then put a knife to him. That is the way any good farm boy in my childhood would have done it, if beset by any ravaging coyote, badger, or wild dog in rural northern Michigan. David thought that God had given him both the courage and the skill to kill that lion.

In any case, it surely is times like that, ringing in the back of his head, that prompted him to express his trust in God in these poetic words: "Even if I am walking in the dark valley where death is lurking, I will fear no evil. You are with me" (JHE trans). Because he believed that was the way life is wired, so to speak, he was confident that the good things of God's provident guidance and care, and God's unconditional grace and mercy, would be the matrix of his existence forever. No wonder he wrote hundreds of psalms of praise to God. No wonder he was a celebrator of God as he sought after God, experienced God, and counted on God being palpably present to him day by day.

Now, of course, personal spirituality does not develop in a vacuum. We are not just isolated persons working out our spiritual quest all alone and on our own. No human being is spiritually that autonomous. We are usually members of a family, of a community, and of a history. David's family was apparently a godly family, at least in the sense that they were genuinely interested in what God is like and how God is involved in history and was present in their own family history and life. David's kind of piety, or psychospiritual quest, and the sensitivity and awareness with which he pursued it, usually is the product of a culture of spiritual quest and religious practice.

It is not accidental that when the prophet Samuel looked for a family in which to find a good person who could be counted on to be a godly king over Israel, he came to David's father's household. Such a candidate would be sought in a family with a long-standing reputation for both wisdom and godliness: God's kind of people, so to speak. There were, undoubtedly, generations of ancestors in David's family, of whom he was consciously aware, who had been busy with serious psychospiritual quests long before him. That is, David had the language of the spirit in his bones, as it were. He had good tutoring about how to look for and perceive God in nature and in God's manifestations of grace and providence in human life.

We are all born with a sense of spirituality, of hunger for the ideal, for the transcendent, for God. We learn what that means and how to handle that as we grow. We are particularly fortunate if we grow up in a family and community that know how to process that quest. Apparently David did. So David was able to borrow or absorb the language of the spirit from his community and the spiritual culture it had created. It does not take an overt decision to take all that in. It seeps into our inner selves as we develop psychospiritually. As this happens, the language of our community's spiritual culture defines our inner selves, stimulating our spiritual hunger, shaping nature, and channeling the direction of our spiritual quest.

As all this is taking place, the religious practices we are walked through as children, participating in our family's and our community's religious life, confirm, form, and inform our spirituality and our religion. Our spirituality and our religious behaviors or rituals are interactive, as indicated in the introduction to this book. Our inborn spiritual natures, given a spiritual language by our families or communities of faith, are certified as real and important. Formed and informed by that language, by the accrued experiences of our personal quests, and by the patterns and practices of our religious rituals, we are progressively shaped and defined in our spirituality. In that way we come to know what the fulfillment of our psychospiritual quests ultimately means.

As a celebrator of God's nature and presence in his personal life, David was a product of a substantial spiritual heritage. Many of his songs celebrate that very fact. He was conscious of all those who had gone before him in this journey of inquiring after God, as it were. He tended to thank God for this heritage, and he perceived that his personal experience of God rang true to it, and perhaps even went beyond it in the clarity of his insight and ability to express it.

David was probably aware, for example, of others who had written songs that celebrated how they thought about God, thought they experienced God, and understood the ways in which God is present to us in daily life and in worship events. Moses wrote a number of famous songs. We have one of those in the form of a psalm (Ps. 90) and it is remarkable for both its poetic form and its profound content. That song starts out celebrating the evidence in nature of the clever creativity of its creator and then goes on to take account of the remarkable providence by which God cares for the human race throughout the eons of its history. It continues with a celebration of the various evidences of God's power as humans can experience it, and it closes with a prayer for God's perpetual favor to prosper us all. A few verses are worth quoting here.

Lord, thou hast been our dwelling place in all generations,
Before the mountains were brought forth
Or ever thou hadst formed the earth and the world,
Even from everlasting to everlasting thou art God

Let thy work be manifest to thy servants,
And thy glorious power to their children.
Let the favor of the Lord our God be upon us,
And establish thou the work of our hands upon us.
Yea, the work of our hands, establish thou it. (RSV)

However, Moses' most famous celebration is in Deuteronomy 32:1–43. That is called the Song of Moses. It is a long celebration of his own psychospiritual pilgrimage and that of the people of Israel, whom he led out of Egypt. In it he recounts all the ways he thought he had directly experienced the presence and behavior of God with him, and all the events in which the Israelites should have been able to see the presence of God in their lives, if they were authentically searching for God, desiring to walk with God. Moses makes it clear that his sense of spirituality is such that he is sure, if a person or community experiences the presence or providence of God in life, that it will affect the style with which that person or community will carry itself before the face of God. God does not need to lay heavy moral or ethical regulations upon us. If we are experiencing the presence and spirit of God in our spirits, we will lay appropriate claims upon ourselves regarding how we ought to carry ourselves in relationship with God. Taking account of the history of our spiritual quests is a way of understanding our own spirituality better. When we look back on the way our lives have been led out in God's providence and grace, it is much easier to see God's presence than it is at the time we are experiencing it. During my 75 years of psychospiritual quest, the things I thought were the most important things in my life, that I would have pushed and shoved into place with might and main, if I could have, proved in the long run to be irrelevant. The events that I thought God should have averted and from which God should have protected me, if God really knew what he or she was doing, proved to be the hinges of my destiny. These realities are hard to see at the time. They can be seen with much more clarity in retrospect.

Moses had a sister, and she had a song. She was a celebrator of God. Miriam sang a song of joy that has become truly famous, and for a very good reason. First, it is a really fine song of praise to God for a benefit she was sure God had provided to the ancient Israelites. Second, it celebrates the successful traverse of the Red (Reed) Sea by Miriam's people, in their escape from oppression in Egypt (Exod. 15:1–18). When Miriam began to sing, the whole congregation joined in, recounting their perception of God's surprising presence to them in an unusual kind of deliverance from danger.

Those are things in life to celebrate, and it is a good thing to savor the flavor of the transcendent nature of such an event, as well as celebrating the simple scientific cause and effect processes we can figure out in a merely horizontal view of it. If we only see the horizontal, we miss all the meaning, and that leaves us without the potential for psychospiritual growth from it. Here are brief excerpts of the best parts of Miriam's Song.

> I will sing to the Lord, for he has triumphed gloriously;
> The Lord is my strength and my song,
> And he has become my salvation.
> This is my God, and I will praise him,
> My father's God, and I will exalt him.
> Who is like thee, O Lord, majestic in holiness,
> Awesome in glorious deeds, doing wonders.
> You have led us in your steadfast love.
> You will bring us into destiny,
> Fulfilling our quest in spiritual sanctuary,
> Establishing us in your intended place for us!
> God will always be God.
> (JHE trans)

One of the special moments in the New Testament that reminds us of Miriam's Song is Mary's Magnificat (Lk. 1:46–55). It is called the Magnificat because of the opening words, "My soul magnifies the Lord, and my spirit rejoices in God." In Latin, the language into which the Bible was translated by St. Jerome in the fourth century and that was used in the Roman Catholic Church for 1,500 years, the first word is Magnificat. That means, "It (my soul) magnifies or praises." Thus, "Mary's Magnificat."

In this song Mary tells the story of her most important spiritual experience. It was a moment of awareness of the presence of God in her life. That was when she realized she was going to be or already was pregnant. She saw the pregnancy as a remarkable gift of God. I am not surprised. I must say that when each of my seven children was conceived it seemed to me at that moment as though God was specifically expressing a focused intention that a life should be created right then. Of course, that will make anyone laugh reading this. It makes me laugh as I think about and write it. If you are not laughing there is something wrong with you or you have never experienced an orgasm. The trouble with being an atheist, or someone not on a profound spiritual quest, is the fact that you have no one to call out to when you are having an orgasm.

However, what I am trying to say here is that on those seven occasions my experience was not just another experience of love making, or intercourse, or orgasm. I had the conscious sense that there was some divine intentionality in that specific moment and event, and I guess I was correct. A magnificent child was conceived every time, each of whom has now become a magnificent adult. I am telling you, I could write seven Magnificats. Mary saw her event as so paradigmatic that she perceived it as a metaphor for the kind of goodness God adds to human life all the time. She was sure that with her pregnancy God had given humanity a good gift that would have universal and permanent value for us. Well, her perception was pretty close to the truth!

Some of us experience our spiritual fulfillment not so much as walking with God or as searching for God, but as celebrating God. I guess that if you are busy with the first two, your spiritual meaningfulness will eventually lead you to the third. Like Mary, when you set your sail close to the wind of God's spirit, you gain more than you expect or can imagine. Listen to the musical excerpts from the Magnificat.

> I magnify God from my deep inner self.
> My spirit is overflowing with joyfulness about God.
> *He* has noticed *me* and come to *me*.
> Everyone who ever realizes this will understand how happy I am.
> Obviously, he responds to our spiritual hunger and fills it.
> This is exactly what he promised to our ancestor Abraham so long ago,
> God's grace is forevermore!
> (JHE trans)

Most people do not realize that Jesus once sang a song. The Bible does not explain it quite like that, so you are probably surprised to think of it in this way; but I like to think that he sang it and intends us to sing it too. In Matthew 11 he gave us his song. It is right in the middle of a rather long sermon that could put you to sleep if you are a little boy in a Dutch Reformed worship service in a hot stuffy church in rural Michigan in the 1930s. Long sermons were common, and the benefit was that they put the restless little kids to sleep. But this song, in the middle of Jesus' long sermon, could wake up an adult, because it is a startling celebration of a special characteristic of God that Jesus apparently was surprised to experience.

In Matthew 11:25, he lifted his eyes to heaven and celebrated, "I am thankful to you, father, lord of heaven and earth, that you have hidden your spiritual illuminations from the smart alecks and wiseacres of this world and have intimated them instead to the trusting, seeking, searching souls who come to you like hungry children to Mickey D's" (JHE paraphrase). Do you agree with me that here we have Jesus' song of praise to God, as he experienced God, and as he experienced the nature of our psychospiritual longing and quest for the transcendent?

It is interesting, is it not, that all of these celebrations of God in the Bible are full of trust, gratitude, joy, optimism, and a secure sense of God's providence and unconditional grace. There are forms of spiritual expression that are not such positive songs or litanies. Much worship and spiritual expression I see around today, and discern from church history, is focused instead upon wringing our hands and hearts in fear, guilt, and shame. Others are filled with complaints to God or against God, or obsessive attempts to placate God or prove ourselves worthy of his goodness and grace, or legalistic ideas of how to be perfect before God. These forms of celebration, religious ritual, theological ideas, or spiritual style are sick. They all imply a conception of God as a threat, a danger, an ogre, or a monster whose main interest in us is to shape us up or beat us into line. I do not know who such folk think they are worshipping or seeking or celebrating. It is not the true and living God whom any one of us can experience if we set our sail confidently close to the wind of life for a lifetime and wait on God to open to us the psychospiritual gains he intends for us.

Many Israelites realized *that* already in the earliest days of ancient Israelite religion. Quite obviously Abraham, Moses, David, and all those ancient celebrators of God perceived the truth about this. The Israelites who were paying attention, with sensitive spiritual quest, got a lot help in this from their religious traditions. They knew very well the report of Abraham's incredible intimations about God's unconditional and radical grace. They sometimes thought it was only for them and not a universal grace of God, but sometimes, as in Solomon's prayer at the dedication of the temple (I Kgs 8:41–43, II Chron. 6:32–33), and in some of David's psalms, the light of God's universal grace shines through.

Moreover, they had a notion that one of the most important things that worship contributed to life was the opportunity to act out how you felt about God. That is still the reason for worship rituals. They took the grace-promises to Abraham at face value and believed these were the gift that God had given to humanity, to eliminate all fear, guilt, and shame from the equation of our relationship to God. Therefore, worship for them was the opportunity to express to God their gratitude for that arrangement. So they brought the first fruits and the best products from their flocks, fields, and herds as gifts to God, to be used in support of the ministry and the ministers.

Later this system turned sour. They forgot the unconditional grace nature of the vision of Abraham and they began to think that their sacrifices were payment for their sins. That was a really erroneous set of theological notions. However, you can run into a lot of Jews, Christians, and Muslims down to this very day who are doing the same thing. If in our spiritual quest we miss the point of grace, we inevitably end up in the ridiculous place of alienation from our quest for God or we turn into legalistic people who think the spiritual quest is a way of trying to be perfect so we can earn God's goodwill toward us. That is a very bad joke.

Celebrating God in terms of the experiences we have is a valuable form of spirituality. The Bible is full of that kind of spirituality. Those experiences may be events or discernments in which we believe we can see God present to us in tangible ways. Those palpable experiences may be perceptions that the way life has unfolded has within it a golden thread of guidance that is best accounted for by realizing that it is the shepherding of God's providence in the way events have developed. Tangible experiences of God may be special moments of blessing, goodness, healing, or protection.

On the other hand, those experiences may not be any more pronounced than a deep inner sense of the meaningfulness and tranquility of life in spite of its generally challenging and often harried course. Usually people whose spirituality is mainly that of a celebrator of God notice that when they celebrate, in a personal tone of gratitude or in a communal worship ritual, they get a lot of inner feedback from such experiences. The event or process itself is pleasurable and gratifying, but the aftereffect is equally reinforcing of our sense of spiritual well-being. They are delighted, once again, that the experience of gratitude or worship rings true to all they know of their spiritual longing and mean by their spiritual quest.

Few things are as important in life as celebrating life itself—and God who gives us life and liveliness.

Psalm 19

The heavens are telling the glory of God;
And the firmament proclaims his handiwork.
Day to day pours forth speech,
And night to night declares knowledge.

There is no speech, nor are their words;
Their voice is not heard;
Yet their voice goes out through all the earth,
And their words to the end of the world.

In them God has set a tent for the sun,
Which comes forth like a bridegroom leaving his chamber,
And like a strong man runs his course with joy.
Its rising is from the end of the heavens,
And its circuit to the end of them;
And there is nothing hid from its heat.

The law of the Lord is perfect, reviving the soul;
The testimony of the Lord is sure, making wise the simple;
The precepts of the Lord are right, rejoicing the heart;
The commandment of the Lord is pure, enlightening the eyes;

The fear of the Lord is clean, enduring forever;
The ordinances of the Lord are true, and righteous altogether.
More to be desired are they than gold, even than much fine gold
Sweeter also than honey, and drippings of the honey comb.

Moreover, by them is thy servant warned;
In keeping them there is great reward.
But who can discern his errors?
Clear thou me from hidden faults.

Keep back your servant also from presumptuous sins
Let them not have dominion over me!
Then I shall be blameless,
And innocent of great transgression.

Let the words of my mouth
And the meditations of my heart
Be acceptable in your sight,
O Lord, my rock and my redeemer.
(RSV)

Psalm 139 (selections)

O Lord, you have searched me and known me!
You know when I sit down and when I stand up;
You understand my thoughts before I know them.
You see my course of life and are familiar with all my journey.

You know the words of my mouth before I do.
You are in front of me and behind me, as though your hand is over me.
All this is absolutely wonderful to me,
It is beyond my comprehension.

Where could I possibly go beyond your presence?
Where, that your spirit would not be present to mine?
When I go to heaven, you will be there.
When I die, you will be there.
If I go to the other side of the world,
Even there you will be leading me and sustaining me.
Should I try to hide in darkness, you will see through it.

For you fashioned me exactly as I am,
In my mother's womb you crafted me.
You know me through and through.
Before anybody knew my mother was pregnant
You already were designing me in detail
I celebrate you because you have made me
So amazingly well and so awesomely

You saw me and recorded it, even before I was me;
When I was going through all the fetal phases.
Your ideas are so precious to me, O God;
So awesomely great, beyond all analysis;

Vaster than the sands of the sea.
Musing upon them practically puts me into a trance
And when I come to again, there you still are!

Check me out, O God,
Discern the intents of my inner self.
Analyze my thoughts and feelings.
See if there are any flaws in my spiritual quest
And lead me into life on your plain of existence.
(JHE trans.)

Psalm 51 (selections)

Have mercy on me, O God
In keeping with your steadfast love;
In keeping with your unconditional grace
Eliminate my transgression.
Clean out of me all my failures
And make me spiritually genuine!

I see clearly my shortfalls and failures.
I cannot get it out of my head and heart.
I have fallen away from you and lost my track.
You see the swath of wreckage I have left behind.
You are justified in sentencing me,
And quite appropriate in filing a judgment against me.

Indeed, you desire inner spiritual authenticity
So invest me with genuine wisdom in my spirit.
Scrub me clean, white as snow;
Fill me with joy and celebration.
Remove my fear, guilt, and shame
From the equation of our relationship

Create a pristine inner self in me, O God.
Put a brand new and genuine spirit in me;
A willing spirit of joyful gratitude for your grace.
Do not alienate your self from me as I have from you.
I have learned that a humbled spirit and a contrite nature
Is the right mode for my quest for you.
(JHE trans.)

Psalm 32 (selections)

That person is fortunate who is forgiven.
Whom God sees as genuine
And who knows himself or herself authentically.

I confessed my failures to God,
I did not hide my real self
And God declared my sin, guilt, and shame as gone.

So, if you are in trouble, pray to God,
God is a safe place, a protection.
God is always surrounding us with that grace-deliverance

Do not act like a bad-acting stud or a jackass.
Steadfast love is the matrix in which we live.
So trust in God, be glad, rejoice, shout for joy.
(JHE trans.)

Psalm 23

The Lord is my shepherd, I shall not want;
He makes me lie down in green pastures
He leads me beside still waters; he restores my soul.
He leads me in the paths of righteousness for his name's sake.

Even though I walk through the valley of the shadow of death,
I fear no evil, for thou art with me, thy rod and thy staff, they comfort me.
Thou preparest a table before me in the presence of my enemies.
Thou annointest my head with oil, my cup overflows.

Surely goodness and mercy shall follow me
All the days of my life;
And I shall dwell in the house of the Lord
For ever.
(RSV)

Psalm 33 (selections)

Rejoice in the Lord, O you righteous!
Praise befits the upright.
Praise the Lord with the lyre,
Make melody to him with the harp of ten strings!
Sing to him a new song,
Play skillfully on the strings, with loud shouts.

For the word of the Lord is upright;
And all his work is done in faithfulness.
He loves righteousness and justice;
The earth is full of the steadfast love of the Lord.

By the word of the Lord the heavens were made,
And all their hosts by the breath of his mouth.
He gathered the waters of the sea as in a bottle;
He put the deeps in storehouses.

Let the earth stand in awe of the Lord,
Let all the inhabitants of the world stand in awe of him!
For he spoke, and it came to be;
He commanded, and it stood forth.

The counsel of the Lord stands for ever,
The thoughts of his heart to all generations.
Blessed is the nation whose God is the Lord
The people whom he embraces as his heritage!

The Lord sees all the thoughts and intents of our hearts.
He observes our deeds.
Power is a vain thing for victory,
Might cannot save.

God keeps a careful eye upon those who stand in awe of him.
They hope in his steadfast love and unconditional grace
My soul is searching for God, my source of meaning and purpose
Shower us with your steadfast love, O God. Our hope is in you!
(JHE trans.)

Psalm 37 (selections)

Do not be upset by wickedness, others or your own.
Trust in God and do good.
Delight in God, who will respond to the longing of your heart.
Commit your way to him, trust in him, and he will act.

Search for God quietly and patiently.
Do not get anxious or angry!
The meek shall delight in abundant prosperity

I was young once, now I am old;
I have not seen the authentically spiritual disappointed.
Such folk are of liberal and open spirit.
Their children are blessed by that and become a blessing.

Wait for God and search for his way.
Salvation is from God.
God is our refuge in trouble.
Take refuge in him.
(JHE trans.)

CHAPTER 6

BIBLICAL SPIRITUALITY AS TALKING TO GOD: PRAYER LIFE

This chapter is about the spiritual experiences of prayer and epiphanies. The list of persons in the Bible who experienced epiphanies or life-changing illuminations is surprisingly long. The list of those who are described as having a very active or extensive prayer life is even longer. As an illustration of prayer life, of course, we have Jesus' apparently frequent practice of spending entire nights alone in prayer. As an example of epiphanies we could study Paul's illumination and his call to ministry on the Damascus road. Paul's experience, as he reports it, is filled with psychological processes and intriguing notions of divine intervention. Such events do not need to be seen as supernatural. The point is that whether they are natural or supernatural, whatever those words mean, such events are of God, as can be demonstrated by their results in people's lives.

Prayer is mentioned 133 times in the Bible, and there are about 200 additional references to the act of praying. In Proverbs 15 we are informed that God hears the prayers of the person who is genuine in his or her spiritual quest; and those prayers delight him. Moses, David, Isaiah, and a number of Israelite kings and prophets were noted for their prayer life. The entire community of godly people in the OT and NT was enjoined regularly to pray continually. The Bible speaks as though prayer is the matrix within which people who are authentic in the quest for God live out their lives of spirituality. Of course, everyone wonders about the nature, purpose, function, and outcome of prayer, because prayer is a mystery, even to those of us who have lived a life of prayer for half a century or more.

Nine times the gospels tell us of Jesus' prayerfulness during his last two or three years of life (Mt 14 and 26; Mk 1, 6, and 14; Lk 5, 9, 11, and 22). Of course, three to five of those are duplicate references, each of the gospel writers offering his own take on one of their memories of Jesus. It is interesting that the gospel of John does not make much of Jesus' spirituality as prayerfulness; but he gives us one long prayer from Jesus, reporting it as though word for word (Jn 17). John refers to it not as a prayer, but as a conversation Jesus had with God, or really a speech Jesus made to God. We call it Jesus' Great High Priestly Prayer because he prayed, as a high priest might, for his disciples and the community of faith that would follow them.

The gospels paint a picture of Jesus as a person whose life was suspended, as it were, between his occasions of intense and extensive meditation and prayer. He regularly meditated and prayed all night long, they tell us. He also enjoined us to pray, just for the spiritual expressiveness of it or when in special need. He urged us to pray for others even if we do not like them. He asked us to pray, as he did, for the world in all its special concerns. Paul tells us to pray for the leaders of the church, nation, and world, even if we do not like them; and probably *especially* if we think they are not doing a very good job.

So spirituality, as talking to God, is assumed and taught by the Bible as though it were the atmosphere in which godly people live, so to speak, the air we breathe. In fact, most of the persons who populate the stories of the Bible seemed to resort to prayer on almost any occasion when they felt strong emotional feelings of any kind. Whether they felt sad, mad, glad, or scared, prayer seems to have been their natural life expression. They talked to God a great deal, almost all of the time in life. Paul says that we should pray without ceasing. That used to mystify me, since I figured there was a lot of work to be done in this world, and how could one responsibly take a lot of time out to pray? However, as I grew older and spiritually more mature, that conundrum resolved itself for me, simply because I began to notice that all the time I tend to be in the spiritual posture of prayer.

That is, I tend to live in the mode of grateful and hopeful consciousness that I am in the presence of God. My spirit is rather constantly, I would say 99 percent of the time, emoting toward God my intimations of gratitude, joyfulness, optimism, assurance, and a sense of the empowerment of God's spirit in my spirit. For 25 years I have been serving as interim minister to numerous churches in the Detroit metropolitan area. Consequently, I live in Farmington Hills and drive fairly long distances to the churches I serve. I find the 30 or 45 minutes on the highway a very good time to ruminate about the cares and concerns of the congregation, and to pray. When I mention this to my parishioners, they quickly ask me to make sure I keep my eyes open. I do not need to close my eyes, of course. My ruminations and reflections, my thoughts and expressions of quandary, imploration, or gratitude are prayer, a conscious and intentional sharing with God's spirit these matters of my spirit. I know what Paul means by praying without ceasing (I Tim. 5:17).

Abraham was clearly a man for whom prayer played a meaningful role. A king, named Abimelech, together with his wives and concubines, suffered from a disease that obstructed conception. He had a dream in which he was sure that God was telling him to ask Abraham, a praying man, to pray for healing. So Abimelech did that, and "Abraham prayed to God; and God healed Abimelech, and also healed his wife and concubines so that they bore children" (Gen. 20:17). Abraham's son, Isaac, is not described as a man of prayer but rather as one who "went out to meditate in the field in the evening" (Gen. 24:64).

In the pilgrimage of the Exodus from Egypt, the Israelites rather regularly complained and were abusive of Moses. Moses generally resorted to prayer as the resolution of the matters, or at least as the source of strength to endure and negotiate the persistently revolutionary spirit of the twelve tribes (Num. 11:2, 21:7; Deut. 9:20, 26). Prayer is a source and method for centering one's spirit, refocusing upon the most important priorities of life, and directing one's life beyond the immediate anguish or travail of life, toward a more transcendent perspective. Whether one explains that as psychological clarification or connection with transcendent sources of energy, strength, or illumination, it makes little difference. In either case it is God's way of mediating to us consolation and clarity for our journey, for our psychospiritual quest for God and God's way for us.

I have already mentioned the spiritual quest of Hannah, Samuel's mother, as she longed for a son; and when he was born she dedicated him to God's work in the world. The entire story of Hannah, as we have it in the Bible, is the story of prayer. The story of her prayerful life fills most of the first chapters of the book of I Samuel. It is not a coincidence that the very next chapters pick up with Samuel as a man of prayer. He talked to God in his nighttime theophany (I Sam. 3) that confirmed his call to ministry. He prayed for the Israelites when they were in trouble and confusion and provided vision and leadership to them. He experienced what seemed to him to be a prayerful conversation with God about whether he should anoint a king in Israel, as the people wished. In fact, once a king had been crowned, Samuel said that he would pray without ceasing for the nation and its people (I Sam. 12:23).

It is clear that everyone in the community assumed that prayer was as natural a part of everyday life as a good drink of water or a good sandwich. In fact, when David was casting about in his mind whether he should build a temple, a national worship center for Israel, it seemed like the normal thing for him to talk to God about it. He prayed, and from that prayer came a surprising insight that David took to be an illumination of his mind and spirit by the spirit of God. He got the clear message that *his* style was for war—securing of the borders and establishing domestic tranquility—while *his son Solomon's* style would be for temple building. David acted upon this insight because, whether the answer to his prayer was just his own rational psychology or divine theophany, the message was God's word, so far as he was concerned.

David prayed when he went to war (II Sam. 7:18–8:18), he prayed when his child was ill (12:1–12:23), he prayed when he alienated himself from the godly way of life and from his own integrity (Ps. 32 and 51), he prayed when he was victorious in achieving peace and prosperity for the nation of Israel (II Sam. 22), and he prayed when he took his farewell from the people and prepared for eternity (II Sam. 23:1–7). David was an adulterer, a murderer, a violent guerilla revolutionary against King Saul, an aggressively bloody conqueror of Israel's neighbor, a king who tolerated no turbulence in his kingdom, and a vicious repressor of other people's violence. He had blood on his hands, and that is why he thought God did not want him to build a sacred temple. Nonetheless, the overall message of the Bible is that David was, all in all, a man after God's own heart, because he was a praying man, walking and talking with God, despite his human flaws and his wicked mistakes (I Sam. 13:14, Acts 13:22). Obviously walking and talking with God reshaped his heart from destructiveness and evil to forgiveness and health.

Prayer does that. Prayer is a process of talking to ourselves as much as it is an experience of talking with God. Therefore, we should expect that prayer will have as much of a psychospiritual affect upon our inner selves as it has upon God. That is one of the mysteries about prayer. It is a way of engaging ourselves and engaging God. We know it is both and not just one or the other because of very simple empirical evidence. Anyone who prays knows that the self-talk has a way of clarifying and cleaning our inner selves of grief, shame, fear, guilt, anger, or confusion.

It is consistently the case with those of us who live life as a prayer process that when we are in a situation in which we need calming, clarity, resolution of an impasse, understanding of a confusing situation, change in a conflicted relationship, or guidance into an unknown future, prayer helps. That is, by the time we finish talking the thing out with God we have, in effect, thoroughly talked the thing through with ourselves. Of course, there are those who would stop right there and say, "Of course, that is the point. It is all simply psychological, or self-hypnosis."

Praying people, however, know that it does not stop there. If that were all there were to it, that would already be a fine gift of God, given us in the way he fashioned us in our evolving creation. However, the evidence makes it clear that our praying not only affects us, but it also affects God. Indeed, those two impacts are inseparable. There is a long accumulated and burgeoning volume of data that demonstrates that prayer has often changed things outside us and not just inside us. That does not always seem to be the case, but it is the case often enough that the data cannot be set aside or devalued. It must be faced realistically.

Hezekiah prayed and it changed his life and healed his body (II Kgs 20). David prayed and it changed his life and healed his body (Ps. 40). At its dedication, Solomon prayed that God would make the temple he built the focus of worship and godliness in Israel, and that anyone from any land who turned his face to God and his temple, God would hear, and bless his land, and heal his people (I Kgs 8). That was a prayer that changed Solomon and his people from their particularistic notion that God cared only for Israelites into a people who, for a time at least, realized that God is the one true and living God for all humankind.

Solomon's long prayer sounds like a lot of redemptive self-talk, and of course it is that much at least; but where did this wise man of prayer get the illumination for such a universalistic theology? That is always the leading of God's very spirit in his spirit. Left to itself the human spirit is inherently anxious and prone to the defensive posture necessary for survival. Egalitarianism is godlike. Universal grace is always the perspective of one who has come to know a lot about how God feels about and deals with humans: radical, unconditional, and universal grace. Nobody wants to believe that. We all want to hold on to a conditional arrangement in relationships. Then we can claim that our merits deserve reward; and most importantly, then we can claim that because the next guy in our opinion has less merit, he should go to hell! To see life as the matrix of God's radical and unconditional grace for all is an insight and illumination from God's spirit alone.

In any case, I was making the point that prayer continues to be a relatively popular thing to do in every culture in the world and apparently always has been. It persisted against great odds, even irrepressibly, in such atheistic societies as the former Soviet Union and contemporary China. People find prayer welcome. They assemble freely and spontaneously for communal prayer everywhere humans are able to do so. Jesus' disciples apparently felt deprived because, while John the Baptist had taught his disciples how to pray, Jesus did not do so until they talked him into it (Mt 6, Lk 11). It is interesting that a person like Jesus, whose whole life seemed to be suspended between seasons of prayer, was so reticent to teach his disciples to pray.

Perhaps there is an indication here that we must find our own time, mode, and inner need to pray; and when we do, praying will come naturally, like a conversation with a good friend or even just a desperate cry like, "God help!" Surely it cannot be the case that Jesus did not think prayer was important in the lives of his disciples. He prayed every chance he got and many times on occasions when he simply had to create the opportunity. He enjoined his followers to make prayer a way of life: talking with God. Moreover, he knew and claimed boldly that prayer has remarkable beneficial consequences. It did in his day, and it still does.

I have a family of friends whose third daughter was born a hydrocephalic. When that baby was born they were shocked, of course, and very anxious. So they did what godly people do. They prayed for their child. Indeed, they laid their hands upon their child's head and prayed for her to be a normal child. Within days the hydrocephalic condition receded and their child is now a wonderful normal adult person, bright, healthy, godly, and a woman with a profoundly prayerful life. Physicians tell me that sometimes such a condition spontaneously cures itself. However that may be, the case is that they prayed and their dear child was healed. What counts for that family is just that, and that is as real to them as the sunshine in the morning. David once said in the Psalms, "This poor man cried, and the Lord heard him, and delivered him out of his anguish." That is enough for me!

My father prayed regularly for rain in times of drought or for the rain to stop and the sun to shine when the fields were too wet to work, and he prayed for my younger brother's healing from pneumonia every winter from the time he was two until he was six. He prayed for my older brother when we thought he had been killed in a hay-baler accident. My father's prayers were answered. Those two brothers are alive and well. One is 60 and the other is 81. We were not wealthy in the Great Depression, and we lost our corn crop and the second cutting of hay to the hot dry sun in 1937, but we managed and lived well enough for that time and setting. Prayer kept us hopeful and secure.

We had a neighbor who was disillusioned with the church, with faith, with prayer, and with God. He thought my father was rather naïve in his life of devotion and prayer. He was quite sure that when the drought came or when the climate was congenial, it was simply the natural cyclical process of nature. Its affect on us was an accident of history and the chance you took at this crapshoot called life. He was not an unhappy man. I really kind of liked his jovial and devil-may-care outlook on life, and he told unbelievably good jokes.

However, there was a difference in my father's outlook on life and that of our neighbor that I found deep, mysterious, and reassuring. The family of friends I mentioned above knew that when their daughter was healed it was of God—a gift of grace. My father knew that when the rain came in the late fall of 1937 and the winter wheat flourished so we had a good crop the next spring, it was a gift of God's goodness to us. He knew that when the year was prosperous, it was not an accident of history but a providence motivated by God's grace. It was the difference in the quality of life that those two different ways of looking at things produced that really interested me. The prayer perspective always seemed quite mysterious to me, but the difference it made in the quality of our life seemed to me to make a life of prayer more than worthwhile.

As I have already noted, the Bible says that Jesus prayed a lot. We discussed above that he is reported to have gone away by himself to some isolated place frequently and to have spent the entire night in prayer to God. It is interesting, therefore, that Jesus seemed to have a great deal of resistance to public and communal prayer. He did not even pray with his disciples, so far as we can tell from the biblical record. He once told a story about two fellows who went up to the temple to pray. One was a genuinely upright person, a learned man of note, a teacher of spirituality. Moreover, Jesus says that he practiced what he preached: "Keep the law and honor God." Well, this man stood at the front of the worship sanctuary to offer his prayers very publicly. It was the thing one did in that communal place of worship at that time.

So this religious leader, as he was expected to do, stood there in plain view, lifted his eyes and hands to heaven, and prayed fervently a prayer of thanksgiving for the fact that God had prospered him, had guided him into a life of righteousness, and had motivated him to keep the law, to care for the poor, to give adequately to any needy charity, and to keep himself in the way of God, as he understood it. He especially thanked God at the end that he had been given such a genetic heritage, such a wholesome childhood, such a successful material and spiritual quest that he was not tempted to be a scoundrel, thief, rapist, drug addict, or womanizer. Casting his eye briefly toward the back of the temple, he thanked God that he was not a low-class lowlife like some other men he knew.

The other man who went up to the temple was a tax collector. He had a license from the Roman government to collect all the taxes he could squeeze out of his fellow Israelites, and whatever he collected in excess of the Roman levee he could keep. These men were usually wealthy, often extortionists, and universally thought of as thieves. They were seen to be in a class with prostitutes. They were economic whores who had sold themselves to the Romans for personal gain. In Jesus' story, this man crept surreptitiously into the back door of the temple, stood virtually unseen in the dark shadows of the pillars at the back, bowed his head, beat upon his breast, and cried quietly to God, "God, be merciful to me, a sinner!" That man, said Jesus, went down to his house justified, rather than the other one.

Jesus' disciples wanted him to teach them to pray, but apparently, because of his reticence about public and communal praying, he was disinclined to do so. He often told them that when they wanted to pray, they should do it as he did, that is, go away to some solitary place and talk to God privately. In fact, he told them to go into their closets to pray in secret, "and the father, who hears in secret, will reward you openly."

The story in Matthew's gospel about Jesus teaching his disciples to pray is very interesting in that regard. It seems that the disciples had been taking this matter up with Jesus for some time, and he refused to give them a formula for their prayers. At least in this story they seem to be coming to him with a certain sense of desperation, since they finally confront him with an argument that he just cannot get around. They tell him that John the Baptist teaches his disciples to pray, so why does Jesus not do so?

Remember that four of Jesus' disciples were formerly John's disciples. Do we hear a little blackmail here? Is there a suggestion in their argument that they might very well return to John and leave Jesus? In Mark 8 the multitudes have forsaken Jesus, and he asks whether the disciples will also abandon him. Obviously the disciples feel that they have some leverage for their request by citing the case of John, reminding him that if they cannot get what they want here they can always get it with John. Well, it looks like they had finally put a gun to his head, so to speak.

So in Matthew's story, Jesus relents and agrees to teach them to pray. It is interesting how he introduces that teaching regarding prayer. He starts out by saying something like, "Well, if you must have a formula for prayer, then pray as follows." However, he then tells them three or four ways of praying that we should assiduously avoid. We should not prayer like the Pharisees, who stand on street corners or in the front of the temple and pray publicly so that they may be seen and praised by the crowds. He declares that people who pray like that only want their prayer to bring them public esteem, and it does, so their prayers are answered; not by God but by the crowd's response.

Secondly, he commands his disciples not to pray like the heathen who prays endless and obsessively verbose prayers, haranguing God with a superfluity of verbiage, sometimes called logorrhea, like verbal (logos) diarrhea. Do not pray like that, Jesus counseled. You will remember that the prophets of Baal on Mt. Carmel with Elijah prayed like that and, according to that story, they were not heard (I Kgs 18:20–46). Such efforts to attract God's attention by compulsive spinning of a prayer wheel, dancing as a whirling dervish, rocking back and forth at the Wailing Wall, or obsessively reciting a traditional ritual are worthless. Indeed, they are obscene in the sense that they imply that God is someone who can be manipulated by such magical methods.

Thirdly, Jesus said that the disciples, if they really insisted on praying at all, should not pray like those who think that they can manipulate God, talking God into doing nice things for them that God would not have the good sense or presence of mind to do if they did not talk God into doing them. Jesus assured them that whether they prayed or not, God knew what they needed before they asked him, and he was always busy giving them everything they needed, so far as it was possible and good for them.

Jesus clearly thought that people should pray as a secret communion with God directly, letting the spirit effervesce, as it were, in the presence of God. Prayer may be more a matter of reflective consciousness than implorations. Jesus seemed to think it was mostly a matter of thanksgiving and celebration of God, rather than presenting petitions. An old hymn says it right, I think:

Prayer is the soul's sincere *desire, unuttered* or expressed,
A *motion* of a *hidden fire*, that trembles in the breast.

Prayer is the *burden* of a *sigh*, the *falling* of a tear,
The *upward glancing* of the eye, when only God is near.

Prayer is the believer's *vital breath*, the believer's *native air*,
Our watch word at the gate of death; we enter heaven with prayer.

Perhaps that is why Jesus urged us that when we pray we should enter into a closet, close the door, and pray to God in secret, confident that God, "who hears in secret," will respond to our prayers in very obvious ways.

Jesus really seemed to be implying that prayer was not a thing that can be contrived, and that a lot of types of prayer were really lousy ways of trying to express our spirituality or relationship with God. He implied that living a life of conscious trust and responsibility before the face of God was the real thing. Prayer was mainly for expressing *that* mode of being before the face of God, so to speak. It was clear from his approach that God consciousness was very good and God manipulation was dumb and useless. In fact, Jesus said about everything one needs to say to argue that petitionary prayer is really unnecessary at best, and at worst is a failure to trust God's continual grace and providence to us, unless we beg him for it.

What is surprising, therefore, is that after his firm cautionary introduction, Jesus did finally teach the disciples a prayer, and in his prayer there are *four petitions*. It is a prayer, admittedly, that Jesus formulated out of already-existing Israelite prayers and a doxology. Nonetheless, the prayer says a lot about Jesus' notions regarding the nature of healthy personal spirituality. He tells us much here about his sense of the nature and importance of our deep inner psychospiritual hunger for a connection with God.

However, why did he add those four petitions, since he had just warned against trying to manipulate God? Moreover, "God knows what we need before we ask him," Jesus had said. He gave us the Lord's Prayer in three sections. The first one extols God and asserts that we know God is in charge, and we know that it is a good thing God is. We are for that and we wish to align ourselves with that reality. "Our father who art in heaven, hallowed be thy name. Thy kingdom come, they will be done, on earth as it is in heaven." That is like saying, "Oh God, we are for what you are for and we gladly give ourselves to it."

The third section of the Lord's Prayer is a doxology, that is, a song of praise. "Yours is the kingdom, the power, and the glory, forever." Jews usually closed all prayers with this doxology. When we pray those words we mean to affirm that we are those who stand in awe of the majesty and magnificence of God in nature and in grace, and of all we experience of God. Those words are a way of saying that we are so very glad that God is God and grace is grace.

It is the center section of the Lord's Prayer that is troublesome or mystifying in view of what Jesus had said at the outset. Here are four petitions: "Give us this day our daily bread. Forgive us our debts since we know what forgiving debtors means. Bring us not into temptation. Deliver us from evil." Why would Jesus build this prayer around four such fundamental petitions when he had just explained so forcefully that petitionary prayer was unnecessary and probably an offensive act of unfaithfulness before the face of God; a failure to trust God for what God knows we need?

This much we know: He did not give us these four fundamental petitions about daily food, daily forgiveness, daily protection, and daily deliverance because he thought God would not otherwise give us these graces unless we talked him into doing so. Jesus had just assured us that such could never be the case. "God knows what you need before you ask him." So there must be another reason. If petitions in prayer are not designed to persuade God, who are they for? Well, then they must be for us. If they do not manipulate or influence God they must influence us in some necessary way.

Edson T. Lewis is a minister in Columbus, Ohio. A couple of years ago I asked him to write a chapter in a book I was editing, *Psychology and the Bible*. He wrote a long and sturdy chapter on spirituality, arguing that spirituality is a matter of our posture toward God. That is, spirituality has to do with how we stand toward God. He reminded us of his experience with his seven-year-old grandson who was taking karate and whose success in it depended upon the posture he was able to hold toward the master, or toward any opponent. Effectiveness in the relationship, friend or foe, depended upon and was a matter of posture.

Lewis explained that he thought spirituality, our relationship with God, was also a matter of posture. It depends upon how we stand toward God, or with regard to God. Jesus seems to have understood that, so he gave us the four petitions, not to talk God into doing nice or necessary things for us that God would not have had the presence of mind or good sense to do otherwise. He gave us those four petitions so that on the fundamental matters of our existence we would stand toward God as needy, or at least expectant, children, lifting up our hands and hearts to God and making it plain that we understand how we depend upon God's good providence and grace.

The petitions are for us, to create a proper posture toward God. They are not for God, who does not need them in order to remember what we need or in order to desire to fill our needs. They are for us so that we will continue to cultivate in our inner selves that sense of living and moving and having our being from God's hands of grace, mercy, and love. These four petitions, and all of our crying out to God in our neediness throughout life, are for the cultivation of our sense of being his children who await his kind largess.

That is what was happening in my father, and in our family and not in that of our neighbor. We knew who we were—God's expectant children—and it felt good to us to be that. It gave us great security and hope in trying times. We were glad, and we prayed the first and last sections of the Lord's

Prayer with joy and trust and celebration, because the middle section kept us properly oriented. When the rain came on us and on our neighbor, we knew it was a gift to us from our heavenly father, and that made all the difference in the world as to how we felt about it. Our friend down the road was glad for the rain, which he considered just a lucky turn in the weather. We weathered the drought in the sure knowledge that the thin thread upon which life is suspended was firmly held on the other end by our provident God. That was our posture. It made all the difference in the world!

So, in the end, prayer is a great—a heavenly—mystery. Who can explain it? Who can account for it all? It blessed my friend's daughter's life with wholeness and wholesomeness. It healed her. It got us through the Great Depression and the war, humble, secure, and joyful people. It blessed us! I do not know that our outer world would have been any different had we not been a praying family. I know that without it our inner world would have been barren and empty.

I am sure I have not so far exploded all the mysteries of prayer. I think it would be unfortunate if I did. The only way to find out about prayer is to do it, to experiment with it, to explore it deeply. Coleridge said wisely, "More things are wrought by prayer than this world dreams of."

CHAPTER 7

BIBLICAL SPIRITUALITY AS SEEING GOD: EPIPHANY

An epiphany is a moment when we realize a new and important thing rather suddenly, as though someone turned on a light in our minds or spirits. My father always liked to mention the conundrum of the man who stayed up all night to be sure to see how the sun rose, and finally it dawned on him. Ok, so you do not like dumb puns. My father liked them for their wry, subtle, and understated humorfulness. However, my point is that an epiphany is a moment when something important, particularly an important meaning of some kind, dawns on you. The ancient Greeks had a festival called Epiphany, which celebrated the appearance of a god to a human, at some specified place. Epiphany is a date in the liturgical calendar of both the Eastern (Orthodox) and Western (Roman Catholic) churches, and it is celebrated on January 6 each year. It commemorates the appearance of the star to the Wise Men who, according to the nativity story in Matthew's gospel, came from Iraq to see Jesus, the Christ child (Mt 2:1–12).

> When Jesus was born in Bethlehem of Judea, in the days of Herod the king, behold, wise men from the East came to Jerusalem, saying, "Where is he who has been born king of the Jews? For we have seen his star in the East, and have come to worship him." When Herod the king heard this, he was troubled, and all Jerusalem with him; and assembling all the chief priests and scribes of the people, he inquired of them where the Christ was to be born. They told him, "In Bethlehem of Judea; for so it is written by the prophet:

And you, O Bethlehem, in the land of Judah,
Are by no means least among the rulers of Judah;
For from you shall come a ruler
Who will govern my people Israel."

Then Herod summoned the wise men secretly and ascertained from them what time the star appeared; and he sent them to Bethlehem, saying, "Go and search diligently for the child, and when you have found him bring me word, that I too may come and worship him." When they had heard the king they went their way; and lo, the star which they had seen in the East went before them, till it came to rest over the place where the child was. When they saw the star, they rejoiced exceedingly with great joy; and going into the house they saw the child with Mary his mother, and they fell down and worshiped him. Then opening their treasures, they offered him gifts, gold and frankincense and myrrh. And being warned of God in a dream that they should not to return to Herod, they departed into their own country another way. (RSV)

Paul had a life-changing epiphany on the Damascus road. I happen to think that Paul, on that occasion of his illumination, may have had sunstroke or some overwhelming psychological crisis resulting from his intense internal dissonance. He must have had a great deal of internal conflict in his psyche because he was spending his life killing fellow Jews merely because they disagreed with his theology as a Pharisee. The thing finally came to an impasse and God used that crisis to bring him to some profound illumination, which had been growing in the back of his head for some time, so to speak. Rather suddenly, for some reason, it reached a critical mass of insight and truth for him that day on the road. In that epiphany, his unconscious served up a set of insights into his right brain; and everything came together in a thoroughly meaningful picture. He realized he was on a terribly wrong track with his life. The psychospiritual experience was such a real vision that he could say of it that he had seen God. Of course he had! We know it was a divine event for him. Just look at how it wholesomely changed his life.

The biblical book of the Revelations of St. John is made up of what, on the face of it, seem like a jumble of really crazy cataclysmic ideations. We can make a little more sense out of the whole thing if we realize the spiritual and religious context in which the author was writing. He may also have had sunstroke, or was high on something, on that remote island of Patmos, but the greater likelihood is that this complicated book is a report on his vision of life and history. Whoever wrote this book was living at a time when the Roman emperor was set upon exterminating all Christians. The author wanted to paint a spiritual or theological picture of history that would help the Christian community, under those dire circumstances, preserve its sense of hope. He had to do it in code, of course, lest the emperor find out what he was up to. So he crafted this very strange set of images that urge Christians to believe that, however unfortunate, hopeless, and helpless they feel, Christianity will triumph in the end because God will triumph in the long haul. Sure enough, that is what happened.

We can *supernaturalize* the book of Revelations, and then we miss the point. The point is that the author sat down and tried to write in code a theological philosophy of history that let the community know that their cause would likely survive and prove to be the hope of the world. We can *psychologize* the book of Revelations, and then we also miss the point. The author may have been crazy, but this book is not an indication of that, so he or she probably was not. The vision the author claims to have had was his own effort to put together a meaningful and hopeful vision of how God is in history, in the Christian community's history, in the author's own history. As he or she was living life in that spiritual quest for understanding the nature and presence of God to him, her, or them, God used that posture to offer some inspiring insights. These insights come to their metaphoric climax in chapter 21:1–4.

> Then I saw a new heaven and a new earth; for the first heaven and the first earth had passed away, and the sea was no more. And I saw the holy city, new Jerusalem, coming down out of heaven from God, prepared as a bride adorned for her husband; and I heard a great voice from the throne saying, "Behold, the dwelling of God is with men. He will dwell with them, and they shall be his people, and God himself will be with them; he will wipe away every tear from their eyes, and death shall be no more, neither shall there be mourning nor crying nor pain any more, for the former things have passed away." (RSV)

If we should supernaturalize or psychologize that strange book and take it apart at the seams or criticize it, for a lot of sensible reasons, that would prevent us from seeing how it functioned for the early Christian community, in its desperate circumstances. It would devalue the consequences the book had in the life of that community just at that time: Its bizarre ideations gave the community what turned out to be a realistic hope. Leave it alone. It was spiritually real for the author and his or her community, and it empowered their lives constructively, just when they needed it.

Such timely illuminations of what turn out to be rather helpful new ways of looking at life, such as the experience of Paul on the Damascus road and John (or whoever it was) on the Island of Patmos, are examples of those frequent epiphanies in life that help us see and understand our calling and destiny in life. For people who walk with God, are accustomed to talking to God, or live out life searching for God such epiphanies are not surprising or unusual. My sudden sense of the meaning of life, that sunny summer day in 1937 when I realized I could spend the rest of my years helping all those around me who were suffering, was for me such a Damascus road epiphany.

The Bible is full of such stories. Jacob fled in fear from his brother, whom he had betrayed. His heart was full of anguish and quandary about his future. He was alienated from his home and family, and he faced a completely unknown destiny as to where he should go and what he should do. At a place called Bethel he fell into an exhausted sleep and in a dream received an epiphany (Gen. 28:10–22).

> Jacob left Beer-Sheba, and went toward Haran. And he came to a certain place, and stayed there that night, because the sun had set. Taking one of the stones of the place, he put it under his head and lay down in that place to sleep. And he dreamed that there was a ladder set up on the earth, and the top of it reached to heaven; and behold, the angels of God were ascending and descending on it! And behold, the Lord stood above it and said, "I am the Lord, the God of Abraham your father and the God of Isaac; the land on which you lie I will give to you and to your descendants; and your descendants shall be like the dust of the earth, and you shall spread abroad to the west and to the east and to the north and to the south; and by you and your descendants shall all the families of the earth bless themselves. Behold, I am with you and will keep you wherever you go, and will bring you back to this land; for I will not leave you until I have done that of which I have spoken to you." Then Jacob awoke from his sleep and said, "Surely the Lord is in this place; and I did not know it." And he was afraid, and said, "How awesome is the place! This is none other than the house of God, and this is the gate of heaven. (RSV)

In his dream he realized that however far he fled from home and country, he could not run beyond the boundaries of God's grace and providence. God was there in Bethel too, and he had the enlightening awareness that wherever he went, God would be with him, undergirding the goodness of his life. This entrenched in Jacob's life the realization that walking with God and talking with God would be a meaningful, spirit-filling way of life for him. Moreover, the sustaining providence of God, even to a scoundrel like him, was following him in spite of himself and wherever he went. In his time of spiritual tragedy he discovered his true psychospiritual quest at Bethel. Beth-El means the house of God or the place where God is present.

Joseph was an intensely intuitive and naively arrogant boy and youth. That got under the skin of his brothers. They decided to get rid of him. Most of the brothers decided to kill him, but one of them proposed an alternative. They sold him, instead, as a slave, to some Bedouins. The Bedouins sold him, in turn, to a highly placed political official in Egypt. Joseph must have felt very badly used and a young man with a precarious future. However, as time passed he rose in honor and fame in Egypt, until he was running the country. His great intuitive capacity empowered him to interpret dreams, and by interpreting a dream or two of the Pharaoh, he came into his favor. That got him the job of managing the kingdom.

All this led Joseph to a set of insights that changed his life. He had always been a person, from childhood up apparently, who searched for God, talked to God, and walked with God. That is, he was aware from an early age of the hunger of his soul for a sense of the authentic transcendent meaning of his life. He wanted a fulfilling nurture for his psychospiritual longing for deep meaning—soul-satisfying meaning in life. So when his life took a turn for the worse, as it were, he continued to look for how God would show up around the next corner.

Regularly God did show up in Joseph's life, and being a man who lived life as a search for God, he was able to notice these moments when they happened. First, in the providential turn that led his brothers to sell him to the Midianites rather than to kill him; second, in the Midianites' smart move to sell him to Potiphar in Egypt; third, in the attempt by Potiphar's wife to seduce him, followed by her accusation against him, which landed him in prison; fourth, in his encounter in prison with the two chief servants of the Pharaoh, by means of which he came to Pharaoh's attention; fifth, in his ability to surprise Pharaoh by interpreting the king's dreams satisfactorily, sixth, in this turn of events empowering him to come into contact again with his family and save them from starvation; and finally, in his restoration of his relationship with all his father's household.

That is the moment of the supreme epiphany for Joseph. Out of his travail came the life-shaping insight that he explained to his brothers when they fell in fear and shame before him because of their abuse of him. He said to them,

"Come near to me, I pray you." And they came near. And he said, "I am your brother Joseph, whom you sold into Egypt. And now do not be distressed, or angry with yourselves, because you sold me here; for God sent me before you to preserve life. For the famine has been in the land these two years; and there are yet five years in which there will be neither plowing nor harvest. And God sent me before you to preserve for you a remnant on earth, and to keep alive for you many survivors. So it was not you who sent me here, but God; and he has made me a father to Pharaoh, and lord of all his house and ruler over all the land of Egypt....Fear not,...as for you, you meant evil against me; but God meant it for good, to bring it about that many people should be kept alive, as they are today. So do not fear; I will provide for you and your little ones." Thus he reassured them and comforted them. (Gen. 45:4–8, 50:19–21 RSV)

What a profound moment of forgiveness and reconciliation! What a life-shaping event for them all! Life is full of these kinds of epiphanies for those who have the eyes to see them and the ears to hear them, when they signal us in life.

We have already taken account of the epiphany in Samuel's life. His epiphany came in a nighttime event, as did Jacob's. It is not clear whether it came in a dream or a theophany. It is possible that it was a combination of both.

> At that time Eli, whose eyesight had begun to grow dim,...was lying down in his own place; the lamp of God had not yet gone out, and Samuel was lying down within the temple of the Lord, where the ark of God was. Then the Lord called, "Samuel! Samuel!" and he said "Here I am!" and ran to Eli, and said, "Here I am, for you called me." But he said, "I did not call; lie down again." So he went and lay down. And the Lord called again, "Samuel!" And Samuel arose and went to Eli, and said, "Here I am, for you called me." But he said, "I did not call, my son; lie down again." Now Samuel did not yet know the Lord, and the word of the Lord had not yet been revealed to him. And the Lord called Samuel again the third time. And he arose and went to Eli, and said, "Here I am, for you called me." Then Eli perceived that the Lord was calling the boy. Therefore Eli said to Samuel. "Go, lie down; and if he calls you, you shall say, 'Speak, Lord, for thy servant hears.'" So Samuel went and lay down in his place.
>
> And the Lord came and stood forth, calling as at other times, "Samuel! Samuel!" And Samuel said, "Speak, for thy servant hears." Then the Lord said to Samuel, "Behold I am about to do a thing in Israel, at which the two ears of every one that hears it will tingle...." And Samuel grew, and the Lord was with him and let none of his words fall to the ground. And all Israel...knew that Samuel was established as a prophet of the Lord. (I Sam. 3:2–11, 19–20 RSV)

As I already noted, Samuel's experience was not very different from the experience that came to me in that night in which I anguished over being tried for heresy. I am not sure whether, in my case, the voice I heard plainly and loudly in the darkness of the night was the end of a dream, the rest of which I do not remember, or whether it was a single divine intervention.

Or perhaps it was some kind of magnificent fruiting of insight in my psyche, derived from a progressive accumulation of unconscious thought processes mixed with a painfully conscious impasse to which I had come that night. What I know is that it awakened me suddenly from a profound sleep, illumined me with an incredibly important new insight, and completely changed my life from that moment on. So I do not care what mechanism God used to serve me that night, natural or supernatural. In any case, it was from God. Samuel seems to have drawn the same conclusion from his moment of epiphany. My empirical experience tells me that he was correct in doing so. He knew God spoke to him, and that set the course of his life—mine too.

Daniel's main epiphany came to him in a "night vision." We do not know whether he meant that it was a dream or something else. It makes no difference. His epiphany was most unusual, but it shaped the thoughts, ideologies, theology, and religious practices of most of the many Judaisms that developed after his day. According to John's Gospel, especially, but confirmed by the other three as well, Daniel's night vision shaped the thoughts, ideology, theology, and religion of Jesus. It formed the basis for the Judaism that became the Jesus Movement and later developed into Christianity.

In Daniel's night vision (Dan. 7–12), that prophet saw a person, who looked like a human being, presented before God in heaven. The report in Daniel 7–12 says that Daniel saw "one like unto a son of man" presented to the enthroned "Ancient of Days."

As I looked, thrones were placed
And one that was ancient of days took his seat;
His raiment was white as snow,
And the hair of his head like pure wool;
His throne was fiery flames, its wheels were burning fire.
A stream of fire issued and came forth from before him
A thousand thousand served him,
And ten thousand times ten thousand stood before him;
The court sat in judgment and the books were opened
. . .
I saw in the night visions, and behold, with the clouds of heaven
There came one like a son of man,
And he came to the Ancient of Days and was presented before him.
And to him was given dominion and glory and kingdom,
That all peoples, nations, and languages should serve him;
His dominion is an everlasting dominion, which shall not pass away,
And his kingdom one that shall not be destroyed.
. . .
The court shall sit in judgment,
And the dominion shall be taken from the empires of the earth
To be consumed and destroyed to the end.
And the kingdom and the dominion
And the greatness of the kingdoms under the whole heaven
Shall be given to The People of the Holy Ones of the Most High;
And all dominions shall serve and obey them.
(RSV)

God gave that one like a son of man the power and authority to throw down all the evil kingdoms and empires on earth and raise up in their place the reign of God—the Kingdom of God. That was to be accomplished by the one like a son of man indirectly, not directly. The field forces of the son of man, operating on earth, would make it happen. They were identified in the night vision as "the People of the Holy Ones of the Most High."

This epiphany gave Daniel the conviction that God was busy in the endeavor of establishing his reign throughout the world, that this was the meaning and purpose of history, and that God's kingdom would achieve its consummation in some finite time frame in history. That vision grew in the mind of the Israelites and became the central focus of Jesus' life and ministry. In fact, it seems to be clear from the Gospels that it was that notion that shaped Jesus' entire sense of personal identity and purpose. He called himself the Son of Man and claimed he was on earth to bring in God's reign of grace that works and love that heals.

Consequently, Daniel's vision is the epiphany that has reigned in the world ever since, in one form or another, for good or ill. It led to the Jewish insurrections that in 70 C.E. brought the Roman extermination of Jerusalem, the Temple, and Judaism as it had been known. It is also the vision that produced the Bar Kochba revolt of the Jews, which virtually exterminated them in 135 C.E. It gave rise to the Jewish rebellion in Egypt that eliminated that large and wonderfully illustrious community in Alexandria in the second century C.E. On the other hand, Daniel's vision gave rise to Christianity, and *reaction to Daniel's vision* gave rise to what we know today as the very rational religion of Rabbinic Judaism.

People who walk with God and live life as a search for God, with their sail set close to the wind, as it were, get intimations and insights like that. Such epiphanies shape history. Sometimes the visions prove destructive and turn sour or get misused and abused—made into excuses for all manner of evil. One need only think of the Christian Crusades or suggest Napoleon's vision of conquest of the Russians or Hitler's vision of the thousand-year Reich, founded upon the carcasses of millions of Germans, Poles, Slavs, Russians, Austrians, Gypsies, and Jews. Sick souls produce sick visions that make for sick shapes for the world. Godly souls often produce wholesome visions that guide and heal the world.

In the late sixth century B.C.E. Zachariah, a leader of the Jewish community in Jerusalem, had a vision that proved to be an epiphany for him. It clarified two things that changed his life. First, he came to realize that good leadership is not by might nor by power but by God's spirit. He was in a situation that seemed to call for a lot of pushing and shoving, but that was going nowhere. The epiphany constructively altered his method and objective. The second insight was even more important and "closer to the bone," as they say. He saw Joshua the high priest standing before God in some kind of transcendental judgment hall. Joshua was being judged, symbolically, as the surrogate for the people of Israel, who were charged with forsaking God and breaking God's covenant of grace with them. Just at the moment that the hammer of judgment was to fall upon God's willful people, God intervened and declared that God's grace was greater than all their sins.

John Bunyan wrote a great Christian classic a couple of centuries ago about the pilgrimage of being a Christian. He called it *Pilgrim's Progress*. It is written as a kind of novel depicting the struggle of the devoted and sometimes tempted and turbulent Christian life. At the critical moment in the unfolding of that drama, John Bunyan depicted Pilgrim facing the ultimate challenge. He stands at the river of death. The noises, rushes, and sounds of the dangerous waters trouble him. It is as though the ultimate enemy is creeping into his soul, and then over the rush of the current he hears a great voice coming from the other side. It says, "God has delivered thee," and John Bunyan says, "Pilgrim then crossed over in safety and joy." That is something like the context of this passage from Zechariah 3.

It was a peculiar time in history, about 525 B.C.E. The children of Israel had been carried off into exile in Babylon in 586. But the Babylonian government was overrun by the Persians, who were, in turn, dominated by the Medes. Cyrus the Great became the ruling monarch in Babylon. Cyrus issued an edict, as the prophets of Israel had foretold, that permitted the Israelites to return to Jerusalem and rebuild the city and the temple. About 10 percent wanted to go back to Jerusalem. The rest had it so good in Babylon that they wanted to stay there. In fact, that Jewish community in Babylon lasted for centuries and was, the whole time, the most scholarly and illustrious theological and cultural Jewish community anywhere in the world.

However, there was that 10 percent, that remnant of people with a very special devotion to the city and to the temple in Jerusalem, who wished to return and re-establish something of the economy and the spirituality of the great golden age of David's kingdom. They returned under the leadership of Zachariah, the prophet; Zerubbabel, the prince and general; and Joshua, the high priest. Joshua stood in the supreme court of almighty God. On his right hand stood his defense counsel, a figure obviously well prepared to present a case in the court. So the case began to unfold. The defense attorney stepped forward and began to read all the facts into the record. These were the facts about the history of God's people.

Joshua was clothed in tattered and filthy garments, representing the sins and iniquities of the whole people. He was not an impressive figure. Worst of all, the defense counsel sounded increasingly like a prosecutor. It was all condemnation. All the facts were against the accused. As the story came to its climax and the hammer was ready to fall, into the courtroom stepped an emissary of God himself. Instead of addressing the court he addressed the defense attorney turned prosecuting attorney. His statement is simple. "The Lord who has chosen this people rebukes you! They are a brand I have plucked from the fire."

The case against them was that they did not look, think, or behave like godly people. The concluding judgment was that God loves and forgives them anyway. Zachariah's epiphany is the same as that of Paul and Luther, "By grace we are saved through faith, and that not of ourselves, it is a gift of God; not of works, lest anyone should boast" (Eph. 2:8–9). God simply declared, "I have snatched them like a brand out of the fire. I have chosen humankind as an old piece of abandoned drift wood and I am going to take this piece of drift wood, for all its knottiness and all of its nastiness, and I am going to polish it by my grace and providence. I am going to set it on the mantle of the universe and nobody will be able again to miss the beauty of the gospel of grace."

That is the sort of epiphany that changes lives. It may come from deep inner psychospiritual insights of our unconscious minds. There we are always cooking the stuff of daily experience, mixing it with the juices of creative reflection, and progressively forming a cumulative critical mass of insight and illumination. It may come directly from an audible voice generated in God's deep spirit. It makes no difference. Those are just two slightly different methods for conveying to us the illuminations of God's spirit in our spirits. When we are tuned for it, the epiphany can happen.

All of us are tuned for it by being created a living human being. The Bible says we are created in God's likeness. That means that all our ways of knowing are fashioned by God and correspond to the channels of God's processes of knowing and expressing. So it makes no difference which channel God uses through which to illumine our lives. It is just a very good idea to keep the channels all open to God by sailing close to the wind of the spirit. Then we will be available for the intimations when we need them, or when God wishes to express them to us.

At his baptism Jesus experienced an epiphany. He perceived God saying to him, "You are my son." It took him 40 days in solitude to sort out what that epiphany could possibly mean. He sensed that it meant that he should line his life up with that Son of Man in Daniel 7–12 and become a significant agent among the People of the Holy Ones of the Most High. That meant, of course, to dedicate his life to replace the forces of political and social evil in the world with the reign of God's kingdom.

As he tried to sort this out, three options presented themselves to him, according to Matthew 4:1–11. He could bow down to the god of power and take charge of the world as the new Alexander the Great, throwing out the Romans and reorganizing the politics, economics, and social structure of the world to institute God's reign of love that works and grace that heals. Or, secondly, he could take Psalm 91:9–12 literally and create some psychologically manipulative spectacle that would captivate the whole world and so accede to the power necessary to impose upon the whole world-order the reign of grace and love. Psalm 91 promises some rather unusual things, which, quite frankly, I would not try myself. I would rather be a sky diver than try to pull off this stunt. This is what that psalm says.

Because you have made the Lord your refuge, the Most High your
    habitation,
No evil will befall you,
No scourge come near your tent.
For God will give his angels charge of you,
To guard you in all your ways.
On their hands they will bear you up,
Lest you dash your foot against a stone.
(JHE trans)

Matthew 4 says that Jesus really considered whether one should take that seriously, whether he should jump from the pinnacle of the temple, expecting the angels to spectacularly save him. Fortunately, he agreed with my view of Psalm 91; namely, that it is a profound truth spiritually but a lousy idea literally. That psalm starts out with words that put verses 9–12 into a sensible spiritual setting, turning what sounds like a ridiculous passage into a wonderful psalm of consolation. Listen to the first two verses. It speaks exactly of the irrepressible, God-implanted, psychospiritual quest and hunger for God with which all of us are born, and which this whole book is about.

He who sets up his home in the shelter of the Most High,
Who lives in the shadow of the Almighty
Will say of the Lord, "My refuge and my fortress;
My God, in whom I trust."

Jesus had a third idea there in his wilderness of solitude, another option regarding what it meant for him to be a son of God. What about a plan to feed all the poor in the world? Would that not be a good interpretation of his epiphany? That would go a long way toward establishing God's reign of love that works and grace that heals. What more practical way could one go about solving the problems of the world? Take over the World Bank and use it to jack the UN around to the point that it starts to do its job right in the whole world? Would that not be the true destiny of a son of God, indeed, even of the heavenly Son of Man? Resolution of all the economic problems of the world by turning the infinite number of stones lying around in all the fields of the world into cost-free bread; or breaking the code for successful nuclear fusion and making infinite amounts of cost-free energy available for the whole world; that should do the job! Jesus was asking himself, "Is that what God has in mind for my role in establishing his reign?"

In the end, Jesus decided that none of those really fit the bill for a proper interpretation of his epiphany. He decided instead for a model that is more like leaven in a loaf. He gathered a few ordinary and rather widely differing kinds of persons together and told them to get the process started by loving and forgiving one another, acting out God's kind of love that works and grace that heals. Well, that is what has been going on ever since, here and there, by fits and starts, now and then. Not efficient, but persistent. And wherever you run into it, the surprise is that it works—seems like it is the only thing that works consistently in this world. To bad we have never been able to mobilize any really massive energy behind this option! I hear people saying, in their ignorance, that Christianity has been around for 2,000 years and has never really worked. Well, the fact is that it has never really been tried on any significant scale at all. In simple local settings where it has really been put to work, it has succeeded spectacularly. The alternative options have brought nothing but the horrors of history.

Peter's most life-changing epiphany follows nicely after our discussion of Jesus' achievement of self-understanding and divine mission. Of course, Peter was a Jew like Jesus, born into a society that was very parochial. They really thought they were the only people of God and that everyone else made up a world of lost souls. Indeed, the Jews considered non-Jews as both alien and unclean. To them we were all the untouchables, and to many of them we still are! Then along came Jesus and sowed into the hearts of his disciples some unconventional ideas. Jesus continued to talk like his divine mission was basically for the country of Israel, but occasionally he gave some evidence that he had a wider vision. He went to visit a Greek woman from Syrophenicia and healed her daughter (Mark 7:26). He had compassion on the Roman Centurion and healed his son (Mt 8:5–14, Lk 2:7–7). John's gospel has Jesus repeatedly referring to his being the savior of the *whole world* (3:16–17, 12:32).

In any case, some years after Jesus' departure, Peter was busy trying to figure out his mission project in this world, for God's reign of love that works and grace that heals. He had been concentrating mainly on converting Jews to Christianity in what we call today the Hellenistic Jewish Christian Church. Paul had already been demonstrating great success in his mission to Asia Minor (Turkey) and Greece, converting Gentiles to the faith. A fairly aggressive interdenominational fight was brewing between the Hellenistic Gentile churches Paul was establishing and the Hellenistic Jewish churches Peter was promoting. The battle was about whether Gentile converts should be required to follow the Jewish laws of diet and circumcision that still prevailed in the Jewish Christian churches.

Right in the middle of this nasty conflict, which, incidentally, came to head at the first ecumenical council of the worldwide church, Peter had a dream which turned out to be a life-changing epiphany. He and Paul had a knock-down, drag-out fight, according to Paul's account of it. The conflict was over Paul's claim that being a believer in Jesus as the Messiah did not require Christians to be circumcised or to be observant Jews. James, who ran

the Palestinian Jewish Christian Church in Jerusalem, worked out a com-
promise in which Paul's churches did not need to follow Jewish law, while
Peter's could if they wished. James' church was thoroughly observant, and
his Jewish Christians still worshipped in the temple in Jerusalem and kept
the Jewish feasts and rituals.

About that time, one would suppose, Peter dreamed his epiphany. In it
several sheets were let down from heaven before him, filled with clean and
unclean meats. A voice commanded him to eat of both. He protested that he
would not eat of the unclean meats because that violated Jewish law; moreover, if the unclean meats had not been kept separate from the clean meats,
the latter were also rendered unclean. Therefore, he would not eat anything
from this heavenly buffet. The voice then declared to him, peremptorily,
"What God has called clean, you better not call unclean." Peter got the point
immediately. He knew this was a metaphoric message about his fight with
Paul, and that he was not on God's side of the issue. He was a man who
had tried hard to walk and talk with God. He wanted to be on God's side of
things. The epiphany changed his life.

Now, were these epiphanies the sort of enlightenment that can come to
twenty-first-century people as well, or were they some kind of other worldly
magic, limited to the Bible stories or Bible times? Of course, there is no difference between all of these epiphanies and our own experiences. Either all of
them come from earthly sources or they all come from heavenly sources, no
doubt about it. However, who can tell the difference and what difference does
it make? Or, to put the matter more succinctly, is it not possible, even likely,
that the dichotomy I just constructed between the earthly and the heavenly
does not exist at all?

Whether an epiphany is generated by electrical impulses in my unconscious or by energy sources in God's transcendent world, both and either
are products of God's divine system for illumining me. The miracle is in the
fact that the insight is initiated at all, that there is an energy source for it in
any case, and that the channel for it to be conveyed to my conscious mind is
crafted just the way it must be to awaken me to a profound new insight. Ingenious insights, registered in our complex consciousnesses, at just the critical
moment that life change is necessary and possible are things of God. Those
who walk and talk with God, live life in the quest for and consciousness of
the presence and spirit of God, experience those illuminations as words from
God. The confirmation of the truth of it is the quality of the life change that
is generated by the experience.

CHAPTER 8

BIBLICAL SPIRITUALITY AS
COUNTING ON GOD

Paul counted on God. From his Damascus road epiphany to the end of his life he counted on God. His entire theology is a theology of counting on God, absolutely. That is, his interpretation of Jesus and his ministry claims without reservation that Jesus' entire intention was to get us to count on God abjectly and at all costs. Of course, it was Paul's interpretation that gave us Christianity as we have known it since the end of the first century C.E. Paul, clearly and urgently, enjoined us all to count on God.

This was not a new message in the Judeo-Christian tradition. The Hebrew Bible, the Old Testament, is striated and held together in a coherent stream of thought and history by its call and encouragement for people everywhere to count on God. However, Paul's emphasis, filled with the spirit that he perceived was in Jesus Christ, promoted the idea of counting on God with a new style and a new urgency. He gave a new focus to the long-standing biblical quest for human life with God.

For Paul, counting on God meant trusting God to be a God of unconditional, radical, and universal grace, and counting on God's grace to be absolutely real and predictably practical. That is, we can count on God to be a God of grace to us and we can count on the experience of God's grace to give us that relief and fulfillment that makes us feel completely whole and tranquil in our spiritual quest, in the midst of the travail of earthly life. Everything Paul ever wrote moves consistently along this trajectory, and always to this specific point. His confidence in counting on God is epitomized in Romans 8:28–39 where his memorable words have accorded Christians immense consolation in triumph and tragedy, sin and salvation, joy and sorrow for

2,000 years, no matter what was happening in their lives and in history. Paul declared in those verses,

> We know that in everything God works for good with those who love him, who feel called to live their lives true to God's purposes.... What then shall we say to this? Since God is for us, who can be against us?... It is God who justifies; who can possibly condemn us? Jesus Christ can; but he died for us, indeed he was resurrected for us, he is at the right hand of God interceding for us. So who shall separate us from the love of Christ?... In all things we are more than conquerors through God who loves us. I am thoroughly persuaded that neither death nor life; neither otherworldly agents nor earthly powers; neither the past, present, or future; neither powers from heaven nor powers from hell, nor anything in all of God's world can separate us from the love of God. (JHE trans)

Counting on God is not a spiritual experience or style of faith unique to the Christian faith quest. Indeed, the Jesus Movement developed out of a type of Judaism, in fact, a rather wild apocalyptic eschatological type of Second Temple Judaism. Likewise, the *style of Christian spirituality* came from that Judaic source. Jesus and Paul were both Jews, entrenched in Jewish history and tradition. Both prized the Israelite pilgrimage in the quest for God, and both valued much of Israelite religion and the Judaisms of their day. It was that Judaic source of both spiritual quest and religious behavior from which Paul drew the essential elements of his theology of grace.

Paul was well aware of the fact that the prophet Micah, six or seven hundred years before him, had championed exactly this same kind of notion about counting on God. As we have noted before, Micah was sure that from long before any of us were born we were already secured in God's promise of forgiving grace and providential goodness to all people. Moreover, Micah grounded his conviction, that God is the kind of God we can count on, in the insights to which Abraham had come in his search for God 2,000 years earlier. Despite the precarious and ambiguous complexity of Israelite history, the tradition that God was a God to be counted on, absolutely, was long-standing in Israelite religion. The Israelites were more inclined toward losing their grip on that confident faith vision than they were toward holding to it with firm embrace, but the tradition persisted resiliently, nonetheless. It formed the mainstream of the message of all the prophets of Israel, with the rare exception of those few who seemed to have nothing more on their minds or in their psyches than bitching and moaning.

One of the ways in which this strong confidence in God is expressed in the Bible is by its frequent reference to our hope in God. Hope is described in many ways and contexts in the Hebrew and Christian scriptures, but seldom so graphically as in the anchor metaphor, especially notable in the Epistle to the Hebrews. This metaphor of confidence in God as an anchor is, admittedly, somewhat limited in biblical usage, but the concept is frequently referred to. In Hebrews 6:18b–20a we have this rather dramatic picture painted for us.

> We who have fled for refuge may have strong encouragement to seize the hope set before us. We have this as a sure and steadfast anchor of the soul, a hope that enters into the inner shrine behind the curtain, where Jesus has gone as a forerunner on our behalf.

Now any person in any faith tradition who lives out his or her spiritual quest in studied consciousness of God's gracious presence and provident guidance should be able to express with confidence that his or her faith is like that anchor of hope. That is a kind of watershed criterion of the fruitfulness and maturity, or authenticity, of any person's spiritual quest, it seems to me. In the Christian tradition the metaphor is always tied to that significant psychotheological notion of a durable hope. That is the very core concept for the Hebrews Epistle, and you could say for the warp and woof of the entire biblical narrative. I believe that the author of the Hebrews Epistle, indeed, all of the biblical authors, would agree with what I have long considered the bottom line of authentic spirituality or religious belief: "Will it bury your child?" That is, is your faith or spirituality of such a kind and quality that you have some kind of meaningful life left after you have been forced to lower your dead child into the cavernous tomb? Nothing ever gets worse than that in life. It is the watershed criterion for authentic spirituality, I believe.

At such a point in life the only thing that counts, the only thing that helps, the only thing that works is some kind of durable hope. That is the import of the anchor metaphor in the Epistle to the Hebrew Christians. The figure of the anchor is also linked here to an interesting but complex model of God and the material universe. In Hebrews 6:19–20 we have a two-storied universe.

The context of the story is important. God is represented in Hebrews 6 as guaranteeing the promise that he can be counted on. His guarantee is twofold: his promise and his character. The author of the epistle argues that surely God cannot lie about either one of these and still be God. So you can see how the mythic confession of faith is unfolding here. That is why, as stated in the passage quoted above, we can confidently flee to that promise as a refuge. We can count on the fact that God can be counted on. That anchor of our spiritual quest is held in the hands of Jesus, who as a forerunner has gone before us into eternity with God.

The author mixes his metaphors a bit here. This produces a complicated framework of symbols. We have (1) the question of the function of the curtain or transcendental veil through which Jesus enters the heavenly world with our anchor; (2) Jesus named as a transcendental high priest; (3) Jesus, as our transcendental high priest, called the timeless Melchizedek; and (4) the mysterious concept of the Christological "forerunner."

The metaphor is mixed in the sense that the concept of forerunner is not a particularly nautical figure, though the main structure of the picture here seems to be nautical, because it is dominated by the anchor metaphor. However, if we think of the forerunner as the person in the small boat who goes ashore ahead of the ship and anchors the rope solidly in the bedrock of the harbor, the picture clarifies and the metaphor is coherent and uniform.

Obviously the writer of this epistle is earnestly trying to create an operational rationale for the psychology and theology of godly hope, of counting on God, in the Pauline sense. Placing the focus of our spiritual hope upon the image of Jesus as an eternal high priest employs a notion, however, that goes far beyond any similar percepts in Paul's writings and in most other religious traditions. Melchizedek is an Old Testament priest of the Most High God, whose birth and death were known to no one, and hence he seemed to everyone to be an ethereal eternal figure. So the author of Hebrews uses that enigmatic figure to emphasize Jesus' eternal priesthood, thus reinforcing the durability and eternity of the concept of hope promoted by the passage.

The prominent core concept, around which the Hebrews Epistle is built, then, is this biblical concept of hope, which is, moreover, universal to all faith traditions. It says that we can count on God and that living the life with our sail set close to the wind is the life of counting on God, in that sense. This is not a wishful notion of some desirable eventuality that might not develop. This kind of hope, which the author describes for the Hebrew Christians, is a confident certitude that the future will provide exactly the same fulfilling and secure experience that our past life of faith has offered. The past life with God has been fulfilling, and the future is secure in the same expectation.

The author would certainly have meant to include the experiences of divine providence, creative beneficence, consolation, meaningful purposiveness, and peace. John Calvin thought that faith was best described as a sure knowledge of God and of his promises, and a *certain* confidence that all things are directed to their appointed end. Christian hope, in this epistle, is *that* kind of palpable and confidently grounded faith, projected forward through all the unknowns of the future, including life after death. This concept of hope, which is emphasized at five key junctures within the epistle, constitutes the set of hinges upon which the entire story line of the whole book turns.

That story line is interesting, and the references to hope in it are illumining for our purposes in understanding the anchor metaphor in 6:19; and so for understanding this epistle's notion about counting on God. The first phase of the narrative encompasses chapters 1–3. It begins with the high view of Jesus Christ that we find in chapter 1. There we read, in words that sound a lot like John's Gospel, that Jesus, the Christ, is identified as the Son of God in whom the full divine nature is evident. Jesus is God's agent in creation. He has the stamp of God's nature. He is sustaining the universe, enthroned in heavenly majesty, and superior to the angelic host. This first phase of the story reaches its climax with the defining assertion in 3:6 that "Christ was faithful over God's house as a son; and we are his house if we hold fast to our confident hope."

The important issue to be noticed here is that Jesus, the Christ, is divine and functions as God's chief of staff, now that he is in heaven. So the believing community has a solid reason for hope for God's grace, mercy, and provident goodness, because Jesus, who is one of us and surely has our best interests at heart, is exalted to the role of divine chief of staff. There he has specific responsibility to manage our affairs for time and eternity. "We are his house, if we hold fast our confident hope" (3:6). Moreover, Calvin emphasizes once again in this context that Christian hope is the certitude of empirically based faith, projected confidently through all the unknowns of future time and eternity.[1] This perspective sets the stage for our understanding of the spiritual model we have in the anchor metaphor of 6:19.

The second phase of the narrative is initiated by the first word of Hebrews 4; "Therefore," we should take serious interest in entering into our eternal rest where Christ is. This second phase closes with the last words of chapter 4, where the author emphasizes, once again, the significant confidence inherent to Christian hope. "Let us then with confidence draw near to the throne of grace, that we may receive mercy and find grace to help in time of need" (4:16). In the Bible, the throne of grace is always a reference to the metaphor of enthronement of God as the God of grace, to whom we turn in prayer. When we experience a biblical kind of spirituality by talking to God, we can do it with confident assurance that we shall receive mercy and grace appropriate to our needs. It is notable that here the content of Christian hope is spelled out concretely, as we have alluded to it already above. It is simply our confident certitude that grace, mercy, and provident goodness are guaranteed us because Jesus, the Christ, has our interests at heart and he is in charge of our destiny. This colorful and inspiring confessional myth of biblical hope has successfully sustained numerous generations of humans through every kind of vicissitude of life for at least three or four millennia. It is the universal human hope against our common human terrors.

The third phase of the story, Hebrews 5–6, reinforces the claim that we are in good hands by introducing the metaphor of Jesus as our transcendental high priest. Who could have more power and authority to look after our interests than our own personal high priest, with the specific priestly office of bringing the needs and cares of God's people to the throne whence God's covenant grace and forgiveness reign? Moreover, he knows our need for grace, mercy, and sustaining goodness, because he is one of us, a human being. "For every high priest chosen from among men is appointed to act on behalf of men in relation to God, to offer gifts and sacrifices. He can deal gently with the ignorant and wayward, since he himself is beset with weakness (humanness)" (5:1–2).

One cannot savor the flavor of these lines without being reminded of Paul's observations in Romans 8, "If God is for us, who can be against us?...Who shall bring any charge against God's people? It is God who justifies, who can condemn us? *Christ Jesus can* (presumably because he lived a human life and did it right); but he died for us, he was resurrected for us, he is enthroned at the right hand of God for us, indeed, he intercedes for us. Who shall separate us from the *love* of God in Christ?" (8:31–35).

According to the author of this epistle, this priesthood is both human, like Melchizedek's (5:6), and divine, that is, heavenly and eternal. Jesus, the Christ, qualified for it by learning obedience to God through suffering as a human (5:8), "and being made perfect he became the source of eternal salvation to all who obey him, being designated by God a high priest after the order of Melchizedek" (5:9–10). This is the main hinge of the argument that makes 6:19 and its anchor make sense in the theological logic of the epistle. Chapter 6 opens with the invitation to leave the elemental doctrines of Christology, that is, the ideas of following the Christ as a kind of model of ideal legalistic human behavior: good works, ablutions, magical spirituality, and fear of hell (6:1–2).

Here the author is writing a critique of his or her fellow Jews who hold to the Old Testament concepts of hope but have not embraced what he or she considers to be the deeper certitude of Christian hope. The author claims that on the one hand, a former law (priesthood by genetic succession) is set aside because of its weakness and uselessness (for the law made nothing perfect). On the other hand, a better hope is introduced, through which we draw near to God (7:18–19). We are enjoined to partake of the illuminations of the Holy Spirit, rather than legalistic striving. We are invited to taste "of the goodness of the word of God and the powers of the age to come   better things that belong to salvation...the full assurance of hope until the end..., imitators of those who through faith and patience inherit the promises," presumably the promises to Abraham and Christ (6:5, 9, and 12).

The stage is now set for our metaphor: the anchor of our hope. The argument is intricate but predictable in the light of the above. God promised to Abraham that he would be a God to him and his progeny forever, no strings attached (Gen. 12 and 17). The promise was made with an oath, "Surely I will bless you and multiply you," a thing for which Abraham had to wait patiently a long time; but the promise was fulfilled and the oath both kept and vindicated. So the climax of this phase of the argument and the illumination of our anchor metaphor is now inevitable. "We who have fled for refuge may have strong encouragement to seize the hope set before us...a sure and steadfast anchor of the soul" (6:18b).

Of course, it is not difficult for an informed Bible student to notice the import of this concatenation of word pictures. The similes or metaphors employed here conjure up the picture of Solomon's temple, of course. Our high priest presents himself on our behalf in the temple's Holy Place and even enters further into the place where only the high priest may go, into the Holy of Holies, behind the curtain. In this metaphor, however, the curtain is the screen between temporal and eternal life.

This word picture is extended through the next phase of the epistle's narrative, in chapters 7–10, in which the image of the progress of the high priest into the temple and into the Holy of Holies is graphically described in detail, and the metaphoric implications are drawn out. This development arrives at its telling climax in 9:11–12, and 10:19–23. Here Christ is depicted as a high priest of the good things that have come, we have confidence to enter the sanctuary by this new way that he opened for us through the curtain, and since we have a great priest over the house of God, we can "draw near with a true heart in full assurance of faith," holding fast to our hope "for he who promised is faithful." The remaining two sections of the epistle celebrate the heroes of faith and hope in chapter 11 and enjoin Christian faith, hope, and love in 12 and 13.

We have noticed how each phase of the narrative turns on the hinge of the spiritual hope celebrated as the climax of each section of the story. This creates a crescendo of hopeful urgency up to the point of our metaphor. The confidence and certitude of godly hope is grounded in the claim that Jesus, the Christ, one of us humans, has been exalted by God to the high priestly role of God's chief of staff and the manager of the affairs of the community of believers. In that role he has presented himself, metaphorically, into the Holy of Holies of the divine presence, where he resolves all matters of grace, mercy, and goodness on our behalf.

But why an anchor in the Holy of Holies? This metaphor as an anchor symbolizing hope is not from the Old Testament but from Greek classical tradition. There it was a long-standing symbol for hope.[2] Hope and anchor in ancient Greek are compatible figures in that both imply strong and steadfast safety and shelter for fugitives. The New Testament speaks of "tossed and troubled spirits, in imminent danger of making *shipwreck of the faith*" (I Tim. 1:19). The heavy anchor of a ship is sunk into the sea bottom; but the hope anchor of the authentically spiritual person is carried to the remote bedrock of eternity and there finds its stable ground. The word picture in Classical literature is built around the shape of the anchor, as a hook, and around its capacity to hook into something solid and hold fast.

The word picture intends to suggest that we are refugees from the sinking ship of this present world order. So our hope is fixed on the eternal world order, where the promises of God are made good to his people in perpetuity. Our hope, based upon his promises, is our spiritual anchor,[3] moored to an immoveable object, the throne of God itself, where Jesus is (1:3). As faith is based heuristically, phenomenologically, and empirically upon the experience of God's past performance, so Christian hope is grounded solidly in the certitude of God's promises for the future. Moreover, this certitude is given tangible and palpable trustworthiness by the fact that one of us, who understands our predicament and has our best interests at heart, has not only gone before us into eternity as our forerunner, but has been accorded the role of our high priest and manager of our temporal and eternal affairs, in the very presence of God. Moreover, he has the authority of one enthroned by God as his chief of staff. Fairly solid ground for ethereal things, to say the least!

So the complex of metaphors comes down to one rather unusual image. The high priest, wearing the ephod on which are the symbols of all the tribes and peoples, enters through the veil into the hidden sanctuary of the Holy of Holies and its unknown spaces and atmospheres, its unknown world. He drags with him a heavy anchor whose cable is tied to the vessel containing the community of believers. Bloodied and battered from negotiating the shoals of crashing waves, pounding surf, roaring tides, and tricky rocks of history, he passes through the concealing mist and bloody spray of transition into the transcendental world. There he sinks the anchor into the solid ground of eternity, wrapping the cable, as it were, around the very throne of God himself, so to speak. Now the anchor holds or God himself is at risk. The promise and oath from the throne endure, or the throne is dragged away into the maelstrom of meaningless human history.

But how do we get a high priest carrying an anchor so that we can get an anchor into the Holy of Holies? The clue is probably in Leviticus 9 and the prophecy of Ezekiel. Marvin A. Sweeney,[4] and before him Margaret S. Odell,[5] have given us great assistance here. Sweeney explains the prophecy of Ezekiel in which he demonstrates that the book is built around the prescription in the Torah for priestly ordination ritual. In Leviticus 8–9, as well as in Numbers 4 and 8, the requirements and procedures for that ordination are stipulated. The priestly ordinand was required to experience seven qualifying ritual steps: (1) achieve the appropriate age and maturity (30 years old) for ordination; (2) ingest a divine gift (a sacrificed ram); (3) endure a spiritual retreat (a period of sacred days); (4) symbolically atone for the sins of the multitude (perform a blood sacrifice, or in Ezekiel's case measure and thus symbolically recapitulate the destruction of the city and temple); (5) experience a theophany (in the tabernacle or temple, as in Isaiah 6:1–13, or as in Ezekiel, the visions of his repeated call by God); (6) proclaim the kingdom of God on the earth; and (7) predict the destruction of the holy places.

It is clear, upon careful reflection, that the gospel writers consciously copied this taxonomy in writing the story of Jesus. He was apparently (1) called and ordained by baptism at age 30; (2) immediately received a theophany at his baptism; (3) spent sacred days (40) in the wilderness immediately thereafter in spiritual retreat; (4) ingested a divine gift in the form of the nourishment that the angels are said to have provided him in the wilderness retreat; (5) made symbolic atonement for the sins of the multitude; (6) proclaimed the kingdom of God; and (7) predicted the destruction of the holy places (Mk 13). Indeed, he effected a symbolic destruction of the temple himself in John 2 (Mt 21, Mk 11, and Lk 19).[6]

Surely this notion of Jesus' conformity to the requirements of priestly ordination is graphically present in the mind of the author of the Hebrews Epistle. The projection of his role as high priest is a very short step from there in the metaphoric narrative. The spiritualization of his struggle for the kingdom of God, through the travail of Gethsemane and Golgotha, to the drama of the resurrection and ascension stories readily formed the matrix in which the author of the epistle employs the concept of secure hope as used in classical Greek literature. The agent of our hope (our high priest) becomes the carrier of our anchor (the transcendent agent of our eternal security, as well as of our other best interests). That anchor is grounded in the bedrock of the eternal authority of God, expressed in his promise and oath. That authority is delegated to God's chief of staff, our representative in the heavenly realm—our guy at the head shed, as we used to say in the army. So the anchor is quite compatibly manhandled by our High Priest and carried through the veil of the future unknown and hooked on the leg of the throne of the Almighty.

Therefore, Ebrard declared, poetically, "The soul, like one in danger of shipwreck, casts forth her anchor; and though she cannot see whither the rope is running, she knows that the anchor itself is fastened to a ground within the veil which hides the future and the heavenly from her view, and feels assured that if she can only keep fast hold to the end, she will finally be drawn by a Saviour's hand upwards and inwards to the eternal sanctuary. *So hope contains within itself a power which draws on its own fulfilment"* [7] (emphasis added). This is the whole point of the spiritual strategy of counting on God!

Certainly the author of the Hebrews Epistle succeeds in his or her intention to conceptualize Christian hope for the unknown future as just as sure and certain a reality as the empirically and heuristically based faith of past experience, in the light of the witness of the prophets and apostles. What a lot of generations of believers of this Christian myth have, in the precarious vicissitudes of life and history, gotten through the travail of burying their own children and successfully negotiating the perplexities of their own morality and mortality by holding fast to this anchored hope, counting on God!

It is possible to tell the entire story of the Bible, in all its 66 books, as the story of God's invitation to humankind to count on God. The counterpoint to the melody in this score, of course, is dissonance and cacophony raised when the Israelite people or the Christian community lost their grip on this anchor rope and wandered off into spiritual confusion. Moreover, as Joseph Campbell and Ninian Smart emphasized, this pattern of spiritual melody and cacophony is not just the story of the spiritual quest of the biblical communities. It is the story of humankind in our hunger for God and our troubled process of finding the experience of God and godliness.

CHAPTER 9

BIBLICAL SPIRITUALITY AND THE HOLY SPIRIT

Any quest for understanding biblical spirituality must take account of the Holy Spirit. Regardless of how one understands the Judaic or Christian theological doctrine about the Holy Spirit, it is the unavoidable case that this figure is a mysterious presence throughout the Bible. The Holy Spirit first appears in the second verse of the Bible.

> In the beginning God created the heaven and the earth. And the earth was without form and void; and darkness was upon the face of the deep. And the Spirit of God moved upon the face of the waters. (KJV)

It is clear that from the outset the Bible wishes to inform us that from the very first moments of the existence of this material universe until this very latest moment in our individual and communal lives, it is the Holy Spirit that constitutes God's creative presence with us. The implication of this is that whatever course we take in our own spiritual quest, it is our hunger for and our response to the divine spirit that drives our spiritual development.

The Christian community has neglected the Holy Spirit. Humans wish for concrete things that can be dealt with tangibly. The Holy Spirit is illusive, subtle, whimsical, wistful, and ethereal. Jesus once said that it is like the wind (Jn 3:8). You cannot really tell where it is coming from nor where it is going, but you can discern the force of it, and its consequences are empirically evident all around us. As I sit writing this chapter, the branches of the big oak trees outside my window are moving rather vigorously. I cannot tell where the forces working on them are coming from or going; that is, I cannot tell, from watching them move, from what direction the wind is blowing. However, that it is blowing is obvious. I can tell that the wind is present in my world right now and is quite forceful. Moreover, I can discern from the kite flying high in the sky beyond the trees that it is a good day with a good wind for a young boy, just free from school, to enjoy the vigorous life the wind brings him.

So it is with our personal spirituality. It is difficult to define, impossible to quantify, but enormously influential in the way our lives are shaped by it. It offers the great delight of experiencing the life that the wind of the spirit can bring us. The Hebrew word for the Spirit of God in Genesis 1:2 is (*ruach*) the breath or wind of God. That is why Jesus' metaphor in John 3 is so apt a description of the Holy Spirit in our lives. One of the reasons why the community of believers, Jewish and Christian, has neglected the pursuit of knowing the spirit of God is that it is so difficult to quantify. In our preference for the concrete rather than the ethereal, we prefer the legal regulations of Moses or the propositions about the history of Jesus.

Such things are possible to define and package in well-dressed religious packages. So the believing communities have spent the last 2,000 years keeping busy with theological definitions about Moses or Christ or the propositions of Mohammed. We have failed to realize that God is not present to us in our day in Moses, Christ, or Mohammed. They are memories that we may cherish, but all we have of them is these memories. For Christians, for example, veneration of Christ will never cease because Jesus is our very best memory. However, the Holy Spirit is our very best present experience of God with and to us in this time in history.

In fact, Christians who have been really serious about their spiritual quest have tended to be preoccupied with Jesus Christ to such an extent that their ideas and memories of him have become a kind of idolatry. This preoccupation has often obstructed their capacity to really connect with God. It is difficult to get modern-day Christians to refocus their spiritual life from Jesus to the Holy Spirit, despite the fact that Jesus instructed us to do so in his farewell address to his disciples (Jn 14). Christians today tend to pray to Jesus. Marcus Borg says that most Christians have simply renamed God as Jesus Christ. The Bible calls God Yahweh. That was the name of God, so far as Jesus and his disciples were concerned. That was true for the early church as well.

We have been preoccupied with Jesus for so long, at the expense of any direct conscious sense of the presence of God, that we have in effect substituted Jesus and his name for God and God's name. So Christians pray to Jesus, meaning to be praying to God. This is understandable, in the sense that the ancient bishops, who formulated the Christian theological statements of faith in the fourth and fifth centuries after Christ, defined Jesus as God. They said that God is Father, Son, and Holy Spirit, a divine trinity. Of course, that may be good and well, but it differs from Jesus' notion. He made it clear that our awareness and experience of God present to us since his departure should be as life with the Holy Spirit. Biblical spirituality is about life lived with the Holy Spirit of God, which Paul always called the spirit of Christ.

My father's cryptic view of all this was very pragmatic. He said, "Work like everything is up to you. Pray like everything is up to the Holy Spirit of God." I believe that the outcome of that kind of spiritual life will be a rich spiritual product of the action of the spirit, realized through that kind of responsible action of the person. Frankly, I still see that as superb advice for sensible and authentic spirituality, no matter what is one's religion or community of faith. I think any truly spiritual Jew or Muslim would agree wholeheartedly. When my father died, the man who gave me the most spiritual help and consolation was a Muslim who spoke to me of communion with the Holy Spirit. He spoke in terms of what had really helped him when his father died.

The Holy Spirit is always a mystery, an intriguing agent of God, full of intimations of God's nature, truth, and grace. These intimations speak spontaneously to our natures as we hunger for God. In this process, the spirit is always evident, sometimes only in retrospect, always better than we thought it could be. One must have the eyes to see and ears to hear, of course. That is, these things are evident to those living life close to the wind, expecting the progress that comes from such a vital spiritual quest. It is an intriguing and exciting thing, indeed, to live life always consciously anticipating how the Holy Spirit of God will show up around the next corner. The spirit always does if we are expecting it.

My son-in-law is an officer at a well-known state prison. Whenever he describes his work to me I become aware again of the fact that the experience of being in prison is, for the guards and prisoners alike, a special way of life. That is, it takes on the shape of a *prison culture*. It is a very different, unconventional mode of existence, but it runs as a community system because the conditions are clear to everyone, the expectations are understood by everyone, and they have a language peculiar to that community. In a constructive way, the same was true for me for the 37 years I served as an army officer. The military culture was as pleasing to me as the prison culture seems to me rather horrid.

Comparably, since the 1970s we have heard a lot of talk about the distinctive kinds of communities in which we live in America. People speak positively or pejoratively about being part of an urban culture or of a suburban culture. Depending upon your value system, you may be pleased or pained by either or both. We hear of people bemoaning the loss of America's rural culture. Most people who grew up in rural cultures do not bemoan its disappearance.

I once lived briefly, as a soldier, in the Bronx, New York, and I have close friends in Brooklyn. There I discovered that people in the Bronx of the 1950s had a Bronx culture and the Brooklynites had a Brooklyn culture quite different from what I had experienced elsewhere. One of the striking things about it was that our neighbor and friend was scared to cross the Hudson River into what she considered the Western wilderness. She was sure that if you crossed the Appalachian Mountains you would find wild Indians riding broncos, with feathers stuck in their hair.

During the 1960s to 1980s we heard much about hippie types going back to nature—a naturalist culture. We do not hear of that anymore because most of those experiments failed when those folks, ignorant of what nature was really like, discovered to their dismay that nature will bite you in all the very sensitive places you have, the first chance it gets, and will discourage and defeat you.

I am interested in emphasizing here what it means to create a distinctive way of life or a distinctive kind of culture, in the sense I have been suggesting. Any community of faith intends to develop a consciousness of being the growing People of God together. That is, regardless of our faith tradition, we tend to experience ourselves as a group of individuals that has formed a social community in which we are busy investing ourselves, spiritually and materially, in developing the consciousness of being God's people. That is who we really are and what we are really about.

You could say, then, that we are creating a distinctive culture, a culture of consciousness that we are a people in communion with God in everything we do and are. For 2,000 years Christian churches have been busy cultivating a Jesus culture. Christians have talked all the time about following Jesus, loving Jesus, living Jesus' example, being Jesus' disciples, and working for Jesus. There was a certain remote truth to that, but it is not exactly in line with Jesus' instructions. You will remember from John 14, as I hinted above, that Jesus said, "I am going away. You cannot come now. I will prepare a place for you to which you can come later; but I will not leave you feeling like orphans. The important thing is that I will send you the Holy Spirit of God, who will testify to you regarding what I was up to; and that spirit will lead you into the truth" (JHE paraphrase). The Jesus culture in the church for 20 centuries turned Jesus into a religious idol and replaced both God and the Holy Spirit in our consciousness, with a historical messiah.

True spirituality, however, would move us toward the cultivation of a Holy Spirit culture. By that I mean that everything we think, say, anticipate, hope for, and experience regarding our relationship to God may be shaped by conscious and intentional awareness of the Holy Spirit. That means that to be a Christian and to be the church means that we expect to experience God present to us as spirit. Thus we should always be expecting to experience that presence. God is always busy trying to relate to us as God's spirit with our spirits.

I think that cultivating a Holy Spirit culture, as a valuable form of biblical spirituality, means 10 things. First, it means expecting to experience the presence of God's spirit in tangible ways regularly. Second, it means that we hold ourselves consciously open to the intimations of God's spirit in our practical daily lives. Third, it means that we notice the manifestations of God's spirit in ordinary and extraordinary moments and events. Fourth, it means that we identify those experiences of God's manifestations or intimations to us individually and communally, as the presence of the Holy Spirit. Fifth, it means that we name those moments as "of the spirit." Sixth, it means that we explain those moments to each other and thus raise the consciousness level of us all regarding the constant ministry of the spirit in our lives. Seventh, it means to continually recall together that those moments have happened and continue to happen. Eighth, it means to become a community of believers who are constantly conscious that we are experiencing God's spirit all the time. Ninth, it requires that we develop an aura of consciousness of being the people of God who live in the matrix of the active presence of Holy Spirit in us and around us. Tenth, it involves our coming to think of ourselves as the body that is constantly made lively by that spirit of God and living in the expectation of the experiences of the spirit's presence to us in tangible ways.

That is what I mean by creating a Holy Spirit culture. We do not need to do anything to make it happen except to cultivate a constant consciousness of the experiences of the Holy Spirit in God's spirit's ministry of presence to us. You could say that we live in a matrix of forces that looks natural and mundane but is in fact transcendental. God is always working by the spirit, from the eternal world in this temporal world. The spirit of God is alive here. We all have stories to tell that testify to that. I have mentioned the fact before that at a most stressful time in my life, when I feared I would lose my ministry, my ordination, my life calling, my livelihood, and my ability to support my family, I was awakened in the middle of the night by a voice that said loudly, "Trust in the Lord and do good!" That was a moment of the Holy Spirit illumining and leading me. From that moment on I was completely relieved of my anguish, and the problem eventually resolved itself. As I have mentioned before, my life has been shaped by about a dozen of those special turning points of the spirit's illumination.

When we (1) notice those kinds of moments, (2) name them for what they are, and (3) celebrate them together, we become a culture conscious of the spirit. They are not always such dramatic experiences as I reported or as the Bible records. They may be an inadvertent meeting with a stranger in the grocery store line that turns into a healing sharing of an important spiritual insight, heartening your life, and his or hers, for the rest of the day. Every time, however great or small the event, it is the breaking in of the presence of God's spirit into your spirit's consciousness to shape your life in the light of heaven. Those moments we must remember and make a part of our growing consciousness, the awareness that we live in that kind of surprising world of the spirit, participating already now in the things eternal. That is the epitome of biblical spirituality and will surely produce healthy and authentic religious behavior.

We express the spiritual implications of such experiences with joyful worship, studying the Bible, fellowship experiences of shared love and cherishing of each other, mission programs, and all the things we can do in ministry. Believing that we live in a matrix of spiritual forces working in and through us, we put ourselves into high gear for the Holy Spirit culture. That is, a Holy Spirit culture is always a culture of gratitude. If God is as busy with us as I say he is, clearly it is appropriate for us to be as invested as God is in joyfully and gratefully making sure that we open all the doors for God to lead us through, in his ministry to and through us.

God has declared God's covenant of unconditional and universal grace to all people, guaranteeing that we are all God's people and God is our God, no matter what. God guaranteed that we can never sin ourselves out of God's grace, nor squirm out of God's long embrace. Therefore, authentic, Bible-based spirituality will be shaped by expressions of our gratitude to God.

Now, the Holy Spirit, and life in or with the spirit, is not magical. As Jesus suggested in John 3:8, it is living constantly with a sense of expecting and looking for an experience, the nature of which we cannot be sure until we are experiencing it. We search for it, not knowing exactly what it will look like, and when we experience it we realize it was right there before our noses. That is, the Bible suggests and experience confirms that the spirit of God is always present, permeating the world. We live in a matrix of divine spirit, as surely as we live in an atmosphere of oxygen, hydrogen, and nitrogen. We are often unaware of just how that is true. As we cultivate the culture of the Holy Spirit, we raise our own consciousness level regarding it, acquiring the eyes to see.

Most stories in the Bible that allude to or describe moments of the Holy Spirit indicate that it was while some human was looking for the spirit, so to speak, that the spirit overtook him or her. The issue at stake always seems to have been whether the person could recognize the spirit of God in such a moment. In Zachariah's dream of Joshua in the divine judgment hall, it was just at the moment of Joshua's potentially greatest danger and despair that the spirit of God showed up to him and set everything right (Zach. 3).

There is no formula for achieving the experience of the spirit in our spirits. It cannot be prescribed as a medication for spirituality. We do not need to craft it and cannot dig it up or search it out. We can pursue it only in the sense of consciously living our lives waiting for God to manifest God's self to us, that is, living life open to the spirit. We can and must recognize it when we experience it. Then we must name it and share it.

How often one hears stories of moments like that experienced by a friend of mine. She was waiting in the checkout line at a grocery store. The lady ahead of her was struggling with her glasses, checkbook, pen, and paraphernalia. As she struggled, she remarked to the clerk that she was upset and confused because her mother was dying. My friend spontaneously expressed concern about how hard that can be. That led to an extended conversation in which she was able to share the burden of that stranger and communicate to her the consolations that my friend experienced in sailing her life close to the wind of the spirit, so to speak. This struck a responsive chord in the stranger's soul, and the upshot of the event was a great sense of strength and renewal for both persons. It is important to name those moments as events "of the spirit" and then share them with others so that they become a conscious culture of the Holy Spirit and are not forgotten.

C. S. Lewis is said to have observed that such experience as my friend had in the grocery line are common for all humanity. At the time they happen we know beyond a shadow of a doubt that they are of God, moments with God. Then we spend the next six weeks rationalizing them away. I think that he is right and the reason we rationalize them away is because we do not name them, share them, establish them in a tradition of memory, and so make them into a conscious culture of the Holy Spirit. For our best growth in the spirit, regardless of our faith tradition, it is imperative that we name, share, remember, and cultivate them, so we may be the celebrating people of God.

When Jesus departed from his disciples on the Mount of Olives, they were wondering whether he was going to set up the Kingdom of God in Israel and throw out the Romans. His response is especially enigmatic, and it reveals much about the nature of our life with the spirit of God. He said, "I will tell you about God's reign being set up here. The Holy Spirit will enter you like a strong force, and you all will become exhibits (*marturion*—witnesses) of what God is like, in the courtroom of world opinion." The reign of God is present where we are living by and with the spirit of God in our spirits. That means living with the confidence that love works and grace heals. Our moments of the spirit are those occasions when something develops in life that graphically or subtly illustrates that love does work and grace does heal. It is important to name those moments and tell others about them, so we become a people of the spirit, cultivating a culture of the Holy Spirit.

Throughout the Bible we continually read about human beings accomplishing great achievements as a result of the spirit of God coming upon them. In Genesis 31 and 35 the ancient Israelites believed that people with remarkable artistic creativity were filled with the Spirit of God. In the book of Numbers and in the later prophets, it is thought that the spirit of God provides prophets the wisdom to speak about the things having to do with understanding God's way with humans. The book of Judges repeatedly refers to the spirit of God coming upon a person, turning him into an inspired leader and successful general, defending the boundaries of the Israelites.

As we have previously seen, the Bible depicts Samuel as being a wise leader because the spirit of God was in him. When Saul was crowned king of Israel, it is reported that the spirit of God was upon him, making him a mighty man of valor. When he crossed Samuel, politically, however, Samuel denigrated him and "turned his back on Saul," and "the spirit of the Lord departed from Saul," and he became psychotic. This is a most interesting story because of what it indicates about the Israelites getting confused about the presence of the spirit.

Samuel, thought by the people to be the spiritual spokesman for God, had charged Saul, the king, with exterminating the Amalikites: men, women, children, cattle, flocks, dogs, cats, and pet skunks. Saul was, however, a rational and decent man, indeed, kingly. He defeated the Amalikites but killed no more people and animals than was necessary. Samuel publicly defamed Saul for this, declaring stupidly that "God wants obedience at all cost." Caught in this impossible crunch between the responsibilities of maintaining good public opinion in support of his responsible kingly rule, on the one hand, and the "divine" defamation of his reputation as king in the public mind, on the other, he cracked. Samuel is the criminal, of course, and the writer of the story did not know the spirit of God when he saw it. The import of this story is not that the spirit came and went. Rather, it is about the fact that the king lost a political contest with a preacher because the people had made an idol out of the preacher and so erroneously identified everything he did with the divine spirit. Samuel was evil spirited on this occasion. That was not the spirit of God—one can tell by the destructive outcome.

In the New Testament there are frequent references to Jesus being led by the spirit or filled with the spirit, promising to send the spirit, and declaring that the spirit of God will fill the spirits of his followers. The pattern is uniform throughout the NT, indicating that the Holy Spirit is an inner power and illumination, experienced within the spirit or psyche of a person, resulting in life-changing insights, understanding, knowledge, and constructive actions. In each case, the consequences seem to be of such a nature that one can step back from the report and observe, "Yes, that does seem like something God would want to get done in the world." Jesus declared of people living their lives close to the wind of the spirit, "By their fruits you will know them." That is the story of biblical spirituality and the Holy Spirit.

CHAPTER 10

VISIONS AND VISIONARIES IN THE BIBLE AND TODAY

Whether Samuel was, in the main, a really good man or a bad one, the editor of his story describes him as a seer. That means that he had the reputation of possessing a remarkable sense of intuition and was something of a clairvoyant. He was a visionary, and he regularly had visions. This special quality or character was thought to be the result of the divine spirit having taken up special residence in him. Of course, Samuel had originally crowned Saul as king of Israel. Saul quickly and efficiently consolidated the kingdom and his rule over it and established a substantial and effective armed force. Thereby he secured the borders of the nation and established domestic tranquility. Samuel began to realize that he was now dealing with a great leader who had the people's endorsement. Saul could no longer be controlled by Samuel's intimidating claims of getting messages from God or seeing visions from the divine spirit.

King is king and prophet is prophet, and Samuel had a hard time giving up his theocratic rule in favor of a successful monarchy. So Samuel set about to undermine the popular base of support for this successful and very able king. He anointed David, son of Jesse, as a pretender to the throne in Israel and as an adversary to Saul. Saul was still alive, still king in Israel, and still doing well. This new pretender to the throne was set up by Samuel as a guerilla leader, a late adolescent wild revolutionary, whom Samuel probably thought he could control. Samuel encouraged David to foment insurrection against Saul, despite the fact that Saul was "God's appointed and crowned king."

As this insurrectionist civil war progressively gained the support of the general populace, thanks to Samuel claiming it was of the spirit of God,

Saul's dominion began to fall apart. The *coup de grace* came when Samuel finally thought he had enough of a margin of power to disgrace Saul publicly. Samuel declared that Saul was acting against the will and spirit of God in not prosecuting the conquest of neighboring kingdoms with enough bloody aggression. Samuel claimed that God wanted Saul to assassinate the neighboring kings and exterminate their people in order to expand and secure Israel's borders. Some visionary! Saul was a more decent man than Samuel, at that point, and Saul thought that God was more decent and humane than Samuel represented God to be. Saul, of course, was right and Samuel was wrong on this count.

Saul is made to look very bad, and Samuel and David are made to look very good, in the final edition of the story. That was inevitable because the editors were on David's staff, or at least champions of his dynasty, and it was their business to tell the story in a way that glorified David, despite his murderous adultery. The story was designed to put down Saul and his heritage and justify David's kingship and dynasty. If it is not apparent to every reader of the Bible that those editor's were David's men, it can be demonstrated by noting the difference between I and II Kings, which are simply royal annals, and I and II Chronicles, which have some of the same David stories rewritten to glorify David and his house. Apparently, we are dealing with the same or similar David-oriented editor(s) in I and II Samuel as in I and II Chronicles.

In any case, Samuel seems to have been something of a visionary. Before Saul was anointed king, Saul came to Samuel's attention when Saul met with this seer to ask if Samuel knew where Saul's animals had wandered off to or who had stolen them. Samuel was able to tell him where to look, and Saul found them there. Either Samuel had a good intelligence network or he was a visionary, a clairvoyant. The Bible speaks frequently of persons who were known as seers or prophets. These were persons of a high level of spiritual intuition and fervency, who frequently spoke as though their insights were given them from some transcendent authority. They were quite sure that the source was the Holy Spirit of God.

However, the Bible struggled with the problem of sorting out which of these was a true and which a false prophet, or which of their deliverances were true and which false. In the end the judgment usually turned on whether the prophecy came true or the vision of the seer proved useful. The main function of the visionary, however, was not to predict the future or find lost cattle or runaway horses. The chief role of the prophet was to make divine claims regarding the meaning of a current situation. The seer or prophet functioned as a person who was bright enough and informed enough to rise above the ordinary parochial perspective and interpret the local events of history and life in terms of "the big picture," so to speak.

Among the prophets of Israel whose prophecies are preserved in the Bible, for example, we have a rather long list of what are know as the ethical prophets. Their work does not involve much prediction of the future. It has to do, instead, with announcing God's ethical claims upon the life and behavior of the Israelite nations, here and now. Chastising the rich for "selling the poor for a pair of shoes," depriving their fellow citizens of basic necessities, exploiting others to enhance themselves, and warning kings against making war for the wrong reasons were typical pronouncements of these ethical prophets regarding the divine will.

Occasionally they made threats that Israel, or this or that king or citizen, would fall into desperate circumstances in the future because of present bad behavior; however, those were not prophetic predictions (II Sam. 24:11ff, II Kgs 17:9–20). They were just judgmental opinions or just plain common sense. They had two objectives, neither of which was magical. They intended to declare that bad behavior was bad and the people ought to quit it, and that behavior has consequences. They were ethical prophets, not predictors of the future.

When a visionary was a person who lived a spiritual life of intense discernment of the presence of God in the world and of the intimations of the divine spirit in his or her personal quest, he or she was usually able to inform the community of behavior or courses of action that seemed in line with and appropriate to God's will in this world. Frequently, such a highly developed spiritual person, living life close to the wind, could also see what the future course and consequences of present behavior or communal actions were likely to be. In that sense, the visionary, seer, or prophet could foresee the future with its potential for prosperity or pain. Undoubtedly there were also ancient times, as there are in our present day, when such visionary folks were so in tune with the Holy Spirit present in the world everywhere that they intuited intimations from God's spirit in their own spirits, bold visions like Abraham's theophany that God is a God of grace and not of threat.

This phenomenon was never limited to the biblical narratives, history, community, or era. In every age and community there have been those identified personages and sources of divine wisdom. While I was a college student, Professor Harry Jellema, of towering fame in our community, was noted for incredibly creative ways of getting at knotty intellectual and scientific problems. As I have mentioned in earlier chapters, I once heard him ruminating about where the insights he had came from. He was sure they were the direct gift of God's Holy Spirit. There is no difference between this claim, universal among the prophetic figures in the history of religion and spirituality, and the similar claims of intimations from the divine spirit, experienced and testified to by key figures in the Bible.

It is not easy to discern the difference, as visionaries, between Samuel, Isaiah, Ezekiel, John, Paul, Edgar Cayce, Harry Jellema, Deepak Chopra, Colin Powell, and similar popular figures of the last or present century. Most likely there is no need to try to do so. The objective is to discern what is paradigmatic in the nature and function of such persons, true visionaries, and how that works.

Biblical forms of spirituality, as we have discussed them in detail so far in this volume, all relate in the final analysis to the role of the prophetic visionary. In I Samuel 9:9 there is something of a definition of this kind of person. There we read that in early Israelite history, when someone wished to inquire of God about anything, he or she sought out a seer "for he who is now called a prophet was formerly called a Seer." The contextual narrative of this passage indicates that this visionary functioned as both priest and prophet.

He was acknowledged as the person who lived intimately with God, was open to the intimations of God's spirit, and performed the religious rites that symbolized the common people's relationship with God and God's with them. There was something discernable about him that made it clear that he searched for God, walked with God, talked with God, had epiphanies of God's presence, counted on God, and celebrated God's presence. Therefore, the people found it natural to expect that he talked *for* God, as well. When his visions proved useful and healing, and his prognostications regarding the future came true, his authority and credentials were confirmed.

There are numerous passages in the Bible, among the reports on David and his kingdom, that indicate that on David's royal staff was a seer named Gad. He came to David regularly to inform him of some problem in a course of action that David or the people of Israel were undertaking. Three seers who were associated with David are reported to have written books, but apparently none of them have survived, unfortunately. In I Chronicles 29:26–30 we are informed:

David the son of Jesse reigned over all Israel. The time that he reigned over Israel was forty years; he reigned seven years in Hebron, and thirty three years in Jerusalem. Then he died in a good old age, full of days, riches, and honor; and Solomon his son reigned in his stead. Now the acts of King David, from the first to last, are written in the Chronicles of Samuel the seer, and in the Chronicles of Nathan the prophet, and in the Chronicles of Gad the seer, with accounts of all his rule and his might and of the circumstances that came upon him and upon Israel, and upon all the kingdoms of the countries.

Implied in this account is the fact that these seers were learned men who were literate and produced literature. Apparently, therefore, the society of the time was well educated and operated with a significant sense of the presence of God and of human capacities to experience that presence and discern what intimations the divine spirit regularly intended to provide humans. This would conform, of course, to the fact that David's royal son, Solomon, was reported to be a man of extraordinary wisdom from God and an author of numerous books, obviously intended for a wide audience of a literate Israelite society.

A similar epitaph is written for Solomon in II Chronicles 9:29–31, and for his son, Rehoboam, in II Chronicles 12:13–16, confirming essentially the same state of affairs.

> Now the rest of the acts of Solomon, from first to last, are they not written in the history of Nathan the prophet, and in the prophecy of Ahijah the Shilonite, and in the visions of Iddo the seer concerning Jeroboam the son of Nebat? Solomon reigned in Jerusalem over all Israel forty years. And Solomon slept with his fathers, and was buried in the city of David his father; and Rehoboam his son reigned in his stead.
>
> Now the acts of Rehoboam, from first to last, are they not written in the chronicles of Shemaiah the prophet and of Iddo the seer? There were continual wars between Rehoboam and Jeroboam. And Rehoboam slept with his fathers and was buried in the city of David; and Abijah his son reigned in his stead.

The visionaries or seers referred to here were just a paradigmatic few of those who continued a ministry of prophetic guidance and counsel to the kings and the people until the time of the exile into Babylon.[1] In fact, II Chronicles 29 tells us that it was such seers who supervised the religious education that the Levites provided the people throughout the nation of Israel. It was seers who wrote the liturgies for worship in Solomon's temple. A seer named Asaph wrote many of the celebrative Psalms that were intended for and used in the formal national worship services. One has the impressions that these prophetic seers were the professors of theology and religion and the leading creative artists of the day. All their fellow citizens seemed to know intuitively that the seers' wisdom and creativity was a result of the fact that "the spirit of the Lord had come upon them." They were visionaries because they were those who lived life open to the Holy Spirit and "close to the wind." They were no different or magically special from those who similarly seek God in our day.

Joel was a prophet and visionary who lived after the Babylonian exile, probably around 400 B.C.E. Like the other minor prophets he is referred to as a prophet and a seer or visionary. From the content of his prophetic book we may conclude that he had reviewed much of the history of Israel from the Golden Age of David to the decree of Cyrus the Great to release the exiled Jews from Babylon so they could return, if they wished, to Jerusalem. Joel's most dramatic and memorable vision is expressed in 2:28, in which he declares that the visionary capabilities of the seers is a thing to be sought and emulated in every age by those who highly prize authentic spirituality. It is not something to be seen as magical and restricted to ancient times or biblical inspiration.

Blow the trumpet in the city of God...call an assembly, gather the
people.
Sanctify the congregation, assemble the elders, gather the children....
Be glad, oh citizens of God's city, rejoice in the Lord your God....
God's people will never again be put to shame.
You shall know that I am in the midst of my people;
That I, the Lord, am your God, and there is no other.
And it shall come to pass...that I will pour out my spirit upon all flesh.
Your sons and daughters shall be visionaries,
Your old men shall dream dreams; your young men shall see visions.
Even upon your hired men and women will I pour out my spirit.
(JIIE trans)

There certainly seem to be no exceptions to the human community that
has access to the divine spirit. It is, apparently, simply a matter of sailing
close to the wind, keeping our spirits open to the spirit of God. Clearly the
invitation seems to be as universal as God's promised grace. That would
confirm the word of the prophet Jeremiah, who has God promising, "If with
all your heart you truly seek me, you shall ever surely find me" (29:13—
G. F. Handel trans).

Do you suppose that applies to the visionaries of today? Almost certainly
we should assume that we can count on the Holy Spirit today as at any other
time. William James reported in his Gifford Lecture that many of the persons he interviewed regarding their experiences with the divine spirit spoke
of several times when they felt the consciousness of a presence that felt as
intense as standing in a fulmination of inner warmth. John Wesley reported
that when he finally came to sense within him the deep reassurances of God's
grace to him, it felt like an uncommon level of intensity and inner warmth.

The person whom William James cited later said that he had not merely
had a consciousness of something present, but sensed "fused in the central
happiness of it, a startling awareness of some ineffable good." This was not
the vague emotional effect that one gets from reading a poignant poem or
viewing a strikingly beautiful scene, nor was it like the sense of transport
one may achieve while listening to magnificent music. It was instead a "sure
sense of knowledge of the close presence of a sort of mighty person, and after
it went, the memory persisted as the one perception of reality. Everything
else might be a dream, but not that" (Jas 63).

James has a very long quotation from a clergyman who reported that he
remembered an evening when he was taking a leisurely walk on a hill when
his "soul opened out" to God, and there the world of the infinite and of the
mundane rushed together. The depth of his own struggle with life opened to
the unfathomable depth of the transcendent world. He stood under the stars
and "all the beauty of the world, and love, and sorrow, and even temptation,
flooded him with a sense of the presence of the creator God." He had not

sought this but felt a perfect union of his own spirit with the spirit of God. He lost all sense of the ordinary things around him. "For the moment nothing but an ineffable joy and exaltation remained." He felt it was impossible to describe the experience, but the effect was like that of some great orchestra "when all the separate notes have melted into one swelling harmony that leaves the listener conscious of nothing save that his soul is being wafted upwards, and almost bursting with its own emotion" (67).

The narrator continued. There in the quiet darkness he felt a presence he could not see, but he could no more "have doubted that *He* was there than that I was. Indeed, I felt myself to be, if possible, the less real of the two. My highest faith in God and truest idea of him were then born in me. I have stood upon the Mount of Vision since, and felt the Eternal round about me. But never since has there come quite the same stirring of the heart. Then, if ever, I believe, I stood face to face with God, and was born anew by his spirit" (Jas 67–68). James fills 25 pages of his book reporting such narrations regarding the reality of the unknown.

My own illumination at age seven when I was filled with an enormous sense of relief and meaning, feeling entirely filled with the new sense of purpose and calling to ministry, is very nearly the same kind of experience as the clergyman explained to James. It was accompanied, for me, by a life-encompassing sense of well-being, light that connected heaven and earth, a joyful fullness of the meaning of everything, and utter clarity. When, in the depths of my anguish during my heresy trial, I was consoled, guided, and empowered by the voice that awakened me in the middle of the night, the epiphany had very much the same effect as that man reports. It rendered my life permanently tranquil regarding the impasse I felt was before me. Such moments have become more rather than less frequent as my life unfolds. Each one of those events has had to do with a remarkable intervention in my life involving an experience and illumination that either changed my life dramatically or drew me into a course of action that radically changed the life of someone else who badly needed just that, just then.

In 1976 Julian Jaynes, a professor of psychology at Princeton University, published a wonderfully intriguing and evocative book with a long and complicated title, *The Origin of Consciousness in the Breakdown of the Bicameral Mind.*[2] Obviously, by the term bicameral mind he means to refer to the fact that our brains are divided into two hemispheres. We have a right brain and a left brain. The left brain is that hemisphere that processes experience mainly in terms of linear logic, problem solving, finely crafted sentences, and bottom-line thinking. It is through these kinds of experiences that people with predominant left-brain function get most of their meaning out of life experiences. They tend to be people who like logical arguments, relatively rigid predictability, fixed faucets, solved problems, law and order, and a well-regulated life. They tend to be rigid, habitual, controlled, and controlling.

The right brain serves another purpose and works quite differently. It is the hemisphere that generates language resources and processes experience in terms of sensations of color, texture, form, shape, a sense of mass, aesthetic qualities, emotions, and relationships. People who are right- brain dominant process the meaning of life in terms of such values, expectations, and perceptions.

Seventy percent of the males in the world are left-brain dominant, and 70 percent of the females in the world are right-brain dominant. The remaining 30 percent of both genders tend to be high on both scales, a capacity that tends to lead to better and healthier adjustment in life and to less turbulent relationships. This pattern is confirmed by many studies of brain preference, but notably in numerous superb works by Restak, Edwards, Springer, and Deutsch.[3]

Jaynes' take on all this information has to do with life in the spirit. He argues persuasively that human beings have always had surprisingly greater parapsychological ways of knowing than people today realize. Since the resurrection and restoration of Aristotle's scientific method to the human quest for knowledge of the material world, humans have been preoccupied with empirical science. The modern Western world was reintroduced to this empirical approach by Francis Bacon in the fifteenth century. That gave rise to the Great Enlightenment, the scientific revolution, the Industrial Revolution, the nuclear revolution, and the technological revolution. The empirical method proved to be very productive. It created the world as we know it.

The difficulties resulting from the Enlightenment, however, were at least two. While formerly people were approximately equally interested in rational idealism and its speculation about the spiritual world, after Bacon the Western world shifted its interest to tangible mechanics and its products. Consequently, the focus of the human quest moved to issues of cause and effect and away from matters of meaning and purpose. This amounted to a very major psychospiritual change. It included a loss of interest in parapsychological ways of knowing in favor of a virtually exclusive interest in empirical psychological ways of knowing: logic, factor analysis, and rational empiricism. The shift left the human spirit hungry for contact with meaning and purpose issues, the domain of the spirit.

Jaynes raised major concerns about this, already decades ago, and it has subsequently become the entire problematic that is addressed by the postmodern movement in philosophy, psychology, sociology, and religious studies. Jaynes' argument centers in his claim that the dominant character of the human meaning quest for most of history was carried out on the spiritual plain. His voluminous evidence warrants his conclusion that humans did not depend primarily upon the analytic or logical abilities until a millennium or two before the days of Julius Caesar, Jesus, and Josephus. They did not trust their left brains primarily, as we do today. They trusted their right brains and, as a result, lived life continually listening to and obeying the voices of the gods that they perceived they heard in their affective brain hemisphere.

This meant that people were primarily interested in the meaning and purpose issues in understanding life, and so they were tuned to the parapsychological ways of knowing more than to the empirical psychological ways of knowing associated with the left-brain function. That is, intuition, extrasensory perception, and prescience had more value to them and were trusted more by them as sources of knowledge that was valuable and useful. Jaynes is sure that it was that orientation that made it possible for the ancient Hebrew prophets, visionaries, and seers to hear the word of the Lord and convey it to the society. They possessed highly functional right brains, which generated the insights of transcendental meaning evident to them in many situations in life. They functioned with high degrees of ESP, intuition, and prescience.

They also lived life close to the wind. They were consciously and intentionally open to the visitations of the divine spirit. They expected to experience revelations, intuitions, and extrasensory perceptions of the presence, nature, and meaning of God; and so when they came to them, they recognized them readily for what they were. They had no scientific resistance to them, but rather considered them more natural and real than conclusions drawn from empirical assessment or analytical problem solving. They heard the word of the Lord in their right brains.

Jaynes insists that these same capacities are still as real in humans today, despite the scientific revolution, but we have repressed them in favor of empirical science. We have allowed them to atrophy, and so we are not awake to their parapsychological and psychospiritual potentials, as people used to be and we should be. We are afraid of them, denigrate them, downplay them, and do not trust them. Thus we do not have an expectation of the spirit's communication with us, we do not create a consciousness of the spirit's presence, and so we do not cultivate a Holy Spirit culture. We are afraid to share with others the moments when we have experiences that can be accounted for in no other way than as a divine illumination. If we do share them, we expect others to think we are psychologically whacky.

Thus we never get to the point of naming such moments as "of the spirit." Consequently, we do not collect the series of memories of such events that have happened to us in our lives. So we lose our collective cumulative awareness of the intensity with which the divine spirit is always present to us. We lose out on forming life into a culture of spirit consciousness. It is imperative that we begin again to value this side of human life, experience, and the meaning quest. We have lost so much of our awareness and experience of the presence of God. We really should try again to live life close to the wind— the (*ruach*) wind of the spirit.

Edgar Cayce was known to those around him as a gifted professional photographer, a friendly Presbyterian Sunday school teacher, and the "sleeping prophet." Hugh Lynn Cayce wrote the introduction to *The Complete Books of Edgar Cayce, Modern Prophet,*[4] a volume containing the "sleeping prophet's," four published works. He makes the following observations.

> His own family knew him as a wonderful husband and father. The "sleeping" Edgar Cayce was an entirely different figure; a psychic known to thousands of people, in all walks of life, who had cause to be grateful for his help; indeed, many of them believe that he alone had either saved or changed their lives when all seemed lost. The "sleeping" Edgar Cayce was a medical diagnostician, a prophet, and a devoted protagonist of Bible lore. (7)

The author of a PhD dissertation about Cayce's life and work referred to him as a religious seer. He was born in 1877 and already in childhood seemed to possess powers of perception that exceeded the normal range of the senses. He reported, as a child, the ability to see and converse with what he called visions, frequently of dead relatives. While still very young he was able to develop a photographic memory of textbook material if he first entered a kind of sleep trance. In his twenties he experienced an affliction of his throat muscles that made speaking difficult. He asked a friend to induce a hypnotic sleep or trance and in that state was able to diagnose his own problem, prescribe medication and physical therapy, and so cure himself.

This event led to physicians seeking him out for diagnostic consultation. If given the name and address of a patient he could telepathically diagnose the condition and prescribe treatment at a distance, wherever he was. This was documented by Wesley Ketchum, MD, in a clinical report to the learned societies in medicine; and a popularized description of these unorthodox medical processes appeared in the *New York Times* on October 9, 1910. Thereafter, he was sought out by suffering humans from all over the country. After his death on January 3, 1945, it was discovered that he had left a record of over 8,000 telepathic-clairvoyant diagnoses over a 40-year period. He called them "readings." They were always produced by him while in a kind of sleep trance.

Hugh Lynn Cayce declares that these readings form one of the largest and most impressive records of psychic perception ever known to be produced by a single person. They are now carefully collated and cross indexed for use in research. Cayce's prophetic work falls into two categories: those that have to do with prophetic insights of a personal nature that apply to a specific individual's well-being and prophecies regarding the world in general. The former have mainly to do with a dramatic history of healings. The latter are, like those of Nostradamus before him, the messages of a seer, delivered in highly mysterious, symbolic, and rather abstract form. The former seem to be taken very seriously by those to whom they apply. The latter seem to be less convincing to the world audience.

The reason why Nostradamus[5] and Edgar Cayce do not receive more credence in our day regarding their world prophecies or cosmic predictions and did not develop a large consistent following in these matters lies mainly in the fact that their cosmic visions had, in every case, the following limitations: They were relatively abstract predictions of an infinitely distant future; they were expressed in vague and highly symbolic metaphors and other figures of speech; and they were impossible to calibrate with any specific facet of unfolding reality. So they could not readily be confirmed as truly prophetic, authentically visionary, or the deliverance of a genuine seer.

Cayce's devotees, however, make much of his predictions of what they claim are major world events that have already unfolded, such as his prediction of the Great Depression, his warning against America entering into WWII, and a new age of glorious expansion and growth in the world, because of God's grace. These kinds of global observations, however, seem rather ordinary prognostications for any fairly thoughtful person who had lived through the era from 1877 to 1937. For example, Woodrow Wilson's proposal of the Fourteen Points plan for post–WWI Europe carried with it similar visions of the various kinds of futures humankind could fashion for itself at the treaty of Versailles. Wilson foresaw much of what Cayce envisioned and warned against it more crisply, clearly, and actively than did the "sleeping prophet."

Nonetheless, in his capacity to discern human suffering from afar, telepathically diagnose and heal it, and focus the eye of the soul, so to speak, upon seeking the will and spirit of God, Cayce seems remarkably like the biblical prophets. Quite apart from his mystical functions as a seer, Cayce was known as a man who lived his life open to the divine spirit from childhood to death at 78 years of age. Sailing close to the wind, in that sense, he seems to have been in touch with the spirit of God, as were Isaiah, Hosea, Jeremiah, Micah, and Joel. He seems to have had experiences of illumination and epiphany of the same sort as Samuel, Gad, and Daniel. The benefit he afforded other people's lives in his trance states of insight, as well as the quality of his own personal character itself, strongly urges the conclusion that his sense of the presence of the divine spirit in his experience was of the same nature as that experienced by Jesus.

> Like prophetic passages of the Bible, Cayce's forecasts could become a relic of the past which generations of the future might remember as a curiosity and a strange myth of the twentieth century. Or they could serve to be a source of hope to generations wiser than we. Unlike most prophets, he spoke in a self-imposed hypnotic trance and did not know what he had said until he returned to consciousness. He depended all his life on others to record and evaluate what he brought forth. It was left to others to present his work to the world, or to forget it. The readings state in one place that, like Cayce, Ezekiel had a secretary or scribe to take down his utterances. Also like Ezekiel, he spoke forcefully of our social ills. (12)

Edgar Cayce's experience fits neatly into the hypothesis of Julian Jaynes, namely, that the right brain, and thence the unconscious mind, are sources of the intimations of the divine spirit. Hypnosis and dreams are the two ways that humans have of accessing the content of our unconscious minds. Dreams are always the processes of the unconscious mind sorting out the chaos of material dumped into that huge seething vat, as life experiences come at us faster or with greater trauma than we can handle at the time, with our conscious minds. All dreams are, therefore, of great importance. All dreams mean something important about our inner psychic state. All dreams are attempts by our unconscious to get time on the conscious mind's "computer," so to speak, to sort out the material the unconscious mind needs to process in order to keep us sane and well ordered in our inner selves.

This is the way our unconscious reduces our anxiety, distractions, emotional confusion, and inner anguish. Running this material on the conscious mind's computer makes it possible for our unconscious to select out the important stuff to store in our memory, discard the unimportant stuff, and call critical matters to our attention. Dreams take place, normally, while we are asleep because that is when the mind's computer is available. Usually when it comes to the critical matters to be drawn to our attention, our unconscious awakens us from sleep so we can remember that material from the dream.

It is completely understandable, in Jaynes' model, that Cayce and prophets from time immemorial, such as Samuel, Daniel (7:13), Ezekiel, Peter, and other biblical figures experienced the revelations from God through their unconscious, processed in their right brains in the form of dreams. That is where the action is. That is the channel through which the spirit speaks.

We are forced to conclude, by reason of the numerous figures like Moses, Samuel, Isaiah, Hosea, Jesus, Paul, Aurelius Augustine, Thomas Aquinas, Julian of Norwich, Deepak Chopra, Edgar Cayce, and the like, with which history is studded, that Julian Jaynes is correct in his claim that the availability of the intimations of the Holy Spirit is no less intense, no less likely, and no less revealing in our day than it was in the biblical era. If we see it less and sense it less it has something to do with the decreased keenness with which we are tuned to the right brain and hence to the spirit of God in our day of empirical science.

The wisdom and operational value of such gurus as Sathya Sai Baba of Putaparthi, India, on the one hand, and many persons of courage and wisdom whom we often take for granted in our present moment in the Western world, on the other, tend to generate confidence and a sense of credibility in their followers because they offer both guidance and counsel that is immediately applicable to daily life. Sai Baba's wisdom is universalistic in that it embraces all humanity, indeed, all the world of living things. He counsels an ethic of passion and compassion. He seems to have distilled the best, the most godly, and the most humane aspects of Hinduism, Buddhism, Christianity, Islam, and Judaism and integrated them into one holistic theological worldview. Can we really avoid saying that such a force for good in the world in our day is not "of the spirit" of God?

In this regard, Sai Baba's message is much like the inclusive emphasis of Ba'hai. It is easy to sense that such a figure really does have something from the Holy Spirit. One can readily sense that he has lived his 80 years with his soul open to God, and with his intentional and conscious life focus set close to the wind of the spirit, so to speak. He himself claims to be a kind of incarnation of the divine spirit, as were Jesus and certain other "gurus," whom he identifies as having lived this same revelatory life before Jesus and between the time of Jesus and himself. Sai Baba refers to such figures as avatars, which apparently means something like completed spirits, fully in touch with and incarnating the divine spirit to as great an extent as a human person can.

The wisdom and instructions of Sai Baba have been published in various forms. A very useful reference to his essential thoughts can be found in *A Compendium of the Teachings of Sathya Sai Baba*.[6] It is an encyclopedic collection of quotations and paraphrases of his thoughts and teaching, compiled by Charlene Leslie-Chaden. In it this seer declares of the spirit which is in him,

> For the protection of the virtuous, for the destruction of evil-doers, and for establishing righteousness on a firm footing, I incarnate from age to age. Whenever disharmony overwhelms the world, the Lord will incarnate in human form to establish the modes of earning…peace. At the present time, strife and discord have robbed peace and unity from the family, the schools, the community, the society, the villages, the cities and the state. The arrival of the Lord is also anxiously awaited by saints and sages. Spiritual aspirants have prayed and I have come. (488)

He then concludes that the best way for us followers of the spirit of God to carry out this work of the spirit is to translate the message into our own lives. Our thoughts, words, and deeds may be saturated with the message. Then it will spread effortlessly and efficiently across the face of this planet, and the world will be transformed (488).

Deepak Chopra is much better known in the Western world than is Sai Baba and is very popular among a large following of disciples or readers today because he has said essentially the same thing as Julian Jaynes. However, he has made his claim on the basis of his own personal experience and spiritual worldview, rather than on the basis of Jaynes' kind of psychohistorical science. His popularity arises out of the fact that when he speaks of the dynamics of spirituality and the divine spirit that humans need so much and miss so easily, his invitation to live life close to the wind of the spirit rings true to the deepest hungers in human hearts, minds, and spirits.

Ken Wilber's assessment of Chopra's work and wisdom is highly positive. Wilber is the dean of all psychologists with an understanding of and extensive research in the human capacity for parapsychological ways of knowing. He declares that "Deepak Chopra has introduced literally millions of people to the spiritual path, and for this we should all be profoundly grateful. In *How to Know God*,[7] Deepak continues his pioneering outreach, showing that God consciousness unfolds in a series of stages, each important and remarkable in itself, yet each getting closer to Source" (flyleaf). Wilber thinks that Chopra's volume is at once a map of the divine spirit and of our own deepest selves, which, in the last analysis, are one and the same. So are his other 25 or so published volumes.

Chopra thinks reality exists as a sandwich, in three layers. The layer of material reality we know fairly well, and our five senses give us that knowledge. The middle layer is the quantum domain, in his words, which names a transition zone where energy turns into matter and vice versa. The third layer is the virtual domain, the place beyond time, space, materiality; and it is the source of the origin of the material world. The human brain, according to Chopra, is designed to apprehend the layer of material reality, but also has a longing and proclivity to explore the other two stages. Because of our limited capacity to do so, we can never know exactly, intellectually or empirically, what we mean when we use the term God. However, we do have the capacity to experience the presence of God's spirit, without being able to define or describe it tangibly; and we do not need to define or describe the experience of the divine spirit in our spirits in order for it to be real.

Chopra offers numerous vivid examples of serendipitous experiences humans have that provide clear messages of guidance or affirmation for us in life. Chopra prefers to think of visionaries as saints rather than just seers or prophets. He makes the important point that such saints, those who live life close to the wind of the spirit, who hold life open to the pressures and presence of God's spirit, are not just *saintly*. We really *are saints*! Saints are folks who live a life full of God, full of love, full of compassion, full of forgiveness, not because they know this is the right thing to do but because they cannot help themselves. They automatically are overflowing with forgiveness, love, and compassion. That is what incarnation of the divine spirit entails.

However, Chopra wishes to say even more than that about life in the spirit. He wishes to go as far as I did in the introduction to this volume and in the first chapter, describing the transcendent quality of life we can achieve if we choose with conscious intentionality to live intensely open to God's spirit and in a posture oriented toward the hungers of our own spirits. Chopra sounds like he is quoting William James, James Fowler, and Robert Fuller when he observes, "Truth has many faces, and when you see a new one, your level of consciousness rises" (195).

The true visionary's perception of divine illumination, says Chopra, is the acknowledgement that "The world has a heart, and that heart is love. In the midst of all struggle, I see that God is watching. He doesn't interfere, but he doesn't lose track, either. He brings a solution to fit every problem, a reaction that suits every action. How he does this is a mystery, but nothing is more real. There is grace in the fall of a leaf. Our deeds are weighed in the balance by a loving Creator who never judges or punishes" (197). The unique experience of the visionary is not belief in, but clarity about these things. Chopra illustrates this with a story of a young man's enlightenment, which I borrow here because it is so exactly the same story of illumination we read repeatedly from every century, culture, and religious tradition. James' work is full of stories so similar to this that one must conclude that this experience is a paradigm of an important and universal form of the experience of the manifestations of the divine spirit to a hungry human soul.

> A young man in his twenties named Bede Griffiths had been going through a period of deep doubt and depression. Being religious, he sought solace in a church, where he prayed without success. One day during service he heard the line. "Open my eyes that I may see the wondrous things out of Thy law" from the 113th Psalm. Deeply moved, the young man felt his melancholy lift away, and he had the overwhelming sense that his prayers had been answered by divine intervention. He walked outside onto the London streets, and later described the experience in the following words:
> "When I went outside, I found that the world about me no longer oppressed me as it had done. The hard casing of exterior reality seemed to have been broken through, and everything disclosed its inner being. The buses in the streets seemed to have lost their solidity and were glowing with light. I hardly felt the ground as I trod...I was like a bird that had broken the shell of its egg and finds itself in a new world; like a child that has forced its way out of the womb and sees the light of day for the first time." (204)

I could recite numerous similar narratives from the files of my clinical practice, as I am sure any therapist can who is sensitive to the psychospiritual dimensions of the human quest. I remember especially the story of a friend of mine, an intensely spiritual and sensitively articulate woman in her middle years, who had spent some earlier time in treatment for depression. After a considerable time of analysis it seemed clear that her condition was not so much systemic and biochemical as it was situational. This led her to review her relationship with her ex-husband from whom she had experienced a traumatic divorce, her unusually difficult relationship with her father in adolescence, and her sense of devaluation, demeanment, and loneliness.

She reported that she had lived in this oppressive psychospiritual state for many years, feeding off the rage she felt to the primary male figures in her life and consequently unable to form any constructive new relationships to relieve her sense of being utterly alone. On the one hand, she wished to resolve the impasse with her father that had developed mainly from her having been a seriously unconventional, oppositional, self-defeating, and rebellious adolescent. She had wasted her life, her sexuality, her education, her time, her health, and her relationships. She felt that she had dug a ditch too deep for her to transcend. She had long since abandoned the religious traditions of her family and the spiritual quest it had offered her.

Then one day, in desperation, feeling overtly suicidal, she walked into Christ Church Cranbrook in the middle of the day, in the middle of the week. The cathedral was empty and cool. She sat in a pew near the back with her head on her arm on the pew ahead of her. She wept pitiably. When she opened her eyes they fell upon the Book of Common Prayer. She picked it up and it fell open to the passage, "Knowest thou not that of thine own self thou canst do nothing?" She began immediately to feel an intense sense of release and relief at the center of her being. This was accompanied by a physical warmth that started in the center of her chest and grew from a walnut to an orange, from an orange to a cantaloupe, from a cantaloupe to a watermelon, and then it pervaded her entire self: material and spiritual.

Just then she remembered words of her father expressing forgiveness and compassion to her somewhere back there in her rebellious years when she was trying to define herself by defying him. Over the next days, she said, she felt like everything in her being had changed. Her depression disappeared immediately and completely. Her sense of enthusiasm for her life sprang up resiliently. Her appetite returned. Her health seemed renewed. She longed for each new opportunity to return to church. She felt in every way like she had finally come home—to her self—and to the divine spirit. Even her sorrow over her wasted life percolated out of her and she felt an immense sense of gratitude for the road along which she had so lately come and for the illumination into which just that rough road had finally come out of the wilderness and into the clearing.

This is not so remote from my own illumination when I heard the voice of the spirit speaking aloud in the night, saying, "Trust in the Lord and do good!" From that moment my body felt light, my spirit clarified, my life hopeful and on a good track. It was not so much as though something was cured; but rather that everything had changed. Everything about me had changed. A new spirit had been injected into me. The Holy Spirit is alive and well in our day.

Such moments of clarity may come and go, rise and fall, intensify and dissipate. Keeping ourselves consciously intentional about opening life and heart to the divine spirit, however, can empower us to maintain a consistent level of spiritual awareness and openness to the intimations from God. Sometimes our experiences of the spirit seem to transcend time and materiality, and when we become aware again of the things around us, we wonder where the time has gone. Frequently, we feel disoriented for a few moments until we catch our breath, so to speak.

Such suspension from time and materiality may happen in the intense experience of making love, in the captivation of a grand piece of music, in a particularly illumining worship service, or in sitting in an art gallery contemplating a truly great painting. All these are moments of the spirit's presence. Chopra says, "The quantum world is a place with blurry edges and uncertain outcomes...the things that seem so well defined in the material world turn into shadowy phantoms the deeper we go into the un-manifest domain. Time is no exception, and at certain levels of reality it hardly exists. When the boundary of time dissolves completely, it is possible to experience a kind of mental time travel called clairvoyance, or the ability to see into the future" (260).

No one was ever wrestled into the kingdom of God by logical argument, but no one ever needs to be. Any human being, given the chance to see the genuineness of his or her own spiritual hunger and the authenticity of the intimations of the Holy Spirit, with the eyes to see and ears to hear, will come away discerning with great relief that this is the source of wholeness for the human spirit—indeed, for the whole person.

Is it possible that when Jesus told his disciples, "Other sheep I have who are not of this fold" (Jn 10:16a) he was saying that the reign of God's love that works and grace that heals was much wider than Judaism and Christianity? Was he suggesting that it included people everywhere and always who are in search of and in touch with the Holy Spirit of God? Anyone anywhere with the eyes to see and the ears to hear! Was he speaking of Mohammed, Sai Baba, Edgar Cayce, Deepak Chopra, or the like?

CHAPTER 11

RELIGIOUS CONVERSION: ITS NATURE AND SOURCES

There is a clear correlation between the various present-day models of psychological development such as those of Piaget,[1] Kohlberg,[2] Erikson,[3] and Fowler.[4] This is particularly true in the light of Massey's[5] claim that adults grow or change mainly under the impact of a "significant emotional event." Spiritual conversion is such an event; and its characteristics can be described and accounted for in identifiable psychodynamic as well as in psychospiritual terms. Some types of "religious conversion" are pathogenic in the sense that they create mental illness or aggravate it when it exists in a person. Other kinds of religious conversion are not pathological and offer life-enhancing influences for our psychological and social health. The pathological forms and healthy forms of religious conversion happen in all faith traditions.

The difference between the two is easy to identify. Spiritual conversion that causes a person to experience a greater sense of freedom, forgiveness, security, and joy is healthy conversion. This indicates on the face of it that the life change is related to an authentic experience of God's Holy Spirit in the converted person's spiritual experience and quest, drawing that person's life into a posture closer to the wind of the divine spirit, so to speak. Spiritual conversion that produces legalism in ideas or ethics or constrains a person with a structure of threat, anxiety, fear of God, and the like, is sick and causes spiritual sickness. That posture, by definition, is not from the Holy Spirit. Sick spiritual change often indicates prior personality pathology—mental illness—which becomes exaggerated or aggravated by the conversion experience. Healthy spiritual conversion, in any religion, produces an experience of God's unconditional and radical grace for humans and is accompanied by the kind of faith posture that is marked by trust, relief, and joy.

TRANSFORMING MOMENTS

James Loder attempted to illumine our understanding of "convictional experiences" in his book *The Transforming Moment.*[6] From his own personal experience and numerous case histories he derived a deep appreciation for human life events that produce remarkable change of direction—real conversion of one's life. These epitomes of human life transitions illustrate his work. He expresses a serious appreciation of parapsychological moments of knowing, such as intuition, extrasensory perception, prescience, and intimations of the divine spirit. His various publications contribute in important ways to our understanding of these aspects of human spirituality. He is interested in decreasing our excessive confidence in empirical science as the exclusive or even primary channel to truth. He is confident that spiritual insight is as certain a kind of truth as the results of laboratory experiments.

In the process, Loder largely avoids reducing our experiences of spiritual conversion to mere psychological events, devoid of any relationship to the presence of the divine spirit. Loder would be best described as a pious Christian with a genuine openness to the presence and intimations of God in human experience. He launches the argument of his book from a traumatic personal experience of temporary paralysis he endured following an auto accident. He interprets this event as a distinctive spiritual conversion because the paralysis was completely removed after intense prayer and supplication to God.

Whether it is the case that Loder here interprets as a spiritual event what may have been a spontaneous remission of classic hysterical paralysis is somewhat beside the point. The real issue is that for him, this was an event in his life that he experienced as a moment of God acting in his life, and it radically changed his life into that of a person vastly open to the intimations and presence of God's spirit. Whether the change in his life, the healing of his paralysis, was mediated by God through natural causes or through other, more transcendental dynamics is hardly the important issue for us.

Such a question is an important issue for a physiologist or a psychologist who wishes to study the extent to which biochemical, physiological, neurological, or psychological forces can be factored out in analyzing what happened to James Loder. That is one narrow aspect of the full story. However, the issue of global importance is that Loder's life was revamped by his experience. He was converted to an entirely new sense of the nature of his life, the presence of God to him, and the possibility of living his life from that point on as a life open to the continuing intimations of God's spirit.

Loder raises the central question about the interface of psychology and spirituality in this relatively common instance of the psychospiritual renovation of a human life. He tries hard to describe the watershed that distinguishes subjective psychological process from true spirituality and personalized divine illumination in human life.

Consequently, Loder's book makes a most useful contribution. It amply illustrates the legitimate quest for understanding psychospiritual dynamics in human development, while demonstrating the precariousness of that process of assessment and the dangers into which some religionists are tempted in their fear of exploring the psychological sides of spirituality and the spiritual sides of psychology. Loder does not denigrate the legitimate domains and contributions of the discrete sciences. He does not fear, as do some Christians, that the natural and social sciences will eclipse theology and spiritual authenticity. He urges us to see all these as corollary and mutually supportive channels for our quest to understand the ways in which God is present in our world and our lives, in nature and in grace.

Responsible people of faith, particularly well-informed Christians, understand that the principle of Occam's Razor applies as much today as in the Middle Ages when Occam lived. His principle asserts that when data or experience can be managed or explained by a simple hypothesis, a more complex hypothesis may not honestly be devised to account for it. When human experience or information can be accounted for satisfactorily by psychology, physics, chemistry, sociology, geology, or the like, it ought not to be spiritualized. Theological and spiritual experiences or data, where they are authentic, can no doubt stand on their own feet as well as these other disciplines can.

STRUCTURALIST MODELS

For that reason the structuralist thinkers have devised models of personality development that offer a great deal in support of Loder's spiritual perspective on life-changing events. Fowler (1981) for example, offers a thorough-going description of the structuralist view of psychosocial development applied to growth in faith and spiritual maturity. He explains such experiences as Loder's personal crisis and other life-transforming moments without downplaying or demeaning sound psychological interpretations and without devaluing the transcendental dimension of such experiences in favor of the natural or social sciences. Fowler grounds his work on human spirituality in Piaget's model of cognitive development, Kohlberg's model of moral development, and Erikson's model of psychosocial development. He correctly perceives that these three models are not in tension but mutually illumine and elaborate each other.

Piaget demonstrated that human development can be described in terms of six stages: infancy, early childhood, childhood, adolescence, young adulthood, and adulthood or maturity. Piaget emphasized that there are distinctive developmental characteristics evident in each stage. His empirical research indicated that these stages can be described concretely as a pattern of movement from mere primal sensory experience and reaction in infancy, to preoperational and intuitive responses to environment in childhood, and then to formal operations in which the adolescent tends to think in dogmatic patterns of right and wrong. Young adults become more dialogical and open to others' opinions, and finally, mature adults tend to receive many different ideas from various sources and synthesize them into their own sense of truth and right.

Kohlberg's model of human moral development correlates precisely with Piaget's notions of cognitive development. He emphasized that in infancy we respond to positive and negative rewards. As we move into childhood we are capable of self-control in terms of a greater variety of principles of good and bad things or good and bad conduct. Adolescence and young adulthood move us to self-assertion and then greater mutuality, concord, and a law-and-order mentality. As we progress morally into adulthood and maturity we operate increasingly on the basis of concern for others and personal conscientiousness. Full maturity normally brings with it a sense of appreciation of the perspectives of others and their claims upon us, as well as an outlook of universal ethical principles and loyalty to all humankind.

Erikson's distinctive contribution focused upon the social development humans experience. We move, according to Erikson, from the trust-mistrust of infancy to hope and autonomy in childhood, during which time we exercise our own will and sense of purpose at the risk of experiences of shame and doubt as well as fear and guilt. In adolescence we struggle with the tensions of accomplishment *versus* inferiority as we reach for competence; and with establishing our own identity versus role confusion as we reach for fidelity or authenticity. We are busy learning what it means to be true to self. Adulthood brings intimacy, love, generativity, creativity, and integrity. If, in this adult development, we fail to achieve intimacy, love, generativity, creativity, and integrity we fall into isolation, stagnation, and despair.

FOWLER'S STRUCTURALIST MODEL OF SPIRITUALITY

Fowler presents a framework for understanding faith development based upon these structuralist models. His work moves to one point: the way in which humans come to a focused sense of spiritual meaning, faith, and self-sacrificial or *agapic* love. This experience leads to an inner freedom, peace, and hope and a palpable sense of the presence of God. Fowler notes that for the human infant the world is limited to primary family relationships, and the child's sense of reality is *intuitive* and *magical*, that is, numinous. Childhood brings a wider social experience and a *literal* and *mystical* sense of reality. Santa Claus never comes down the chimney, and it is not clear he could ever make it through that small pipe, but he is real and does come and brings fine objects of delight. God and Santa Claus are undifferentiated. Parents *versus* Santa Claus as the source of Christmas presents, is not a tolerable question. It violates the necessary mysticism.

Fowler continues by pointing out that in adolescence we begin to analyze such myths and move comfortably into a humorous revaluing of Santa Claus, and to some extent of God, and begin our *symbolic* thinking about issues of meaning and commitment. We are able to make this transition by becoming very dogmatic about our new perceptions of reality in which things are usually rather starkly true or false, right or wrong, black or white. Dogmatic, literalist adult religionists seem never to have moved beyond this adolescent stage.

Adulthood should bring with it that spiritual growth that moves us to see that our perception of the world of divine transcendence and the essential meanings attendant upon that are always experienced in terms of symbols and their meanings. Maturity brings us to value a universalistic appreciation of the variety of symbolic meanings humans have contrived for capturing their understanding of their own spirituality and the presence of God in it.

Westerhof (1976) thought that we are socialized into our religious convictions and growth in faith through the influence of our religious environment.[7] The influences of the community and its training programs were dominant in his model of faith development. Joy (1983) claimed that faith development was a direct influence of the divine spirit upon an individual human spirit, and that the structuralists were not only on the wrong track but were rendering spirituality godless by failing to emphasize the power and role of the Holy Spirit more emphatically and exclusively.[8]

Fowler disagreed with both Westerhof and Joy, claiming that faith development depends more upon the built-in structures of human personality development demonstrated by Piaget, Kohlberg, and Erikson than upon mere socialization. Moreover, it is the central point of Fowler's model that in faith development, as in all other aspects of this world, God works, by means of the Holy Spirit, through the functional structures and natural laws inherent to the created world. God works in us according to and by means of the laws that he has laid down in the very structure of the universe—and hence the structures of our unfolding lives.

In this emphasis, Fowler does not undervalue the experience of God in a life lived close to the wind. That is, he does not claim that immediate and direct experience of God's illumination in our spirits, when we live our lives with a consistently high level of consciousness of God's presence, is unlikely or unnecessary. He simply points out that these experiences, and the life of intense consciousness of the presence of the Holy Spirit, are shaped and empowered by our place in the structural developmental process. God moves in mysterious ways his wonders to perform, as Loder experienced, but the mysteries are not altogether ethereal. There is also mystery enough in how the divine spirit that fills this world uses the natural processes built into the structure of life to lead us into transcendental illumination in our experiences of faith and religious conversion.

STRUCTURALISM AND SPIRITUAL EXPERIENCE

Humans are inherently spiritual; that is, we irrepressibly seek meaning in everything from the moment we are born until we die. Harry Jellema was sure this quest and our growth in it goes on for all eternity. He believed that when we step across the threshold into eternity, we pick up the quest and the process of our growth where we left off here in this life. Our quest for meaning deals with everything we experience around us and everything we can imagine. As we progress in life we reach increasingly toward transcendental meanings that deal with the major matters of our morality and our mortality: the meaning of life and death issues. We grow through the natural patterns that the structuralists outlined. As we move from one stage to the next, each gain opens us to the needs and potential patterns characteristic of that new stage. The content of the spiritual growth at each stage will depend, in important ways, upon the information, attitudes, values, and faith commitments of the community in which we live, as well as upon the personal experiences and events that befall us personally. Our personal experiences of the intimations of God's spirit, present to us and in our spirits, are critical or watershed factors.

Whether our experiences in life are painful or pleasurable, they may prove to be destructive or constructive, depending upon how they are integrated into our selves. That integration process depends upon the characteristic pattern inherent in the particular stage of structural development in which the experience is received, the outlook of the community upon the kind of experience we have, and the information we have about such an experience and what it might mean. Christian conversion, or any religious conversion, is an integration *process* or *event* that sets our individual experience in a context that allows and prompts faith. That is, it prompts a sense of God's grace to function as the center and ground of meaning, purpose, hope, and relationships. It is crucial, therefore, in keeping with the point made repeatedly above, that if we are to have healthy conversions we must have a healthy God. A sick notion of God will produce a sick conversion into a sick faith perspective, shaping our life and thought in a destructive way. For example, a notion of God as legalistic or a threat will produce a conversion that makes us rigid, fear motivated, and stuck in an adolescent-like dogmatism about things spiritual.

If Christian conversion takes place as a dramatic integration *event*, rather than a developmental *process* over time, the manner in which it recapitulates or reprocesses all the previous stages of the person's growth is usually intensely obvious. This recapitulation gives a new grounding for our orientation to life. It provides a new foundation for our values and our sense of virtue. This new foundation is shaped in the "light of faith's new center of value, images of power, and decisive master story... When the recapitulative process has done its work, the person has a new foundation of inner integration from which to move decisively toward the next stage" of personal development (Fowler, 1981, 290–291).

As I indicated above, Morris Massey (1972) observed, in keeping with our analysis thus far, that humans continue to grow largely as a result of "significant emotional events" that stimulate movement to the next stage of built-in development. Sometimes persons may experience arrested growth at one of the childhood, adolescent, or early adult stages. Massey may have discovered the trigger mechanism that usually moves us from one stage of growth to the next. "Significant emotional events" may be generated by deep inner needs or by profound outer stimuli.

Robert Fuller believes that it is our capacity to trust the unknown, and hence the transcendental that lies beyond each stage in our development, that makes it possible for us to grow from one structural stage to the next. It is that trust in, among other things, the divine spirit that empowers us to reach out to and embrace the next stage of our growth.[9] He argues that at each stage of growth from infancy to mature adulthood, we develop a paradigm that explains our current experience to us and manages it without undue anxiety. As we grow to the point that we are taking in a lot of experience or learning data that is no longer managed well by our current paradigm or worldview, we need a new framework for understanding our expanded world of experience.

As we grow in our knowledge, for example, between ages 12 and 20, we find our adolescent dogmatism to be too limiting a worldview. It does not provide enough flexibility to handle all the new and apparently ambiguous facts of life and community we accumulate. We are not automatically handed a larger paradigm or a new way of thinking about things, though it becomes increasingly clear to us that we need to think about life in broader and more flexible categories. Others seem to have different ideas about many things than we do, and some of their notions seem to have some truth in them. So we need to expand our paradigm, that is, the basket in which we are carrying our worldview or philosophy of life and its meaning.

We must be able to trust God and the universe that if we transform our set of principles for understanding our world we will be able to find a new paradigm, and new system, in terms of which to manage our life without excessive anxiety. Fuller declares that such trust in the unknown is a religious act and experience, and only such religious acts of faith, or of belief that the universe or God can be trusted to afford us a new paradigm or framework, empowers us to take on the unknown experience of growth into the next natural stage of our development. Only by such an act of trust can we go from infancy to childhood, from childhood to adolescence, and from there to the stages of maturity.

The inner pressure to reach out for a new framework rather than stagnate in an immature stage of growth comes from new interior insights and new exterior stimuli. In any case, what usually forces us across the boundaries into new structures for handling and interpreting experience and reality is a new set of insights or information, a new relationship, or a new trauma. These are experiences that take place in our minds and in our hearts, affecting our cognitive psychosocial and our moral-spiritual levels of knowing. Such events are significant in size or value when they are life changing. They provide us with a new or renewed sense of meaning, outlook, and being. They constitute what Massey called significant emotional events, and they might as well be called significant spiritual events, as Fuller suggests.

ROBERT C. FULLER'S THESIS

Fuller provides a well-developed and persuasive heuristic argument for his outlook, backed by a wealth of convincing evidence and rational analysis. He demonstrates that religious insights and ideas function crucially to mediate the healthy movement of human personalities through the transitions we make from one developmental stage to the next and through the life-shaping stresses and strains that often confront us. Indeed, he contends that religious ideas and experiences facilitate these growth transitions better than any other forces shaping our sense of meaning and our worldviews. For him, life lived close to the wind—that is, open to the intimations of God's spirit and with a deep sense that the Holy Spirit of God—can be trusted and counted on. It facilitates the maturing process in life better than any other factor. Wholesome, conscious, and intentional spirituality enhances healthy maturity, independence, and freedom in God's grace, rather than sick dependency upon sick notions of the nature of God.

So Fuller makes it plain that human maturation, fulfillment, and self-actualization depend upon values and experiences that are spiritual in character. Using psychological theory and clinical research he created a model of the structure and development of the human life cycle, giving particular attention to Erikson's eight states of psychosocial process. Fuller places great emphasis upon the way spiritual awareness emerges in the lives of individuals and the role it plays in our unfolding lives. He has a rich appreciation of the spiritual dynamics that are necessary for our growth in order to achieve wholeness and completeness as persons. Translated into biblical language, Fuller's thesis is that faith in God and in the providence and grace of God, to which the Bible testifies, is the key outlook that incites our health and growth in the adaptive process of achieving a mature and creatively fulfilling life.

Fuller applies his model to spirituality in childhood development, belief and identity formation, values and midlife transitions, integrity, aging, dying, and spiritual self-transcendence. His concern is to locate the place of spiritual illumination within the overall structure of maturing personality and to reexamine and critique modern attitudes toward human nature by investigating the spiritual aspects of personal development. We are here concerned with the way psychological understandings of human fulfillment enable us to understand the role that faith and spirituality play in our lives.

Science and technology have, on occasion in the last two centuries, devalued the role given to spiritual considerations, largely because spiritual function is less easily quantified in cause-effect equations than are the more tangible things we study or experience. In the effort to use the empirical model of physics, the social sciences have sometimes overlooked their significant linkage with theology or philosophy. The structuralists have given us a great advantage in providing a framework within which psychology and the other social sciences can study the issues of cause and effect (hard science) in human development while at the same time giving adequate honest attention to matters of meaning and purpose (philosophy and religion). In the end, it is the resolution of meaning and purpose issues that people seek and hunger for in our irrepressible spiritual quest for meaning It is these meaning and purpose matters of life in terms of which we fashion life's satisfying psychospiritual solutions and that provide the force that moves us from one structural stage of development to the next in our growth process. These meaning and purpose factors, as illustrated by Loder's personal life-changing experience, are the ones that drive true conversion in our lives, towards God's constructive way for us.

The original aims of the empirical method that the natural and social sciences employ are "shaped by the desire to derive public and definitive information" by selecting out those data from life's total range of experience that can be objectively discerned, weighed, and measured (Fuller, 1988, 5). Structuralism, particularly as articulated by Fowler and Fuller, provides a mechanism for reenlisting those sciences in the task of giving us a well-rounded vision of human nature and its complex functions, including those of faith and spiritual desire.

A comprehensive appreciation of how humans function and how religious factors influence the course of human development requires us to focus upon the "extent to which humanity's pursuit of happiness and fulfillment is contingent upon 'adapting' to a spiritual environment beyond the limits of our physical and social worlds" (7). The evidence currently available demonstrates an inherently and inescapably spiritual and religious dimension to human experience that is accessible to and consistent with the methods and spirit of scientific inquiry.

David Tracy, in *Blessed Rage for Order* (1975), makes a point of special usefulness at this juncture in our discussion.[10] He raises the notion that in our process of growth and development we frequently arrive at locations in the unfolding of ourselves at which we confront what he engagingly calls "limit experiences." Such experiences arise when we reach those points in any stage of our growth at which our rational or doctrinal framework, our worldview, will no longer adequately explain or interpret the actual data of our experience or learning. Fuller expands upon this idea by noting that such a limit experience is a knowledge horizon at which we realize, for example, that rational or empirical explanations do not account for our experience.

A limit horizon is reached at the moment when the voice in the night lets us know that there is something going on that cannot be accounted for within the outlook we had before that moment. Limit experiences may be times of calm reflection that generate breakthrough insights, or emotionally charged and dramatic events of ecstasy or despair. In any case, the thing that marks out the moment as a limit experience is that its content forces us to realize that rational methods and earthly perspectives no longer adequately interpret the experience we are having or the new knowledge we have acquired (Fuller, 1988, 10). When we come to that realization, we are ready for a conversion experience: event or process. Life is about to change, and that will be a profoundly spiritual experience of growth, vision, understanding, and sense of the presence of the spirit.

Positive limit experiences, as in rewarding worship, conversion, or significant bursts of illumination, have a revelatory character insofar as they afford persons an experience of God or the transcendent world. Positive limit experiences give us a sense of pleasure, wholeness, joy, and contentment. They provide us a conscious conviction of the reality and accessibility of an ethereal world beyond our cognitive analysis. This generates our faith in God and the divine providence and grace insinuated into our lives and experience as we grow. Remember that in this regard, William James declared that the "heart of religion...is the conviction that (1) the visible world is part of an unseen spiritual universe from which it draws its ultimate meaning or purpose, and (2) that union or harmonious relation with that higher universe is our true end as well as the key to achieving personal wholeness and well-being."[11]

Limit experiences confront us with the awareness that there is some power, some dimension of reality, some potential experience, or some higher level of consciousness beyond our mundane sense of things. This awareness is a reflection of our hunger for and perception of God's grace and providence in life. This and this alone can resolve those disharmonies and feelings of incompleteness that occur in us when we are at the *limits* of our human comprehension and condition.

> They bring us to the conviction that *if* our lives can continue to be meaningful, *if* we can successfully handle the full gamut of mental, emotional, and moral challenges that typically confront humans over the course of their lives, and *if* we wish to interpret the relevance of a religious or mystical experience for our everyday life, *then* we must recognize that the "secret" to a life of maximum richness and fulfillment lies beyond the limits of the world known by (natural and social) science and beyond the limits of the self known by academic psychology. (Fuller, 1988, 11)

Fuller's conceptualization of spirituality and religion will not satisfy those who think of it only as a formal process of ritual behavior or as a functional process of adherence to dogma. Fuller's perspective, as that of James, anchors *religion* "not in God but rather in a certain dimension of experiences common to individuals as they pursue their various courses of life" (12). He is quite correct in this approach since notions about God that make up the formal structures of religion are the content of second-level abstraction in our spiritual experience.

Such religious structures may be (1) learning the biblical story in Sunday school, (2) reading theology, (3) worshipping, or (4) personal conversation. That is, concepts about God are the human experiences by which we name and structure our deeper, primary-level spiritual hunger and revelatory perceptions and intimations from the divine spirit. These primary-level forces are anchored in God, after whose spirit's nature our spiritual hunger is fashioned.

The primary-level structure and content of spiritual perception is that afforded by our direct experiences of faith, trust, and assurance from the Holy Spirit. These primary spiritual experiences produce the hunger engendered in all of us by our being created in the image of God. Aurelius Augustine was psychologically as well as spiritually accurate in his doxological confession, "You have made us for yourself and our souls are restless until they rest, O God, in you!"

THE THESIS APPLIED

True faith always exists in the context of honest and profound doubt. Fuller helps us focus the fact that the personal empirical approach to religious conceptualization "permits us to view religious faith not as a set of unproven beliefs that we either do or do not hold but rather as a style of living influenced by the kinds of insights that occur just beyond the limits of either reason or sensory experience" (12). This is why a life lived close to the wind, consciously open to the presence of God and the intimations of the Holy

Spirit in all facets of our lives, is so important. Such a life lived in expectation of the spirit will be the life with the experience of the spirit. As indicated earlier in this volume, and confirmed by James' research, among others', there is ample empirical evidence for this fact. Thus the pragmatic application of Fuller's thesis is persuasive.

Our happiness and self-actualization or self-realization in life does not depend so much upon our ability to handle the material world with which we must deal. It depends much more upon our capacity to handle the ethereal world we need to be aware of in order to achieve a sense of meaning. Dealing with the physical and social aspects of life is important, or course, but the source of meaning and happiness lies in the world beyond that. As we age from stage to stage we are more and more in need of understanding this spiritual orientation (Fuller, 1988, 12–13).

Fuller recognizes Erikson's structuralist framework as a model of the way humans gain skills to cope with the expanding experience, opportunity, and responsibility that this challenge affords. Erikson rejects Freud's emphasis on instinctual drives and focuses instead upon conscious ego formation. He credits the ego with the capacity to regulate a person's relationship with the mundane and ethereal environment so as to promote maturity and wholeness in ourselves and others (17). This gives our attitudes much more influence in shaping our well-being, adaptation, growth, and faith. If our attitude is rooted in a spiritual orientation, sailing life close to the wind of the spirit, that will directly affect how we develop and negotiate the transition steps at our limit boundaries.

SUMMARY AND CONCLUSION

Each of the structural stages describes how a person is presented with a new developmental challenge, requiring a new developmental method for relating with the internal and external environment in order to successfully resolve and integrate the perplexities and growth possibilities of new experiences. In our progress from one stage to the next we discover dimensions of reality that do not integrate well in terms of our previous framework of understanding. We arrive at the horizon of our understanding and perception—a limit experience. This crisis requires a rethinking and a "refeeling" of our framework of understanding and meaning—our worldview.

At the first level the human infant must resolve the crisis of trust versus mistrust and so acquire hope: "the belief that our wishes can be obtained in spite of difficulties. Hope is the virtue that makes faith possible, and adult faith in turn nourishes hope and inspires us to care for others." At the second stage we must process a crisis of will: "the unbroken determination to exercise free choice as well as self-restraint, in spite of unavoidable moments of shame and doubt." The third stage deals with personal initiative and with rising above a sense of guilt. It resolves the crisis of purpose: "the courage to envisage and pursue valued goals without being inhibited by fear of punishment or guilt." These three initial stages are the crises of infancy and early childhood that we negotiate during the ages of birth to two years, two to four years, and four to five years, respectively (Fuller, 19–23).

The fourth structuralist stage confronts us at 6 to 11 years with the crisis of inferiority *versus* industry, and challenges us to acquire the virtue of competence: "the free exercise of intelligence and physical skills to complete tasks unimpaired by feelings of inferiority" (23–24). This completes the childhood process. The progress from stage one to four is a progression from coping with primal physiological to more advanced psychological and spiritual maturation. The further we go the more likely we are to reach a limit experience.

The notion of God is a cultural-symbol concept, but it rings true to our irrepressible inner spiritual hunger and quest. We have an inherent appetite for the meaning that the symbols afford us. The late teens and twenties afford individuals their first opportunities to make the somewhat turbulent transition from the imitative faith we get from our parents and culture to a firsthand religious faith of our own fashioning.

Thus stage five, ages 12 to 22, leads humans to deal with the crisis of identity and the acquisition of the virtue of fidelity: the ability to sustain loyalty to an important commitment over time and under the duress of life's temporal and eternal challenges. Fuller says, "Fidelity is the cornerstone or foundation of identity and the mark of maturity It is also the precondition of true love" (1988, 38). Infants use transitional love objects such as teddy bears to find security as they try new experiences. Adolescents must employ "nonrational mental processes" to form an outlook on life that "can make life appear trustworthy and true." Religious faith is *the* primary source by which the young person can preserve in his or her world a sense of it being a coherent and vital place in which growth can continue in insight and relationships.

When we are facing the "limiting" questions concerning the origin and meaning of human existence, what we need most is certainty and security, or the safety-affording faith that allows us to move comfortably into the next stage of our understanding of reality. Healthy spirituality and meaningful religion provide exactly that assurance. They tap into the "deepest yearnings humans have for aligning their lives with that which is central to existence and symbolizes what feels profoundly true even though it is not demonstrable. From a psychological perspective, religious faith can thus be viewed as an ongoing expression of those psychological processes that make it possible for humans to venture forth into life on the basis of trust." That is, our spiritual confidence is a force shaping our developing sense of self. "Because religion roots the meaning and purpose of life in the transcendental reality of God, it makes it possible for individuals to locate themselves and their actions within a larger frame of reference." That is why spiritual faith and religious doctrines makes it possible for us to develop confident choices about what we are for and against, and why we take those stands. Such faith and religious doctrines set us free "from being at the total mercy of events in the outer world" (Fuller, 38).

Such a posture is the formation of mature self-control and the responsible behavior that the psychologist Gordon Allport calls "propriate striving," that is, behavior resulting from inner decisions rather than outer influences or instincts. Spirituality gives us a sense of self-assurance and optimism as it coordinates our sense of who we are with our moral values and our understanding of God's mode of operation in our world and life.

Serious doubt is the essential matrix of great faith, as noted above. The human personality that is encouraged and stimulated to full maturation ultimately experiences faith resurging and reasserting itself over doubt under the suasion of pragmatic, mystical, or intellectual-contemplative-reflective experience. Personalities that do not come to this fulfillment are, in effect, arrested at one of the stages prior to full self-actualization or maturity.

Spiritual faith or religious behavior impart zest and meaning to our lives, as William James emphasized so strongly. In that process they really do certify their value for us. The psychospiritual usefulness of a faith conviction does not prove that it is true, but it does demand our consideration of the fact that it, in some way, corresponds to the structure of reality. Likewise, as we know, everyday human experience continually confirms a very practical or pragmatic truth, namely that religious beliefs alone are often sufficient grounds to prompt us to act in terms of them even without logical proof.

Fuller is at pains to get across the point that the mystical validation of our faith is clear when we are confronted with reality that transcends our five senses but is profoundly real to us, and when acted upon, holds up as a legitimate and workable basis of our actions. An illustration of this might be the experience of a person who reads Genesis 1 and 2 as a 14-year-old and comes away with the dogmatic conviction that the evolutionists are crazy and ungodly and that a literal notion of six 24-hour days of creation is the only faith posture true to "God's truth" in the Bible. After arguing this position with dogmatic vigor for seven years, he becomes 21 years old and notices two things. He is less dogmatic about everything than he used to be, less absolutely sure, and his information base now includes a number of alternative ways of looking at Genesis 1 and 2.

At that point this young man must find the resources to think in larger terms without losing his absolute confidence in God and God's truth. He needs a sense of assurance that he can get an adequate grip on the truth. That means he needs the equipment to enlarge his paradigm, walk across the boundary of his limit experience, and make the transition to a new worldview. To do that with a sense of security, assurance, and truth, he must have a faith in God and the universe that will assure him that he will not step off the edge of God's world of truth if he thinks in a radically new way about God, himself, the created universe, and ultimate truth.

When I was a college student making exactly this very transition, I spent a lot of my time with my uncle, Henry Kortman, a man of profound informed faith and a churchman par excellence. He had been raised in the very conservative Christian setting in which I too grew up. He had, at one time, thought of going into the ministry. When I discussed my process of transition from a literalist understanding of the creation story to a view of evolution as God's method of creating this world, his response was, eventually, "This new view of things makes God seem so much grander and more magnificent!"

These were my sentiments exactly. Both of us had enough trust in God and assurance of *God's* grace and good sense that we were able to move across that limiting boundary into a wild new world of possibilities, knowing all the while that we could not step out of God's grace nor squirm out of God's long embrace. "Our faith had made us whole," to quote Jesus. We both thought of God as wise enough and of such a disposition as to allow what for us were challenging new ways of thinking about God and knowing God. We had the faith that God would be in favor of such a transitional move, either as an exploration into truth or as an acquisition of God's truth. Fuller draws the following conclusion from all this:

> Insofar as an individual has direct experience of a presence or power beyond the limits of rational or sensory knowledge, he or she possesses empirical evidence for considering this nonphysical reality as a clue to the nature and meaning of life. Undoubtedly the strong importance that religion places on prayer, meditation, ritual, and various altered states of consciousness is precisely owing to their ability to afford individuals a firsthand experience of a spiritual More beyond the limits of ordinary waking thought. (Fuller, 1988, 45–46)

Intellectual or contemplative validation of religious experience is made up of rational insights that the properties of reality that are empirically perceivable are not self-explanatory. Reason then contradicts its own limits when it confronts itself with the question as to why there is a universe at all. Reason can wonder how it can exist, in itself, but it never can reach deep enough to answer its own question. Realizing that reason is an inadequate tool for explaining reason and explaining our connection to the "intrinsic meaning and purpose of life" compels the acknowledgment of the "validity of concepts that do not confine themselves to the limits of logical reason" (46).

CHAPTER 12

RELIGIOUS CONVERSION: ITS IMPORT AND CONSEQUENCES

As can be seen clearly from the previous chapter, a life conversion is a psychodynamic phenomenon that may form a significant stage in the development of a human personality. It involves a "change of mind" and of life direction. That usually involves a discernable shift in the goals, values, allegiances, and sense of purpose toward which a person, or even a community, is directed. It is a fundamental shift in the meaning of everything, a new way of looking at most everything.

The original biblical word for this change is derived from *metanoia*, which means, of course, to turn one's mind toward a new direction. Conversion may be a purely secular event in which a person shifts from one nonreligious value system or philosophy to another. One might be converted, as was the French writer and philosopher Jean Paul Sartre, from Communism to Existentialism. This is a spiritual shift but not a religious process specifically. It is a philosophical conversion, we might say.

Conversion may, however, be a religious process in which a person shifts from atheism or agnosticism to a belief system that involves a faith commitment to a religious orientation such as Christian, Jewish, Islamic, Buddhist, Taoist, or the like. Or one may be converted in the opposite direction. *The conversion process is psychospiritual*. Its content in a given case is spiritual, theistic, or otherwise. This chapter provides a further development of this theme and a more comprehensive explication of personal and practical cases and applications.

Gordon Allport is one of the noted psychologists who, throughout his life's work in the research laboratory and in the clinic, took seriously the spiritual possibilities of human personality and tried to track them down. He thought that mature faith must be a well-differentiated and dynamic experience, productive of a consistent morality, comprehensive, integral, and heuristic.[1] That means that spiritual and religious experience must provide us with a firsthand faith, it must not be eroded by the ossification of dogmatism or traditionalism, it should imply coherent ethical principles, it must afford an integrated meaning for the whole of life, and it should possess the suasive quality of an appealing belief system and worldview. If it is to provide the foundation for mature identity it must afford us ideological direction for continuing personality development at each stage.

The more dramatic growth changes in life appear between the ages 20 and 35, 35 and 60, or 60 and death. In the first of those, we face the crisis of intimacy and our quest for the virtue of true love. The second contains the crisis of generativity versus self-absorption and the quest for the realization of care for what we have created and for the world context of that creation. The final stage of old age, from 60 to death, is the universalizing phase in which we expand our capacity for understanding and caring to embrace all truth, and all reality dominates our experience.

If we mature to this degree, we are mellowed with the assurance that all the productivity of the mature human quest is "of the spirit" and leads to a universal embrace of all truth and all persons. These stages of development are dominated by the quest for a profound, warrantable, and durable sense of the meaning of life and existence, and for an ethical-moral maturity in which we take responsibility for ourselves, for our world, and for communicating a caring perspective to those who follow us.

The capacity for a strenuous moral and spiritual life, of authentic and transcendent quality, is a developmental achievement and not an inherited disposition. It reaches out toward the reality and existence that transcends our selves, our time, and place. If our faith in God and in God's eternity for us is authentic to our real inner self—a genuine firsthand religious spirituality—we will spontaneously reach out to a "God through whom we can come to feel intimately identified with our fellow living creatures and in terms of whose demands we are prompted to take seriously the requirements of the remote future," indeed, of eternity (Fuller, 1988, 66).

In the words of William James,

> When...we believe that a God is there, and that he is one of the claimants, the infinite perspective opens out. The scale of the symphony is incalculably prolonged. The more imperative ideals now begin to speak with an altogether new objectivity and significance, and to utter the penetrating, shattering, tragically challenging note of appeal. (1956, 212)

James believed that the emergence of "religious faith in the fully rational adult is...justified by its own evolutionary-adaptive functions." That is, religious faith is justified by the manner in which it empowers us to negotiate successfully our way through our limit experiences into the next stage of our development and growth, and on into the broadening of our doctrinal or philosophical framework. This in turn makes it possible for us to integrate healthily our ever-expanding world of understanding, truth, and experience. In this way we acquire the resources to be a wholly ethical personality. "Every sort of energy and endurance, of courage and capacity for handling life's evil, is set free in those who have religious faith, (and thus for) this reason the strenuous type of character will, on the battle-field of human history, always outwear the easy-going type, and religion will drive irreligion to the wall" (13).

Whitehead's reinforcement of this notion is expressed in his claim that religion emerges out of the "longing of the spirit that the facts of existence should find their justification in the nature of existence" (Fuller, 1988, 67).[2] Fuller connects Viktor E. Frankl's "will to meaning" to this proclivity of the human spirit and demonstrates how this process is the vital driver of Fowler's "universalizing" quality of the mature adult.[3] In the end Fuller makes it very plain that he believes that our standard understanding of psychological process, centered in the function of the human ego, cannot "fully center" our personalities when we confront the limit experiences in life, particularly the final horizon of death.

Life urges us to develop a sense of ourselves that is not bogged down in the flow of history but stands in a certain sense above it. That has to do with what we see reality to be, temporal and eternal, and how we understand our psychological response to it. At least it implies that we live in a world that goes beyond the physical world, or at least has dimensions that cannot be explained in terms of this material creation.

We can perceive this material world with our five senses. Therefore, we can study it by means of empirical science. But our encounter with the limit experiences of life always raises in us the sense that the world of real truth and meaning is just beyond the boundaries of what we can account for in this way. "This is precisely the issue raised most poignantly in the prototypical limit experience—the confrontation of death in old age" (Fuller, 72–73).

Developing a basic sense of trust in life and in the meanings that really count to give us emotional stability rests upon a sense of the world of reality that reaches beyond our senses. Likewise, the "acquisition of wisdom depends upon accepting life in its totality rather than its specifics. One cannot find integrity in one's own life unless the integrity of the whole of life can be affirmed. It is not the extrinsic utility of this or that thing we have done that is at stake, but whether there is any intrinsic meaning to the human enterprise itself. This is a religious rather than a scientific or ethical issue" (78).

If we take this seriously, this is a challenge in our development that affords life a meaning that goes infinitely beyond mere rationality. Science cannot tell us of the inherent quality or integrity of temporal and eternal existence. The quality of our spirituality called for at the final stage of life must transcend the doctrines, creeds, and official faith statements of our traditions or faith communities. In this most challenging of all of life's moments of limit experience, our spiritual vitality and scope of insight needs to have that kind of mature transcendence that sustains our feelings of assurance in the face of the doubts and frailties we have when we face great trauma or walk through the "valley of the shadow." Wisdom has been achieved when we can look all these doubts and fears, ambiguities and frailties in the eyeball, so to speak, "while continuing to affirm the intrinsic meaningfulness of life in all of its human ambiguities" (78).

True maturity, then, can finally arrive in the stage from 60 to death, and transcendent religious insight and formative worldview ideas are the crucial maturing dynamic of this old age. This ultimate maturity and self-actualization means (1) the achievement of *detachment*—"The refusal to confuse the quality of our being with the quantity of our having"; (2) *hope*—emotional strength and desire to look forward continually, despite the adversities of life and the certainty of death. The challenge is to look forward with the confidence "that there is a will or power central to the universe that is receptive toward our efforts, and will in the end, bestow wholeness upon our lives"; (3) *humor*—the ability to preserve integrity amidst the incalculable loss of loved ones and of life; and (4) *vision*—the ability to see "beyond the limit or boundary of the finite self and disclose a supersensible reality that envelops or surrounds the physical." This is a vision that shifts the focus of our selfhood from the material to the spiritual, from the physical to the metaphysical, and "from the finite to the infinite, . . . this vision gradually 'invites us to a total, selfless surrender in which the distinction between life and death slowly loses its pain'" (81–82).[4]

Elizabeth Kubler-Ross emphasized that the person with intrinsic faith has relative ease in accepting death. In her interview of aging people she found acceptance of death long before those persons faced serious illness. Their firsthand faith had long since brought them to the point of identifying their intrinsic self with their spiritual dimension. They conceived of themselves as a soul that had a body, rather than a body that had a soul. Their acceptance of death was a function of their vision of light beyond the end of the tunnel, so to speak. Death did not look to them like a final barrier but like a kind of healing release from a body of decreasing use and value. Death confronts us in a way that discloses a limit dimension of life that can be handled best by learning to identify ourselves with a "supersensible reality beyond the limits of our finite personalities."[5]

In the light of all this, it is obviously not possible for us to consider the full scope of our life span authentically without noting how central is the psychospiritual character of life's most crucial and profound developmental challenges, and the spiritual understandings that empower us to meet them. The hunger of our hearts is for God. Moreover, it is the significant emotional events of life, which occur at the limits or boundaries of our growth stages and paradigms, that are crucial in making the spiritual forces urgent and effective.

THE CENTRAL CLAIM

The unfolding of the Christian self is a precarious and enchanting thing to see in others and to experience in ourselves. It is a mystifying, though not altogether mysterious, process of growth and development, as we have begun to see. It includes the entire person, body, mind, and spirit. It always drives toward perfection in the sense of wholeness or completeness of personhood. It has mainly to do, however, with the spirit, that is, with those aspects of our persons to which we usually refer with such terms as spirituality and psychology, because things of the spirit have always to do with our sense of meaning and understanding.

Undoubtedly, we were correct in the introduction to this work in the suggestion that we should learn more and more to see human psychology and spirituality as involving the same domain or operation of the human spirit. The two terms should likely be interchangeable, each encompassing all of what we have historically meant by both. Surely this is the biblical way of referring to and dealing with the functions of the psyche.

The development of the psyche, in all of its aspects, is mystifying in the sense that it is so wonderfully distinctive in each individual human that it is never possible to predict just how the world of the inner person will take its shape for each of us. On the other hand, the process is hardly mysterious. We know a very great deal about it, particularly in terms of the history of psychological research. We can, in fact, predict a great deal about the patterns our development will take and the behavior individual persons will manifest at various ages and stages of the unfolding. These predictable patterns are present in the growth we customarily call spiritual as well as that which is referred to generally as psychological.

Therefore, it is the claim of this chapter that the dynamics at work in our spiritual transitions and in our significant emotional events are approximately as follows. When a person experiences a significant new life-shaping insight, relationship, trauma, meaning, or challenge, that event experience cuts down through all of the patterns and defense processes of our personality structures and developmental formation and reaches all the way down to the characterological level. There, at that level, the cognitive, psychosocial, and moral-spiritual content of the significant emotional event or the challenging limit experience produces a paradigm shift in the values and belief system we have previously formed. The assumptions, commitments, loves, values, and beliefs that have prevailed until then are changed by the new insight, relationship, or trauma. These structures, which heretofore functioned as the ground of our being and our integrating perspective, are now all illumined in a new way with the new light of the new significant event of the psyche.

As in the shift of the visual patterns in a kaleidoscope when one turns the barrel a few degrees, so also at the values and belief level of the psyche the shift in experience produces an alteration in the paradigm and a significantly modified system of valuing and believing. The change does not alter the inherent nature of the crystals in the kaleidoscope or the inherent nature of personality dynamics. The person, gender, and mood may remain essentially the same in a person. But while everything is essentially the same, everything, nevertheless, is wholly different—seen in a different light, from a different perspective, forming a different sense of truth and reality. As the turn of the kaleidoscope has converted one pattern of crystals to another and caused the light to fall upon the whole in a whole new way, so also the person just described has experienced a life conversion.

RELIGIOUS CONVERSION

Authentic religious conversion is a life-changing significant emotional event, provoked by arriving at a paradigm boundary and its limit experience. It is produced by the impact of a new insight, relationship, or trauma. It involves a new personal *relationship* with God, as the God of unconditional, radical, and universal grace. For Christians, this experience usually includes a new sense of the meaning of the person and work of Jesus Christ in the world. The converting forces include a new *insight* regarding the truth about God and oneself. It often includes the *trauma* of facing a new world of moral claim and vocational destiny.

Sometimes conversion starts in *trauma*—moral, physical, or psychological—and then moves through new insight to a new relationship. At other times it starts with a new sense of *relationship* with God, often mediated through a new quality of relationship with another human, and then moves on to new insight and the trauma of a revision of one's personality or worldview. At still other times it starts in new *insights* and grows to include the other two factors. Sometimes it takes place mainly on only one of the three levels.

In any case, Christian conversion is psychodynamically and sociodynamically like any other conversion and can be accounted for wholly as a significant emotional event of the psyche in terms of standard psychosocial models, such as those we have discussed above. Humans are converted from other faiths and from the lack of any faith at all. People are, likewise, converted from Christian faith to other faiths or to atheism and agnosticism. Humans are sometimes converted from hope to hopelessness, cynicism, or existential despair, and vice versa. During the last half century conversions in all these directions and many others have been a common event.

The crucial insight here is that all of these shifts are the same kind of psychodynamic and spiritual event. The key differences are differences in the content of the insight, relationship, or trauma—the content of the conversion. Sometimes the conversion experience is of such a sort that the paradigm shift constitutes a new integration of the person's nature in terms of God and his grace, particularly revealed in Jesus Christ. That is Christian conversion, and we correctly speak of it as redemptive, since it can be demonstrated empirically that such conversion, when it is not distorted by psychopathology, frees, heals, motivates, renews, and embellishes human life.

If, on the other hand, it is "Christian conversion" that is poorly worked out in a personality fraught with psychological illness, as we sometimes see, the "conversion" experience may well enlarge neurotic guilt and compulsivity, exaggerating anxiety and social dysfunction and deepening narcissism with its manipulative egotism. That is hardly a Christian conversion and surely is not redemptive, even if the person's confession is profusely about God and Jesus Christ. Spiritual crises may worsen mental illness rather than improve it.

Other conversions can also be redemptive: from Fascism to humanitarianism, for example. Or other conversions can be sick: from benign American civil religion to obsessive addiction to a cult, with its arbitrary authority figure and enslaving structure. The content of the conversion and the direction of the psychological and spiritual reintegration of the personality of the converted person make all the difference regarding his or her health and usefulness. Any given conversion may be Christian, non-Christian, anti-Christian, or have nothing whatsoever to do with Christianity. Each of us experiences a conversion every time we reach a limiting boundary in the life paradigm in which we are working and need to expand our world of insight and experience to make room for our expanding values and beliefs. Each time we move from one stage in the life cycle to the next we are converted and reintegrated, with more or less efficiency.

Fundamentalist conversions, in any religion, tend to lead the convert to a more structured system of legalist ethics, a rigid belief system, and a value system emphasizing worthiness and affirmation based upon achievement, obedience, conformity, dogma, and self-justifying strategies. Such conversions are self-defeating, and they are psychologically sick. They frequently make people mentally ill. Conversions may take place suddenly or in a growth process over considerable time. What distinguishes one conversion from another is its content, not its dynamic, form, or process. The process of all true conversions is a psychosocial and psychospiritual process, accountable wholly in psychological, sociological, and spiritual terms.

This is a critical point for numerous reasons. First, it compels all humans to recognize that we take the position, perspective, or commitment we hold in life because of the initial faith assumptions that underlie our worldview and hence our behavior, whether we are atheist, agnostic, secular, or religious. Second, it compels us to recognize that such a perspective is held for psychospiritual reasons, not merely for rational, supernatural, theological, or cultural reasons. Third, it compels us all to acknowledge that the psychodynamics that impel us spiritually, as well as in every other way, form a growth continuum that we can shape in important ways by the insights we seek, the relationships to which we give ourselves, and the trauma to which we are willing to open ourselves without denial or repression. Fourth, it compels us to recognize that the growth continuum runs through a structured matrix of psychosocial growth stages, no matter what we do, which shape our destiny by the providence of God who created us that way. Fifth, it compels us to insure that the content and conditions of that growth continuum, matrix, and process, in the lives of those for whom we have responsibility in home or clinic, are profoundly fraught with the good news and personal manifestation of God's healing grace.

Sixth, it compels us to remember that when pathology appears in Christian life we must look for its sources in psychosocial and psychospiritual factors. Seventh, it compels us to reject the supernaturalizing of conversion, typical of some literalist Christians; self-defeating as it is in its three main implications: (1) that spirituality is somewhat apart from and different than ordinary life; (2) that the spiritual world is antipathetic to the natural world; (3) that being God's people means being a little strange, culturally, socially, and spiritually. Eighth, it compels us to remember that God's world is one world and comprehends all processes together as a unity and not schizophrenically, that the whole process is natural and not supernatural, and that God's preferred modus operandi throughout history, in nature and in grace, has always been to use the established forces of his natural processes for all things.

Thus the taste of salt and its chemical reasons, the falling leaf and its gravitational guide, the physics of snowflake crystals, or the formation of coal are all as supernatural as the work of the Holy Spirit is supernatural. To put it the other way around, the work of the Holy Spirit, the processes of Christian conversion, and the forces operative in our transforming moments are no more supernatural than the formation of coal under the physiochemical laws of hydrocarbons under pressure. All are natural, moved by forces natural to the experience of humans, whether material or spiritual.

Only on that view will we have the motivation and creativity to create the models for understanding what happens to persons in conversion and, therefore, how to enhance that process for healing growth; an undertaking to which religious institutions continue to give so much time and treasure in such apparently naive ways and about which psychologists continue to be so ignorant and ambivalent. Ninth, it compels us to eradicate all remnants of suspicion about the authenticity or quality of each other's conversions, because they differ from our own in event or process.

Benedict J. Groeschel (1983) has provided an interesting model of spirituality conceived from the perspective of the contemplative monastic ideal.[6] He appreciates appropriately the essential psychodynamic drivers of spiritual growth. He notes that we move under the urges of anxiety on the one hand and the lust for peace and freedom on the other. We move through three phases: purgative, illuminative, and unitive; and on two levels: faith and practical life experience. He notes that the further we move toward the unitive phase of maturity, namely, unity with self and God in contemplation, the more we achieve a reintegration of personality and personhood through a progressive conversion process with the same essential dynamics as are indicated above for the "significant emotional event."

This is also, I sense, the primary manner in which Fowler sees conversion functioning within the structuralist paradigm. However, conversion to a new style of faith and life is experienced in all manners and forms imaginable. They range from the process of a general structuralist psychosocial growth over a lifetime within a believing community on the one hand to sudden life-altering events on the other (Kerr and Mulder, 1983).[7] All forms function in essentially the same psychodynamic way with essentially the same psychosocial and spiritual outcomes.

Fowler and Fuller, particularly, help us to appreciate the ideal ultimate outcome of the growth event or process of Christian conversion. True conversion leads to the universalizing stage when we are able to embrace all God's universe in the joy and freedom of realizing that all God's universe is embraced by God in his universal grace and redemptive love.

SUMMARY

As we have seen, there is a broad stream of literature in pastoral psychology and Christian education, as well as in transcendental and structuralist psychology, that relates directly and deeply to the thesis and argument of this chapter. Fuller's understanding of the crucial role of spirituality in human psychological growth and Fowler's perspective on the nature of faith are among the most important insights available regarding the function of our perception of God in the unfolding of our Christian selves.

Fowler's concept of faith is wider and deeper than just religious content or context. It exceeds the bounds of our theological commitments or creedal or dogma-based belief systems.

> Faith is a person's or group's way of moving into the force field of life. It is our way of finding coherence in and giving meaning to the multiple forces and relations that make up our lives. Faith is a person's way of seeing himself or herself in relation to others against a background of shared meaning and purpose.... Prior to our being religious or irreligious, before we come to think of ourselves as Catholics, Protestants, Jews or Muslims, we are already engaged with issues of faith. Whether we become nonbelievers, agnostics, or atheists, we are concerned with how to put our lives together and with what will make life worth living. Moreover, we look for something to love that loves us, something to value that gives us value, something to honor and respect that has the power to sustain our being. (1981, 4, 5)

With Wilfred Cantwell Smith (1963), Fowler insists that words such as "religious" or "belief" refer to the cumulative traditions societies collect from the faith of people of the past.[8] If "religious" and "belief" refer to those cumulative traditions, then *spiritual* and *spirituality* are correctly used, as indicated in the introduction to this volume, to refer to Fowler's definition of faith or the capacity and experience in individual humans from which faith springs. Faith is the inner human dynamic that reaches for meaning. Religion is the cumulative fruit of the history of past expressions of that inner dynamic as it was experienced, formulated, and testified to by our antecedents, and which history we recapitulate in traditions of doctrine, liturgy, perspective, and practice.

Without question, the faith perspective of Smith and Fowler can be clearly seen as the backdrop to Fuller's understanding of faith. Faith is the accumulated meaning insights that modify our worldview and make successful coping and growth possible. This is especially true at those crises points when we stand before the emotional and conceptual limits of our experience and need a personal inner vision that leads us beyond ourselves and our world of understanding to the More, to the Beyond: to God. In this view, faith or spirituality and religion are reciprocal. Each grows and is dynamically vitalized by interaction with the other. Each generation makes its contribution to shaping the cumulative tradition, as it in turn focuses and sharpens the faith experience of the new generation. The tradition awakens faith in a person, and that person's unique expression of it extends and modifies the tradition.

Fuller agrees and thinks that what marks religion off as different from philosophy, psychology, or sociology, as an inspiration and pathway to human maturation, is its outlook upon the sacred as "the principle sphere to which humans ought to adapt themselves . . . human fulfillment cannot be understood totally in terms of our ability to adapt successfully to the social and economic spheres of life." The life cycle develops in a context of moral and metaphysical considerations, so living life must take seriously the religious "hypothesis that, in the final analysis, wholeness is dependent upon the degree to which we can locate our lives within a wider spiritual environment." Religious symbology, in the form of doctrinal systems, confessional documents, or personal formulations of belief, can be empirically demonstrated to enhance human negotiation of the limit experiences of life. Effectiveness in that process is clearly essential to maturation and wholeness (117, 149).

CONCLUSION

The communities of believers throughout history have called humanity to face the crises of our limit experiences at each stage of life with the faith response of conversion.[9] The Bible itself poses the challenge of *metanoia*, conversion, a change of mind. Conversion is a good term for the remarkable moments, events, or processes we encounter, those significant changes of mind and worldview that occur when we are at the boundary of our growth in any given state and must enlarge our framework of insight and understanding in order to take in and integrate the expanding volumes of truth that are bearing in upon us as we grow.

To mature from one stage to the next we must be converted; that is, we must be awakened to a new dimension of faith in or experience of a transcendent vision that enlarges our paradigm, revises and expands our worldview, and reintegrates our selves and our experience within a new framework of conviction and perspective. When we reach the limit experiences that challenge us to this conversion and then resist the demands of the new and expanded vision of truth, faith, or perspective, we regress and entrench ourselves in the immature worldview of the previous stage of our development. Usually we then proceed to idealize that retarded outlook or formulation and become very dogmatic and even violent regarding our convictions.

It seems clear, then, as indicated above, that what really happens in conversion is this: At a crucial and formative moment in a transition through the psychological stages of structural development, a person experiences the impact of a profound new insight, relationship, or trauma. This impact cuts down through the defensive structures of our personality, through the conceptual framework of our worldview, through the formative coping patterns that have shaped our nature and function. There it disturbs, reorders, and reintegrates our values and belief system at our characterological level. This reintegration takes its shape around the new insight, relationship, or traumatic force we have experienced at that boundary or limit horizon.

As we are cracked open by new insights of truth or relationships with others and with God, particularly in those times when we are at our wit's end, at the boundaries of our present stage of development, we are available for the leaps of growth that faith affords and that bring us into our next stage of growth. Those are the moments when we know beyond proof the truth beyond the data, that our souls are restless until they rest in God and in his incomparable grace—and that we cannot sin ourselves out of his grace nor squirm out of his long embrace!

CHAPTER 13

MODERN PERSPECTIVES
ON SPIRITUALITY

As may be noted from what we have addressed in previous chapters, much has been written about spirituality in recent years. Americans have shown great enthusiasm for the subject of spirituality and have purchased millions of books in this field of interest. Presumably, a large number of those volumes have actually been read, perhaps even with some care and reflection. That is not a surprise in view of the main point of this book. Such an interest in reading about spirituality is an important dimension of our universal human hunger to know more about our own personal inner spirits and to know as much as we can about the transcendent or divine spirit, present to us in the universe.

A number of categories of spirituality have been identified in the literature. They describe and organize the various patterns of religious behaviors and spiritual styles that function for humans in our quest for God and godliness. One of the more interesting notions, describing typical, essential, and universal patterns in spiritual style and religious practices, is the idea that there are intrinsic and extrinsic kinds of spirituality. These are concepts discussed by such notable theorists as William James, Gordon Allport, Donald Capps, and others. We now turn to an exploration of that construct and various other perspectives regarding spirituality, which one finds in the rich trove of literature on the subject today.

My father was a person of great religiosity, a devoted churchman, and informed of a vast theological knowledge. He served with vigor and wisdom in the leadership of our country church, the Christian school board, community government as township treasurer, community service as the manager of the township telephone system, and in numerous other ways by which he believed he was insuring the better future for his family of seven surviving children. William James and Gordon Allport would have defined him as a person characterized by extrinsic spirituality. That is, he was very busy with the programs and projects of being a devoted Christian; and it gave him a great sense of gratification, meaning, and purpose. He felt strongly that he was squarely in the way that God wished for him and to which he was called.

The world of religious devotion is full of people with this kind of devotion. Sometimes it becomes rather mechanical and we end up with a lot of "project Christianity," as I see it. However, that was not the case with my father and need not be the case for anyone. My father was at the same time a man of deep personal piety and prayer. I have seen Christian communities, as well as individuals, however, who understand Christianity merely as programs of charity projects or entertainment events. I guess they really think that is the kind of spirituality that the Bible promotes. The truth is that such forms of religiosity can all be escapes from grappling with the way of the spirit of God in our spirits, avoiding the challenges that living life close the wind of the spirit require.

Project religion is inauthentic if it does not come up from the deep wells of our hearts, formed and informed by personal spirituality and devotion. It must be generated by the heat and light of personal communion with God. In the 1960s and 1970s Presbyterians and others were marching on Hobart Street in Detroit as a revolution against some poorly defined grievances having to do with racism. Meanwhile the denomination was funding Angela Davis in her communist ambitions in California and supporting Jane Fonda's defiance of the U.S. State Department. Jane Fonda, together with her card-carrying communist husband, Tom Hayden, formerly a neighbor of mine, was fomenting revolution against the Vietnam War. In the process, Jane eventually became guilty of betraying our POWs in Hanoi. However one may have felt about the war, surely treason is not condoned, and betraying persons in such abject circumstances as our POWs was evil and self-serving.

The sort of project Christianity that promotes such activities is misbegotten if its reasons and motives are trivial. Christian action in the world is important, but not if it arises out of superficial or perfidious motives rather than out of sound theological reflection and genuine personal spirituality. In such cases it comes to nothing because it does not derive from our walk with God and has no genuine spiritual or theological foundation under it. Jane Fonda committed treason. She has the blood of my own troops on her hands. Those fine young people were, as I was, citizens of this country who answered the call of their country to do their duty.

While my father was overtly extrinsic in his spirituality, with deep undercurrents of personal piety, my mother could have been a Zinzendorfer

Rhineland pietist. Her spirituality was all intrinsic. She lived her daily life in a matrix of conscious personal devotion to God and openness to the spirit. I regularly observed her doing her work in the home while singing melodically the hymns of the church. Her favorites were the psalms that had been set to music as hymns for the worship liturgies. This was a joyful activity for her. She was capable of ecstatic experiences in her times of meditation and prayer. These were the energies that empowered her to survive the Great Depression, live without modern facilities such as electricity and plumbing, bear 9 live children in a very rural setting without benefit of physicians, endure the loss of 10 pregnancies by spontaneous abortion, bury 2 of her offspring in infancy, and send 4 sons off to war.

My father addressed the issues of spirituality from the perspective of theological questions. He fed his inner world by examining matters of religious truth and biblical teaching. My mother was much more interested in what she got out of her experience of the presence of God in her life of prayer and meditation and the times when she could simply sit and savor the flavor of favorite passages of scripture. Extrinsic spirituality is much more a left-brain operation and expression. The right brain constantly calls us to intrinsic spirituality and the experiences of intimations and intuitions, rather than logical propositions and cognitive formulations. My father might argue for a point of theological truth describing God or God's way of operations with us. My mother would smile knowingly, agree or disagree, and indicate, for all the world, that she knew the secret behind that with which my father was grappling and had her wisdom from a higher authority.

Not only was my mother's spiritual life full of song, prayer, humor, and gratitude; but together with my father, she made the life of the spirit seem both accessible and desirable, not remote, esoteric, or something one would want to resist. Living with our lives open to the divine spirit, holding our hearts close to the wind, seemed as natural as eating "meat, potatoes, and apple sauce," or drinking a refreshing glass of water on a hot day. It was not necessary for our parents to compel us into the kingdom, so to speak. There was no command, obligation, or burden in it; it was all invitation, opportunity, and gratification.

I have had the distinct privilege of serving four military congregations, three congregations in the Christian Reformed Church, and eight Presbyterian Churches (United States). I have found the congregations and the individual Christians in these communions, for the most part, very committed to the challenges and personal costs of extrinsic spirituality while at the same time evincing a profound quality of genuine piety, that is, intrinsic spirituality.

Most scholars and popular writers who address matters of spirituality testify to the same experience. Moreover, this is not limited to the Christian communities in today's world, but rather tends to be the character of genuinely spiritual communities in all faith traditions. Carl R. Rogers grew up as an Evangelical Christian and later moved away from that conservative perspective on biblical truth into what he thought of as a basically secular posture of thought and life. Nonetheless, when the time came for him to set down his essential outlook on life, this great psychologist made a number of observations that reinforce the line of thought developing in this chapter.

Rogers asked himself how his life trajectory had unfolded and where it had led him with regard to his view of the objective world of reality. He then observed that the meaning of his journey did not lie in the things that we can see, feel, hold, or possess, nor in the technology with which we are blessed in our day. Neither does it arise, he thought, from the relationships we have with others, or the traditions, organizations, customs, and rituals of the culture with which we identify ourselves. He could not find in logical analysis or theological propositions the essence of what really spoke to his spirit. He did not find that meaning for life even in his own personal world. He found it, he said, in the mysterious and unfathomable realities that lie beyond the boundaries of the tangible world, and are "incredibly different" from it.[1]

In a brief but instructive chapter, "The Meaning of Spirit," Joseph McMahon, in his book, *Discovering the Spirit, Source of Personal Freedom*, reflects upon the usefulness of such spiritual experiences.[2] He remarks, "Although we may be convinced that the reality of spirit underlies our important concerns... the reality of spirit comes home to us most forcefully" in personal spiritual experiences (97). Then he cites two descriptions of spiritual experience from *The Spiritual Nature of Man*, by Alister Hardy.[3]

1. I have had, especially during my childhood, several experiences where I felt strongly that a power in which I could be wholly confident was acting for and around me, even if at that time I was too little to give it a divine explanation.
2. One day as I was walking... I was suddenly seized with an extraordinary sense of great joy and exaltation, as though a marvelous beam of spiritual power had shot through me linking me in rapture with the world, the Universe, Life with a capital L, and all the beings around me.

McMahon's insights relate well to the perspective of James and Allport. He indicates that people tend to describe spiritual experiences as intrinsic spirituality, as in the two cases cited from Hardy. In doing so, the descriptions include both sensory and quasi-sensory experiences. They include, typically, visual and auditory events; more the former than the latter. Visual spiritual experiences include what the persons themselves describe as "visions, illuminations, a particular light, and a feeling of unity with surroundings" and with people (98). Auditory events include voices or music that is designed to have a calming or consoling effect: messages of consolation or guidance. A third set of intrinsic spiritual experiences include healing touch, comforting presence, warmth, reassurance, and the like.

Both Hardy and McMahon operate with a model of 10 cognitive and emotional experiences of spirituality that they rank in order of frequency as follows. The higher an experience is on the list, the more frequently it is reported. The first on the list, and thus the most frequently reported, is a sense of security, protection, and peace; second, a sense of joy, happiness, and well-being; third, a sense of presence, which is not human but transcendental; fourth, a sense of certainty, clarity, and enlightenment; fifth, a sense of guidance, vocation, and inspiration; sixth, a sense of prayers answered in events; seventh, a sense of purpose behind events; eighth, a sense of harmony, order, and unity in all things; ninth, a sense of awe, reverence, and wonder; tenth, a sense of new strength in oneself.

Those who described these experiences indicated that they amounted to a new quality of truth and awareness for that person. While Hardy's and McMahon's research indicated that these kinds of spiritual experience occurred most frequently in childhood and adolescence, they were also common in adult life. My own experiences of illumination conform to this pattern. They occurred when I was aged 7, 23, 37, 43, 50, 65, 72, and at moments of lesser intensity in between. My experiences were life-changing illumination at age 7 and at age 23; a sense of presence and guidance at age 37, 50, and 65; an audible voice expressing guidance and consolation at age 43; and an experience of being physical awakened from deep sleep by a strong and repeated rap on the hand combined with or followed by a truly remarkable illumination that set my inner self at ease at age 72.

For me all of these experiences were intensely encouraging, consoling, guiding, and affirming. They gave me the sense, in each case, that I was directly in touch with the transcendent world and that the spirit of God was filling the moment with incredible meaning, exactly adapted to the particular need in my life at that time. Hardy and McMahon indicate that the important information they derived from the study was that the *initiative* for the spiritual experience came from inside the respondents themselves and that the *response* to their initiative came from transcendent sources, or at least from beyond themselves.

In this regard my own parapsychological or psychospiritual experiences with the divine spirit, throughout my life, have been exactly the opposite, without exception. In every case, for me the initiative came to me from elsewhere and required no response from me except to savor the gratifying quality of the experience; feeling filled as I did in each case with an immense consoling, clarifying, and illumining presence. It was clear to me in each case that the presence was the presence of a life-filling spirit. I had the direct sense, immediately, without needing to reflect upon it, that it was the spirit of God intensely present to me, purposive and transcendent.

That sense of presence was apprehended by me in two dimensions, so to speak. On the one hand, it seemed to be a glow of intense warmth and wisdom and well-being that filled my entire self. On the other hand, it seemed like a glowing celestial aura that took me up into it, as though it had become the matrix within which I was held for the timeless time of the spirit's presence. The residual experience, after the transcendental event or process had passed, was always a sense of strong, very pleasing, and undisturbable well-being. It left me with a sense of relief, security, consolation, and comfort. I always came away with an awareness of the rightness and coherence of all things in life and the universe: peace with God, my situation, and myself. It settled something central and life encompassing in my soul.

From my earliest conscious moments I have never had any feeling of being in any way outside of the matrix of God's embrace and the domain of God's spirit. The trauma of my early childhood called out for strength and solace that was well beyond me. I sensed that my parents lived in the same kind of world of the spirit. I must honestly say, therefore, that openness to the spirit seemed like a natural part of my life, and waiting for its manifestations did not ever seem like something otherworldly or unnatural to daily experience. McMahon quotes Hardy describing a similar state as a feeling of oneness that often passed over to a state of listening for the spirit. "I mean by 'listening' that I was suddenly alerted to something that was going to happen. What followed was a feeling of tremendous exaltation in which time stood still. I heard nothing, yet it was as if I were surrounded by golden light and as if I only had to reach out my hand to touch God himself who was so surrounding me with his compassion" (104). In this quote, I think both Hardy and McMahon betray the fact that the experience was often in their case, as it always was for me, an event initiated from the transcendent spirit and not from their side. James confirms the same direction of flow in these experiences of the spirit, when he makes the important point that we may have a very real expectation of the presence of God's spirit, and we may prepare for such experiences, but we cannot cause them to happen. God is the ultimate source and cause.

McMahon wondered if there are specific triggers that prompt such intrinsic spiritual processes. Hardy believed his data demonstrated that there were 21 such initiating factors from the human side. The most frequently appearing triggers were (1) situational depression and despair, (2) conscious and intentional prayer and meditation on some kind of spiritual content, (3) an experience of natural beauty and its wonder, (4) participation in religious worship of especially meaningful quality, (5) intensely engaging exposure to literature, drama, or film, and (6) illness. These experiences usually produced a new sense of purpose and meaning for one's life or a new and altered attitude regarding others.

McMahon concludes that Macquarrie and Berdyeav are correct in their perceptions that spirit is not a thing and cannot be objectified.[4] Even when we have had numerous experiences like these modern writers report, and as I have described from my own spiritual odyssey, we cannot identify or describe the spiritual presence as an object or person. McMahon's way of saying it is interesting and serves us well, "If we really want to know what spirit is we have to be involved in spiritual activities, just as if we really want to know what music is, we have to play music…The road to becoming a spiritual person is discovered within ourselves through the spiritual activities of self-reflection, intuition, ultimate choice, and creativity" (100 and 102).

As McMahon notes, and I have described in detail in the introduction to this volume, William James says that spiritual experiences, as we have described them in this work, amount to a shift in energy in our inner person. "What was peripheral in the life of the person, such as God, salvation, and eternal life, becomes central" (104). Rudolph Otto in *The Idea of the Holy* says that in these experiences we are seized by God, confirming what my personal experiences with the divine spirit indicates, namely, that the initiative is from the transcendent side and not specifically expected or requested as to time, place, and situation.[5]

On the question of why some people experience these events, even frequently or regularly, while others do not, James thinks we develop intellectual inhibitions that keep our spirits in check, preventing the required openness of our inner selves to the divine spirit. This is a failure to trust what we cannot predictably control. I think that may be part of the problem, but I think there is another part. I believe that the capacity to recognize the visits of the spirit and to take in the meaning of the event requires conscious intentionality, on our part, to live life with a spirit open to the transcendental experience—open to these kinds of moments of the presence of God. Then we have eyes to see them and ears to hear them for what they are when they come to us from the Holy Spirit. The realm of the human spirit and of the divine spirit is subrational and subvolitional, deeper in us than our minds and wills. McMahon says succinctly, "The irony underlying the lives of people that refuse to let go of their rational inhibitions out of fear of losing control is that they get in their own way of reaching a source of power that would give them greater control and direction in their lives" (104–5).

Abraham Maslow lists numerous characteristics that come to a person from the spiritual experiences we have been discussing.[6] Those that ring true to what happened to me, personally, in the experiences of direct connection with the divine spirit that I have had are the following. First, the universe seemed, as a result, a coherent unity. Second, I became less ego-centered in my perception of everything. Third, I saw everything in life "under the aspect of eternity." Fourth, the world seemed unqualifiedly good and beautiful. Fifth, I was far more receptive to the divine spirit, more humbly awaiting God's presence, and much more consciously ready to receive the intimations and experience of the spirit.

We have been concentrating mainly in this chapter on intrinsic spirituality. Philip Sheldrake reminds us that spirituality is not limited to our interior persons but also involves our external religious behavior, including biblical studies, theological thought, worship rituals, ecumenical reflection, and sharing of the faith. Such spiritual operations erode obstructive boundaries between people.[7] His book describes the forms spiritual life took in each of the ages of the last 20 centuries in the Western world, heavily influenced by Christianity since the time of Christ himself.

Sheldrake thinks that to describe all these phases of Christian spirituality for the last two millennia requires that we understand the context—the theological influences that were prevalent in each age, the forms of worship and liturgical music that shaped the thought and feeling of the congregations, and the large themes shaping history at the time. His main thought about extrinsic spirituality is that the programs and projects that give meaning to the religious practices and spiritual life of many people are more than merely achieving a work objective or following a traditional form of worship. Such religious behaviors embody substantial spiritual wisdom and self-expression for the extrinsic person. Patterns of religious behavior are not merely traditions that people keep for their own sake. Frequently, they are or become for that person deeply meaningful forms of personal communion with the divine spirit because they express a willful and consciously intentional desire in that person to work out the objectives of the spirit of God, as they understand them.

One of the most prolific scholars in things related to Christian spirituality and the life of the Christian Church in the world is Alister E. McGrath. In his work, *Christian Spirituality*, he makes a crucial observation that is particularly relevant at this point.[8] He emphasizes that spirituality is closely tied in with the internalization of religious faith. By internalization he means the process of swallowing down into our inner spirits the content of our faith experience, actions, rituals, knowledge, programs, projects, learning, and explorations into the divine spirit.

I say that this perspective is relevant here because it applies equally to the value and fruitfulness of both intrinsic and extrinsic spirituality. McGrath's outlook illumines the development of any person and of that person's life open to God's presence. He observes rightly that there "need be no tension between an inwardly appropriated faith and its external observance, in that the latter naturally leads to the former." I would add that the extrinsic religious behavior also follows, in turn, from intrinsic experiences of the faith. It is the hermeneutical circle of the human and divine spirit, so to speak.

McGrath cites the pietist movement, and particularly Zinzendorf, to the effect that religious conversion is the wording the Christian community has used historically for describing the internalization of our experiences of deep and genuine spirituality. Zinzendorf was concerned that people should achieve what Martin Luther, the sixteenth-century reformer, called "the divine work within us." This work renovates us and produces a person with a different heart, spirit, mind, and emotion.

Walter Brueggemann is a notable Old Testament scholar who confirms the foregoing line of thought in his little manual entitled *Praying the Psalms, Engaging Scripture and the Life of the Spirit.*[9] His point is that using the psalms as devotional reading, to focus our prayer and meditation, results in the psalms being progressively internalized and shaping the perspective and content of our inner awareness of God. What McGrath points out about internalizing the faith specifically confirms the reality of my own experience with the divine spirit, as well as the knowledge I have of my parents' spirituality, and of what I have noticed in the congregations I have served. This rings true for all people of faith and of spirituality, I believe, whether their preferred form of psychospirituality is intrinsic or extrinsic.

The most important implication of this empirical reality is the fact that if a person is not tuned to the openness to God that is required for encounters with the divine spirit, and he or she wishes to be, that person can do something about creating that openness. There is a method for setting one's sail close to the wind. It is possible to take Brueggemann's advice and fill one's inner world with the rich spiritual nurturance of the psalms or other biblical theological content. One must be selective, of course. There are psalms celebrating the goodness of God, celebrating the grace and forgiveness of God, imploring the help of God, deploring God's silence, complaining about enemies, and calling down awful things upon one's adversaries. There are healthy psalms, sick psalms, sad psalms, penitential psalms, angry psalms, fear-filled psalms, grateful psalms, and psalms of praise. For the sake of cultivating a wholesome and deep inner spirituality, it is probably a good idea to concentrate upon the first three and last two types of those mentioned. These are songs written by a person with life wide open to the divine spirit, with the sail of life set close to the wind of God's breath.

Beverly Lanzetta has given this notion a global scope in a book she calls *Emerging Heart, Global Spirituality and the Sacred.*[10] She emphasizes that the human community is now in the birth pangs of a global development in spirituality. This cross-cultural and ecumenical stimulation of spiritual illuminations is creating a new set of spiritual expectations, language, categories, and heart. It is enlarging the spiritual challenge and invitation to all of us to greater openness to the divine spirit in ways that parochial and denominational perspectives cannot offer us.

It is Lanzetta's notion, following her mentor, Ewert Cousins, that in the fifth century B.C.E., when all at once there appeared upon the cultural, psychological, and religious horizon Socrates, Confucius, Buddha, Zoroaster, Lao Tzu, the Hebrew ethical prophets, and Isaiah, the human ways of thinking about things and experiencing things, mundane and transcendent, were radically and permanently changed. New paradigms were framed for every-thing. Cousins is sure that we are now experiencing another such global spiritual change, "exemplified by the convergence of religious traditions and a right brain mode of consciousness.[11] He may be right.

He thinks we are making a spiritual paradigm leap, mutating our conscious-ness into life that is primarily spiritual and heart inspired. Lanzetta styles this a "new age unfolding in our midst" that "points toward the emergence of a spiritual renaissance" in the culture on our entire planet. She envisions this new age as one in which a heightening of global spiritual consciousness will usher in a "greater appreciation for the intersection of the sacred and secular" (6). It is not clear that we are near achieving that global spiritual conscious-ness, but it is surely an ideal state for which people of the divine spirit should be delighted to pray without ceasing.

It is gratifying to bring this chapter to a close by citing some recent em-pirical evidence regarding the practical value of cultivating a culture of the Holy Spirit in one's life. Simpson, Newman, and Fuqua undertook empirical analysis of genuine spirituality and psychological health.[12] They observed at the outset that "generally speaking, research has suggested that more posi-tive spiritual functioning is related to more positive functioning on a variety of dimensions of psychological health." Their study of 190 spiritually mature adults, living life consciously open to the divine spirit, "completed 11 scales designed to measure different dimensions of spirituality, and a measure of the Five Factor Model of personality A principal components analysis in-dicated that the 11 measures of spirituality could be reduced meaningfully to three underlying components. These components were found to have a substantial relationship with the personality measures. Generally, the results are consistent with previous research suggesting that those individuals with a healthier spiritual orientation tend to display greater health on personality dimensions as well" (33).

We need not be surprised or triumphalist as a result of this scientific outcome. Such data has been accumulating now for half a century or more. Moreover, persons of the spirit, who have experienced personally the pres-ence and mystical ministries of the spirit of God, have lived with and from this wisdom or knowledge since time immemorial. Rudolf Otto said, in his book noted above, that some of us are tempted to shut our eyes to that which is quite unique in a life lived close to the breath of the spirit of God. But the experiences offered us by the divine spirit are so real and so much a gift that they might as well provoke astonishment and amazement in us rather than merely to give rise to admiration. For if there is any aspect of human experi-ence that offers us spiritual wisdom that is unmistakably specific and unique, peculiar to itself, it is the gifts of a life in the spirit.

Walter Houston Clark epitomized the modern perspectives on spirituality that we have been teasing out in this chapter.[13] He declared that he thought it possible to reduce the authentic spiritual quest and religious practices of any person to one "essential principle, namely *the inner experience of the Holy*. This experience grows out of mystical states of consciousness. If it is present, then we have religion, at least in embryo. If it is absent, then religion exists only in a truncated, attenuated form.... Though religion can permeate every act and attitude of [a person], essentially it derives from [a person's] living and immediate encounter with the Holy, the fruit of mysticism" (14).

Donald Capps informs us that biblical spirituality has to do with our being a *responsible self*, a *believable self*, and an *accessible self*.[14] The first is a self that is faithful to our life's vocation and so open to God's leading. This self expresses itself in being an instrument of healing relationships with others. The second is a self that looks for "congruity between one's personal sense of identity" and the roles one plays in life. This self discerns the presence of God in ordinary human events and acts authentically. "The *accessible self* is one who is making new self-discoveries, who is profoundly aware of his or her dependence on other selves (including God), and who is concerned to find ways to become more emotionally accessible to other persons" (239).

Each of these forms of self is characteristic of God. Since we are made in the likeness of God, it is our destiny to grow in our progress along the line of these three qualities, thus becoming, in character or inner being, increasingly like the character of God. If we set our sail so as to be open to the ministries of the divine spirit, we will discover that in early adulthood we achieve an increasingly clearer perception of ourselves. This is the phase of growing the responsible self. As we progress toward middle adulthood in the experience of being open to the spirit of God, we find in ourselves the development of the believable self. We grow in increasing coherence and inner unity between who we are and how we believe and behave. When we reach the third phase of spiritual progress we find established in us a sense of spiritual awareness in which we mirror the very relational life of God (243).

All these insights from modern scholars about developing a life open to the Holy Spirit of God quite obviously ring true to everything we have learned about biblical spirituality in our journey to this point in our reflections.

CHAPTER 14

NEAR DEATH EXPERIENCES: THEIR NATURE AND SIGNIFICANCE

The veil that separates time from eternity, the mundane from the transcendental, and the material from the spiritual may well be thinner and more permeable than we generally think. It is not surprising that we believe it to be thick and impenetrable, since we do not experience very clearly the flow of insights or communication from one realm to the other. However, narratives of surprising moments, when that veil was opened briefly, have been reported ever since humans began to keep track of such things.

The reason we are not more aware of that, apparently, lies in the fact that the human experiences of such moments have been readily discounted as impossible, improbable, strange, or downright dangerous. That arms-length distancing from the paranormal, at least, and the categorical denial of the very existence of the paranormal, at most, has been especially prominent in the Western world since the rise of scientific research in the seventeenth and eighteenth centuries.

Our need to deal honestly with these psychospiritual realities, together with their long-standing presence in human experience and in the human record, can be discounted only at significant cost to us. The price we pay for such closed-mindedness is that we will fail to come to terms with a comprehensive understanding of the nature of our own selves and of the psychospiritual potentials of the human community. Wherever the flavor of truth and reality can be savored, we should develop a lively appetite for it and drink from the wells of wisdom to the extent that they will offer refreshing insight and knowledge.

My grandmother died in her late eighties. Her husband, my grandfather, died a number of years before her. They had been married for nearly 60 years and had been the parents of 15 children, 14 of whom survived childhood and lived long lives. Because of the nature of this large immigrant family, my grandmother always referred to her husband as "Pa," and he referred to her as "Ma." I never remember hearing them use each others given names.

Grandmother was her vibrant, jovial, and warmhearted self until the last months of her life. During the last six weeks or so she was mainly in a coma in a nursing home. The day came when it seemed certain that she would die. Her large family gathered round in her room. As is frequently the case with coma victims, at the very end she suddenly awakened and became her old self again for a half hour or so. She conversed with her children, now growing old themselves. She expressed her love and warmth, and shared her typical humor about the situation.

Her conversation was lively to the very last. While busy talking, she suddenly stopped in mid-sentence, gazed upward toward her right, then with an indescribable look of joy on her face she reached her hand heavenward, and called out, "Oh, Pa!" And in that moment she was gone. If that were a singular or unique event, we would find it difficult to comment upon it. Nonetheless, we could not discount its empirical reality. However, a physician, Raymond A. Moody Jr., has published an entire volume of reports of such experiences people have had at the threshold of death, the access point to eternity.[1]

Of course, there are those who discount such visionary events as the side effects of what happens to brain chemistry as the organism of a person's material self begins to shut down and mental operations close themselves out. It is my personal conviction that proposing such a hypothesis is quite unscientific, particularly without any demonstrable proof. Sometimes, as Freud declared, a cigar is just a cigar. The hypothesis that such an event is pretty much what it looks like should be given at least as much credence as the reductionist hypotheses of materialistic empirical science, which may wish, sometimes, to rule out notions of the ethereal spiritual operations in a human being.

Moody's work, together with numerous others that have flowed from his hypothesis, cites a surprising body of evidence for "near death experiences" that cannot be honestly set aside without thoughtful analysis. Moreover, the evidence has a couple of facets that add greatly to its warrantability. First, the near death experiences cited by Moody, and in the testimony from numerous other sources, are largely the same kind of experiences, taking place in a great variety of circumstances. Secondly, these psychospiritual or ethereal events have a number of internal components, most of which are shared by all the near death experiences, cross-culturally and regardless of the nature of the person involved. On the face of it, there seems to be a substantial replication of the tangible experiences reported.

My grandmother's experience typifies one sort of near death experience, namely, that in which the person experiencing it actually dies and does not recover from the experience. The more typical experience reported in the data is that of persons who have experienced some form of traumatic near death experience from which they have returned to life. Of course, the reason for this latter form of near death experience appearing more prominently in the literature lies in the fact that those who experience the former type of such an event, as my grandmother did, are not able to tell their story. Those who return from a death or near death experience are able to report it. Most of the literature reporting these experiences is made up of collections of case histories.

In her introduction to Moody's volume, Elizabeth Kubler-Ross, also a physician, observes that it "is evident from his findings that the dying patient continues to have a conscious awareness of his environment after being pronounced clinically dead." She asserts that this is the same result that her own research in this area produced. Both her research and that of Moody "used the accounts of patients who have died and made a comeback, totally against...expectations, and often to the surprise of some highly sophisticated, well-known and certainly accomplished physicians."

The reports of this phenomenon are consistent in describing the experiences of the patients involved. All the patients indicate that they experienced a floating out of their bodies and a feeling of an enormous sense of peace and wholeness. In this ethereal state, the near death experience included encounter with another ethereal person who appeared to assist them "in their transition to another level of existence." As in the case of my grandmother, "most were greeted by loved ones who had died before them, or by a religious figure who was significant in their life" and was congruent with their faith perspective.

Moody noted in the introduction to his book that his hope was that it would "draw attention to a phenomenon which is at once very widespread and very well-hidden..." (5). Moody reported on 150 cases of persons who had experienced what they and/or their physicians described as death, but who either reported their experiences while dying or returned from that state and recovered. Their reports of the experiences were, of course, remarkable. Moody organized them into three categories in his attempt to subject them to scientific scrutiny and analysis.

The first type of event was that of "persons who were resuscitated after having been thought, adjudged, or pronounced clinically dead by their doctors." The second type was that of persons who, in the course of severe trauma or illness "came very close to physical death." The third was that of persons who died, and while they died they told their experiences to other people who were present and who later reported the story for posterity (16). Moody decided in the end not to include in his book the data on the third category, since this was a secondhand report, at best, and there was, probably for that reason, less consistency in that set of data than in the other two categories.

His book, therefore, treats the cases in which a person died and returned from that state to report the experience himself or herself. Then Moody focused his work on a further, in-depth analysis of the 50 prominent cases that typified the patterns in the entire set from the first two categories.

Moody found that the similarity of the various reports is so great and consistent that "one can easily pick out about fifteen separate elements which recur" repeatedly in the stories (21). His description of the paradigmatic or typical story is as follows.

A man is dying and, as he reaches the point of greatest physical distress, he hears himself pronounced dead by his doctor. He begins to hear an uncomfortable noise, a loud ringing or buzzing, and at the same time feels himself moving very rapidly through a long dark tunnel. After this, he suddenly finds himself outside of his own physical body, but still in the immediate physical environment, and he sees his own body from a distance, as though he is a spectator. He watches the resuscitation attempt from this unusual vantage point and is in a state of emotional upheaval.

After a while, he collects himself and becomes more accustomed to his odd condition. He notices that he still has a "body," but one of a very different nature and with very different powers from the physical body he has left behind. Soon other things begin to happen. Others come to meet and to help him. He glimpses the spirits of relatives and friends who have already died, and a loving warm spirit of a kind he has never encountered before—a being of light—appears before him. This being asks him a question, nonverbally, to make him evaluate his life and helps him along by showing him a panoramic, instantaneous playback of the major events of his life. At some point he finds himself approaching some sort of barrier or border, apparently representing the limit between earthly life and the next life. Yet he finds that he must go back to the earth, that the time for his death has not yet come. At this point he resists, for by now he is taken up with his experiences in the afterlife and does not want to return. He is overwhelmed by intense feelings of joy, love, and peace. Despite his attitude, though, he somehow reunites with his physical body and lives.

Later he tries to tell others, but he has trouble doing so. In the first place, he can find no human words adequate to describe these unearthly episodes. He also finds that others scoff, so he stops telling other people. Still the experience affects his life profoundly, especially his views about death and its relationship to life. (21–23)

This is a composite model of all the stories reported by Moody. Each element was present in numerous stories. None were present in all. Most were present in most of the stories. The longer the person was in the state of having been pronounced dead, the deeper into the experience described in the model he or she seems to have gotten. Moreover, the deeper the experience was the more detailed, complete, and colorful the person's report of it consistently proved to be. Each person had virtually the same difficulty describing the experience through which he or she had come. Their common testimony was that the words we generally use and the conceptual categories familiar to human discourse just do not provide useful resources of thought and language to describe adequately the death or near death experiences.

The remarkable uniformity of four or five categories of ethereal experience in Moody's case studies is particularly noteworthy. First of all, the experience in each case included being out of one's body and viewing the scene from afar as a spectator. This suggests that some ethereal aspect of the person involved was able to objectify the death experience as something happening "out there," so to speak, and separate from the essential self. It makes one immediately think of the reports in the gospels of Jesus' appearances to his disciples and others after his death. It is clear in those stories that it was not the dead body from the cross and the tomb that the disciples were seeing.

Paul calls it Jesus' glorified body, like that which we shall all possess after death (I Cor. 15). Both Paul and Peter declare that Jesus died in the flesh and was resurrected in the spirit, as shall all of us be one day. In any case, Jesus is reported as coming and going without restrictions of time, space, or materiality. He could enter and leave rooms without opening windows or doors. He needed no material food, though he could ingest some food in order to demonstrate to his disciples that he was real and not just a figment of their hysterical imaginations.

Similarly, persons who describe their death experiences say that they were able to see their own bodies lying in some place external to their real selves. Their reports indicate that there was a certain singular quality of relief, freedom, joy, consolation, and pleasure associated with their release from their material bodies. Most of them resisted any return to their bodies, though that was required in every case, of course, for the person to return to this state of mundane material life.

A second common element of note is the fact that in each case the "dead" persons found themselves in a tunnel or narrow valley which led to some unknown destiny. The similarity and variety of this element are both interesting. The similarity lies in the fact that in every case the person faced a journey through a narrow way, through or beyond a barrier, and into a place unknown. The variety of characteristics of this valley or tunnel included the fact that some persons experienced the tunnel as filled with light, some found it dark, some found the valley mysterious and awesome, some found it pleasant and inviting.

Virtually all the persons experienced a third feature of the event, namely, a dramatic and unusual kind of sound, accompanying them in the valley or tunnel. Here again the variety is interesting. Some heard a repetitious beating sound, something like the rhythm of a heart beat, or a train passing over the joints in the trestle. Many heard music, sometimes somber and ominous, sometimes like the joyful ringing of bells.

The fourth aspect worth noting, especially, was the almost universal experience, in these cases, of a person or a number of persons coming from "the other side," so to speak, to meet the "dying or dead" person, for the purpose of protecting, assisting, or guiding him or her. Such persons were always people who had died sometime before and who were familiar to the "newly dead" person. Usually they were loved ones.

Moody reported that in two cases the person telling the near death story indicated that a familiar and congenial person or voice came into the tunnel and instructed him or her to go back into his or her body, declaring that he or she was not yet dead and had further purposes to accomplish in life. The two cases in which this was explicit typified all the others in which something of this sort was implicit.

For good and obvious reasons, Moody drew his book to an end with explanations and impressions, not conclusions. He carefully analyzed supernatural explanations, natural explanations, and psychological explanations. Under natural explanations he explored how near death experiences might be induced by medications or biochemistry changes, physiological changes, and neurological or brain changes associated with trauma. The psychological possibilities for explaining the near death experiences, such as dreams, hallucinations, and delusions, were also carefully studied. None of these options, for a variety of solid reasons, could account for the nature, consistency, frequency, and uniformity of the reports of near death phenomena.

A Gallup Poll, conducted in the early 1980s, indicated that over eight million Americans have had near death experiences.[2] Plato recounted a story of a soldier, named Er, who was injured in battle along with numerous comrades. The bodies lay for 10 days on the battlefield before relatives could come to reclaim them. When they arrived they were surprised that the bodies were all badly decayed except for the body of Er. He was carried home and placed upon the funeral pyre, at which point he revived, stood up, and recounted what he had learned while "on the other side."[3]

The story of Er reminds one of the strange events associated with the death of Alexander the Great. He was declared dead, and so his generals divided up the empire. Ptolemy took his emperor's body and carried it to Egypt, where he buried it in an alabaster tomb. The amazing thing, of course, was that Alexander's body did not decay for a long time after he was discerned to be dead. One wonders what sort of near death experience he might have reported to us, had he not been closed up in a box and trundled roughly in a primitive wagon over undeveloped terrain for a few weeks, from Babylon to Alexandria in Egypt.

Atwater, in *Coming Back to Life: The After-Effects of the Near-Death Experience*, indicates that the author had a near death experience and was professionally interested in the residual effects of these experiences in the subsequent lives of those who had them. Not all such persons reported the positive and empowering processes that most of Moody's cases show. Atwater categorizes the near death events as positive and negative. In the positive category eight items are listed, mainly the same as in Moody's taxonomy. There we have the sensation of (1) floating out of one's body, (2) passing through a dark tunnel or black hole, (3) ascending toward a light at the end of the tunnel, (4) being greeted by and having conversation with friendly voices or people and feeling overwhelming acceptance and love, (5) seeing a panoramic review of one's life, (6) feeling a heavenly warmth and the reluctance to return to the mundane material world, (7) perceiving an altered sense of time and space with sensations of incomparable beauty, and (8) feeling disappointment at being revived.

However, there are those reporting near death experiences who found them to be a wretched process of (1) seeing lifeless apparitions, (2) passing through barren or empty expanses, (3) enduring threats or overwhelming silence, (4) perceiving danger and the threat of potential violence, and (5) having a sense of hellish coldness and isolation. Persons who have had these negative experiences, of course, have no fond memories of the experience. They do not wish to return to the other side and want to stave off death as long as possible. Atwater reports persons who contemplated or attempted suicide who after a negative near death experience of some kind lost all inclination to self-termination.

On the other hand, Kubler-Ross, Moody, and Atwater all report that those who have survived near death as a positive experience might be considered in a certain sense, at least, to be nonsurvivors. That is, the residual effect is often a resistance to settle back down in the reality of this mundane material world, always longing to return to the sense of utter blessedness the near death experience meant for them. Not all, but many, apparently wish to return to the other side sooner rather than later. They feel that they are no longer really citizens of this world, but have entered into participation in another, more inviting state of life.

Atwater's personal experience with the near death process was a positive one, and the acclimatization to living life again in this present world required a major adjustment. That in turn required a conscious and intentional effort to find a way to integrate the meaning of the experience into the spiritual processes of daily life. In this quest, what proved to be of immense help were the liturgies of religious behavior and the effort to find at their center the spiritual wellspring that produced those liturgies, meanings, doctrines, and behaviors in the first place. This was an effort to recover the original spiritual experience of those persons from whose lives and spirits the forms and functions of those liturgies arose. Atwater makes a telling observation at this point, "Spirituality is based upon a personal, intimate experience of God.

There are no standards or dogmas, only precedents, for individual knowing or gnosis is honored" (232).

My thesis in this book and the spirituality promoted throughout the Bible align with Atwater's wisdom precisely. Atwater declares, in keeping with our theme, *"There is no system of spiritual enlightenment that can guarantee spiritual attainment.* Just because someone thinks he or she is spiritual does not mean that person is. Always look to the results, the consequences, for after effects cannot be faked....If you cannot live what you know to be true, then it is not worth knowing" (233).

Moody originally wrote his book on near death experiences in 1975, referring to 150 such events. He continued his research in this specific area, and 20 years later he could testify to having studied 20,000 such reports. The most dramatic and most complete he had ever encountered, he stated, was that of Dannion Brinkley.[4] In 1974 Brinkley was struck in the head by lightning while speaking on the telephone. Moody interviewed him in 1976. Brinkley's story seemed preposterous, and Moody initially discounted it. His narrative included the typical out-of-body experience. He saw his dead body while leaving it and upon returning to it. He was also drawn along the usual journey. A tunnel came to him, so to speak, and in the process his dominant experience was that of moving toward a brilliant light. The encompassing beauty was marked by the singular "sounds of seven chimes ringing in rhythmic succession" (8).

Brinkley felt like an unencumbered spirit with an infinite lightness of being. He seems to have achieved greater progress than the average person in near death experiences. He passed through the barrier to a spiritual realm where kind and powerful beings illumined him with a full review of his entire life and allowed him to assess his successes and failures. The review of his life carried him into deep experiences of guilt, shame, and grief, all of which the Being of Light brought to his consciousness and also gave him complete forgiveness and consolation.

Thereafter he found himself in a beautiful city of crystal and light where he "sat in the presence of thirteen Beings of Light who filled him with knowledge" (x). The spiritual beings imparted esoteric knowledge to him about the future. It was this element that eventually persuaded Moody of the authenticity of Brinkley's report and experience. In 1976, Brinkley indicated that the spiritual beings informed him that the Soviet Union would break up in 1989 and that a Middle East war would take place in 1990 in the desert in which a small country would invite a large country. "According to the Beings of Light, there would be a clashing of two armies, one of which would be destroyed" (xi).

For Brinkley, the residual effects of his death experience include an unprecedented clairvoyance in which he can read minds, foresee things that will happen, and know things about other persons' lives by extrasensory perception and intuition. That is, Brinkley's capacity for parapsychological ways of knowing seems to have been heightened, strengthened, expanded, and clarified. He was not aware of any of these capacities in himself prior to the near death event. His clairvoyance is focused mainly on being able to predict the future and read the mind of anyone immediately upon encountering him or her.

It is mystifying as to why anyone who has had a near death experience should be able to exercise such clairvoyance. No one knows why that should be or why it is the case. However, Melvin Morse and Paul Perry, in *Transformed by the Light*, demonstrated from their research that people who have been through a near death process are three times as likely to experience verifiable and empirically measurable parapsychological events (ESP, prescience, intuition) as the average human being.[5]

The authors focus on qualitative assessments of the near death experiences. Their work is a rich view of the aspects typical in such events. They are particularly interested in the aftereffects. Their model consequently resembles that of other such studies. Their findings include the following: feelings of peace (77 percent), out-of-body experiences (65 percent), brilliant light (72 percent), life review (17 percent), unearthly realm (24 percent), tunnel (51 percent), feelings of joy (31 percent), ESP (33 percent), and visions of the future (13 percent). Among those with visions of the future, the visions referred to the world's future (22 percent), to the person's own future (48 percent), or to both (29 percent). Approximately 72 percent experienced some change in their nature or feeling world after their recovery from the near death event. Particular changes included changes in attitude toward death (82 percent), conviction of survival of bodily death (48 percent), becoming more spiritual (42 percent), becoming more socially conscious (40 percent), and becoming a better friend and person (90 percent).

Morse and Perry expanded their research to include the near death experiences of children and found that the data is essentially the same as that in adults. They published the results on children in *Closer to the Light, Learning from the Near-Death Experiences of Children*.[6]

The works of Michael Newton regarding near death experiences and spirituality have become the most popular in the field very recently. He is considered by some to be the current dean of this research and its interpretation. He is a licensed counselor and a certified hypnotherapist. He is interested in assisting people with behavior modification and accessing their spiritually central selves. His *Journey of Souls, Case Studies of Life between Lives* is a most gratifying read and confirms all of the foregoing.[7] While his concept of spirituality derives more from Eastern Religions and New Age thinking than from the three Abrahamic faiths (Christianity, Judaism, and

Islam), there is much in his ruminations and research from which Christians can learn regarding the nature of our authenticity as spiritual beings potentially in touch with the divine spirit.

Let me close this chapter with some observations of Morton T. Kelsey on parapsychological ways of knowing and their relationship to spirituality. He wrote many books related to this question, but two of them are of particular note. One is *God, Dreams, and Revelation*, in which he takes standard dream interpretation theory from Freud to the end of the twentieth century and demonstrates that it is an empowering enhancement of our understanding of spiritual experience that humans have been dealing with throughout human history. He elaborates the fact, moreover, that this psychological process is also a spiritual process and relates directly to much of the biblical message on spirituality, revelation, intimations from God's spirit, and growth in our openness to that divine spirit in our own.

His other relevant book is *The Christian and the Supernatural*. He makes a considerable point of the fact that if Christians are not open to the empirical reality of ESP, prescience, and intuition as legitimate forms of parapsychological knowing, we miss a vast field of data and experience that is enmeshed with our spiritual vitality and with biblical teaching. Kelsey's central point is one I endorse enthusiastically, and this present volume assumes it as a fundamental underpinning of its argument. That central point is that the world is replete with the pervasive presence of God's spirit in all forms of life and existence. That spirit functions in every aspect of human life and experience and is perpetually endeavoring to access the communication lines with our spirits.

In that enterprise the divine spirit is capable of employing any and every potential of human experience as a channel for intimating to us the meanings and consolations of God's presence and grace. If we close ourselves off to the potentials of the parapsychological, a special aspect of the God-given right-brain function, so as to limit ourselves to the rational and empirical, we foreclose a vast domain of potential encounter between God's spirit and our own. Our best option, instead, is to open ourselves to God's spirit in whatever form it may choose to come to us, by whatever channel it may employ, and so live the life of the spirit more intentionally, consciously, expectantly, and hopefully.

The Holy Spirit of God can speak to us in ESP, intuition, prescience, rational thought, near death experiences, empirical science, heuristic analysis, and phenomenological investigation. All truth is God's truth, wherever we find it and from whatever source. If we find it in the Bible or another sacred scripture, it probably makes sense to call it a special revelation. If we find in nature, science, or our own mystical experiences, we may do well to recognize that such revelations appear to be natural and common.

Undoubtedly Ken R. Vincent is correct in his epilogue to *Visions of God from the Near Death Experience*.[8]

The Spirit of God is over all the earth, and in all things;
It is in God that we live and breathe and have our being.
All that is is God,
And while we are here
There is only one rule:
Never hurt anyone,
And there is only one commandment:
Love one another.

CHAPTER 15

A FEW CONCLUDING OBSERVATIONS

1. We have explored a variety of aspects of spirituality, keeping an eye on the biblical record regarding it, in the hopes of ruminating about a wide variety of facets of religious experience. Our focus has been upon the challenge of living life open to the spirit of God and to its potential for and intention to provide intimations of meaning and truth to our spirits. We all observe persons of great religious character around us for whom the life of piety seems so authentic and inherent to their being the very persons they are that we come away with a sense of awe. We wish the life of the spirit were as rich for us. This book is an intentional challenge to every person to live the spiritual life with his or her sail of life set close to the wind of God's Holy Spirit.

2. In this study of spirituality, I have carefully avoided the use of such terms as natural and supernatural as defining terms for the experiences of everyday life and for the contacts we have with the ethereal or divine world. In God's perspective all is natural. The oxygen and other chemical exchanges in the function of our hearts and lungs are downright supernatural from our point of view; but it is, nonetheless, the most natural thing in the world. Dreams, visions, and theophanies seem to us utterly supernatural when they deliver to us revelations and divine intimations, but this is the most natural thing for God to do, I am sure. These two terms are probably virtually useless. In a world in which God is alive and active everything is natural to his system, however miraculous it may be. At the same time, in such a world, everything is wholly supernatural because it is his system, however natural the process under consideration. It makes little difference which term one

chooses, since each refers to the entire world of reality. It is probably best to avoid both terms and speak of our earthly or mundane experience and our connections with the ethereal world of the divine spirit.

3. Religious narratives, belief systems, rituals, and personal modes of piety are formed and informed by mythic ideation. That does not mean that these are unreal or untrue. It only means that they are cast in symbolic forms. I want to make one more effort to make sure that my use of the term "myth" in this work is not misunderstood, for that could undermine the central line of thought I have tried to share. Myth, in its authentic meaning, does not refer to legend, fairy tale, or fable. It is the key word for referring to a belief system or worldview held by a person or community. Thus it refers to the comprehensive narrative into which a person or community has packed as much as possible of the meaning of life, mundane and transcendent, earthly and heavenly, that has been learned from the experience of that community over time. Our mythic confessional statements are our creeds, our "I believe" documents and expressions of the meaning of things.

4. Since most of the truth we discern from experience and from history is only an approximation of what is ultimate truth, only an approximation of an absolutely pristine report on any given event, all of our personal and communal worldviews are formed from derived data and from our interpretations of that. That interpretation becomes our story, and we incorporate into our stories the stories of others whom we esteem or trust. We even incorporate into our stories reports about God's stories, that is, the ways in which other persons perceived that they had experienced God in their lives. It is important that we continually critique this store of confessional stories in terms of our own personal experiences of intimations from the spirit of God.

5. The quality of our interpreted worldviews depends upon how rigorous we are about our collection and critique of the information that forms them. It also depends upon our evaluation of that information in a scholarly and scientific fashion. The quality of our worldviews also depends upon how well we have critiqued, analyzed, and integrated into our story the information we use from the stories of others and the stories of God that come from others. The development of religious mythmaking requires the rigor required for producing a warrantable and authentic belief system and worldview.

NOTES

CHAPTER 1

1. Christopher Lasch (1978), *The Culture of Narcissism, American Life in an Age of Diminishing Expectations*, New York: Norton. See also his (1991), *The True and Only Heaven, Progress and Its Critics*, New York: Norton.

CHAPTER 2

1. Charles P. Henderson, ed. (2003, Fall), "Religion in this Way is Absolutely Indestructible," William James on the Gifford Lectures, *Cross Currents*, 464–5.

2. William James (1958), *The Varieties of Religious Experience*, New York: The New American Library, Mentor, 367–391. See also Frederick Burkhardt and Fredson Bowers, eds. (1985), *The Works of William James, The Varieties of Religious Experience*, Cambridge, MA: Harvard.

3. Jonathan Edwards (1746, 1959), *A Treatise Concerning Religious Affections*, Vol. 2 of *The Works of Jonathan Edwards*, John E. Smith, ed., New Haven, CT: Yale.

4. Karen Horney (1937), *The Neurotic Personality of Our Time*, New York: Norton.

5. The more familiar set of early psychological categories is Choleric, Melancholic, Sanguine, and Phlegmatic. These constituted the four humors theory of Hippocrates (460–370 B.C.E.) who thought certain human behaviors were related to predominance of certain body fluids in a person's physiological system, i.e., yellow bile, black bile, blood, and phlegm. This notion is not unrelated to the somewhat comparable ancient Greek concept of the constituent elements of the universe: fire, earth, air, and water. The Roman physician Galen (131–200 C.E.) developed what was probably the first typology of temperaments in his work *De Temperamentis*, in

which he attempted to organize physiological reasons for different human behaviors or personality tendencies. Nicholas Culpepper (1616–1654 C.E.) was the first to dispense with this ancient idea, but Immanuel Kant (1724–1804 C.E.) and such other notables as Erich Fromm (1947 C.E.) theorized on the four temperaments, using different terms for each and influencing the development in modern psychological of the set of four cited in this text. Hans Eysenck (1916–1997) seems to have been the first psychologist to base his analysis of human personality on a psychostatistical or factor analysis methodology. Consequently, he concluded as well that personality or temperament is biologically based. His categories were Neuroticism and Extraversion, which he perceived as pairing in various degrees and thus creating patterns similar to the four ancient temperaments of Hippocrates. Modern psychology is increasingly moving to an appreciation of the critical relationship between biochemistry and psychological states.

6. Catherine Madsen (2003, Fall), What James Knew, *Cross Currents*, 329.

7. Huston Smith (1994), *The Illustrated World's Religions, A Guide to Our Wisdom Traditions*, San Francisco: HarperSanFrancisco.

8. James George Frazer (1890, 1900, 1981), *The Golden Bough, A Study in Comparative Religion*, originally published in two volumes in 1890 and again in 1900, republished in one volume as *The Golden Bough, The Roots of Religion and Folklore*, New York: Gramercy Books of Random House, 1959; again republished by Theodor H. Gaster, ed., as *The New Golden Bough, A New Abridgement of the Classic Work*, New York: Criteron Books, 1965.

9. Joseph Campbell (1949), *The Hero with a Thousand Faces*, New York: Bollingen Foundation and Princeton University; reprinted by New York: MJF Books. See also Joseph Campbell (1959–1968), *The Masks of God*, 4 vols., New York: Viking.

10. Barbara Mertz (1966), *Red Land, Black Land*, New York: Dell, Delta, 367.

11. Mircea Eliade (1959), *Cosmos and History, The Myth of the Eternal Return*, New York: Harper and Row.

12. Ninian Smart (1969), *The Religious Experience of Mankind*, New York: Scribner.

CHAPTER 3

1. Revised standard version, hereafter RSV.

2. For an extensive explication of this perspective, see J. Harold Ellens (2006), *Sex in the Bible, A New Consideration*, Westport, CT: Praeger.

3. J. Harold Ellens, hereafter JHE.

CHAPTER 5

1. Judges 14:5–6: "Then Samson went down with his father and mother to Timnah, and he came to the vineyards of Timnah. And behold, a young lion roared against him; and the Spirit of the Lord came mightily upon him, and he tore the lion asunder as one tears a kid; and he had nothing in his hand" (RSV).

CHAPTER 8

1. John Calvin (1963), *Calvin's New Testament Commentaries, A New Translation, Hebrews and I and II Peter*, D. W. Torrance and T. F. Torrance, eds., W. B. Johnston, trans., Grand Rapids, MI: Eerdmans, p. 37.

2. Franz Delitzsch (1952), *Commentary on the Epistle to the Hebrews*, Volume I Grand Rapids, MI: Eerdmans, p. 319.

3. F. F. Bruce (1990), *The Epistle to the Hebrews*, in *The New International Commentary on the New Testament*, Grand Rapids, MI: Eerdmans, p. 154.

4. Marvin S. Sweeney (2001), *Ezekiel: Zadokite Priest and Visionary Prophet of the Exile, Occasional Papers* 41, Claremont, CA: Institute for Antiquity and Christianity.

5. Margaret S. Odell (1998), You Are What You Eat: Ezekiel and the Scroll, *Journal of Biblical Literature. 117*, 229–48.

6. Donald Capps (2000), *Jesus, A Psychological Biography*, St. Louis: Chalice. See particularly chapter 8, Utopian-Melancholic Personality: The Temple Disturbance, pp. 219–266.

7. Delitzsch, *Commentary on the Epistle*, p. 320.

CHAPTER 10

1. See II Chronicles 16:10, 33:18–19, 35:15, Isaiah 29:10, Isaiah 30:10, Amos 7:12, Micah 3:7.

2. Julian Jaynes (1976), *The Origin of Consciousness in the Breakdown of the Bicameral Mind*, Boston: Houghton Mifflin.

3. Richard M. Restak (1979), *The Brain, the Last Frontier*, New York: Warner; Restak (1991), *The Brain Has a Mind of Its Own, Insights from a Practicing Neurologist*, New York: Harmony; Restak (1984), *The Brain*, New York: Bantam, Restak (1994), *Receptors*, New York: Bantam; Restak (1994), *The Modular Brain*, New York: Scribners; Betty Edwards (1989), *Drawing on the Right Side of the Brain*, Los Angeles: Jeremy P. Tarcher; Sally P. Springer and Georg Deutsch (1981, 1985), *Left Brain, Right Brain*, New York: Freeman.

4. Hugh Lynn Cayce, ed. (1990), *Edgar Cayce, Modern Prophet*, New York: Gramercy.

5. Nostradamus is the assumed name of Michel de Notredame, a Jewish astrologer, born in France on December 13, 1503. He is reported to have had the abilities of a psychic or seer, prophet, and visionary, similar to those of Edgar Cayce. Nostradamus studied philosophy and literature at the University of Avignon and then graduated as a doctor in medicine at the University of Montpelier in 1529. He distinguished himself as an ingenious physician while successfully treating victims of the plague. In 1555 he published a book of prophecies in poetic form, entitled *Centuries*. That brought him to the attention of Catherine de Medici, whereupon he published in 1558 an enlarged version that he dedicated to the king. Some of his prophecies were thought to prove authentic over time, and Charles IX honored him as *Physician Ordinaire*. His works have been published frequently, even more frequently debated, and occasionally, though rarely, actually read. They are mysterious, metaphoric, dense,

confusing, confused, and remote, partly because of difficulties of translation, partly because they belong to a distant culture with its own figures of speech and points of view, and partly because of their author's vague and esoteric references, descriptions, and prognostications. He died July 2, 1566.

6. Charlene Leslie-Chaden (1996), *A Compendium of the Teachings of Sathya Sai Baba*, Prasanthi Nilayam: Sai Towers Publishing.

7. Deepak Chopra (2000), *How to Know God, The Soul's Journey into the Mystery of Mysteries*, New York: Harmony.

CHAPTER 11

An earlier version of this chapter appeared as part of The Psychodynamics of Christian Conversion, in the *Journal of Psychology and Christianity* (JPC), a publication of the Christian Association for Psychological Studies (CAPS), Volume 3, Number 4, Winter 1984, and is used here by permission in this revised, updated, and expanded version. Another early version appeared as part of J. Harold Ellens (2007), *Radical Grace: How Belief in a Benevolent God Benefits Our Health*, Westport: Praeger, and is used here by permission in this further revised, updated, and expanded version.

1. J. Piaget (1967), *Six Psychological Studies*, New York: Random House; (1969), *The Psychology of the Child*, New York: Random House; (1977), *The Development of Thought: Equilibration of Cognitive Structures*, A. Rosin, trans., New York: Viking. See also Mary Stewart van Leeuwen (1983), *The Sorcerer's Apprentice*, Grand Rapids, MI: Baker; (1985), *The Person in Psychology, A Contemporary Christian Appraisal*, Grand Rapids, MI: Eerdmans.

2. L. Kohlberg (1963), Development of Children's Orientation Toward a Moral Order, *Vita Humana* 6, 11–16; (1973), Continuities in Childhood and Adult Moral Development Revisited, in *Lifespan Developmental Psychology: Personality and Socialization*, P. Baltes and K. Shaie, eds., New York: Academic Press, 202ff; (1974), Education, Moral Development and Faith, *Journal of Moral Education* 4.1, 5–16; (1976), Moral Stages and Moralization, in *Moral Development and Behavior: Theory, Research, and Social Issues*, T. Likona, ed., New York: Holt, Rinehart, Winston.

3. Erik H. Erikson (1959, 1980), *Identity and the Life Cycle*, New York: Norton; (1963), *Childhood and Society*, 2nd ed., New York: Norton; (1982), *The Life Cycle Completed: A Review*, New York: Norton.

4. James W. Fowler (1976), Faith Development Theory and the Aims of Religious Socialization, in *Emerging Issues in Religious Education*, G. Durka and J. Smith, eds., New York: Paulist; (1980), Moral Stages and the Development of Faith, in *Moral Development, Moral Education, and Kohlberg: Basic Issues in Philosophy, Psychology, Religion, and Education*, B. Munsey, ed., Birmingham, AL: Religious Education Press; (1981), *Stages of Faith: The Psychology of Human Development and the Quest for Meaning*, San Francisco: Harper and Row; (1984), *Becoming Adult, Becoming Christian: Adult Development and Christian Faith*, San Francisco: Harper and Row.

5. Morris Massey (1972), *What You Are Is Where You Were When*, Video Tape Series on Life Cycle Development, Boulder: University of Colorado.

6. James E. Loder (1981), *The Transforming Moment*, New York: Harper.

7. John Westerhof (1976), *Will our Children Have Faith?* New York: Seabury.

8. D. M. Joy (1983), *Moral Development Foundations: Judeo-Christian Alternatives to Piaget/Kohlberg*, Nashville, TN: Abingdon.

9. Robert C. Fuller (1988), *Religion and the Life Cycle*, Philadelphia: Fortress.

10. David Tracy (1975), *Blessed Rage for Order: The New Pluralism in Theology*, New York: Seabury.

11. William James (1956), *The Will To Believe*, New York: Dove; (1958), *The Varieties of Religious Experience*, New York: Morrow.

CHAPTER 12

An earlier version of this chapter appeared as part of The Psychodynamics of Christian Conversion, in the *Journal of Psychology and Christianity* (JPC), a publication of the Christian Association for Psychological Studies (CAPS), Volume 3, Number 4, Winter 1984, and is used here by permission in this revised, updated, and expanded version. Another early version appeared as part of J. Harold Ellens (2007), *Radical Grace: How Belief in a Benevolent God Benefits Our Health*, Westport: Praeger, and is used here by permission in this further revised, updated, and expanded version.

1. Gordon W. Allport (1937), *Personality: A Psychological Interpretation*, New York: Henry Holt; (1950), *The Individual and His Religion: A Psychological Interpretation*, New York: Macmillan; (1960), *Personality and Social Encounter: Selected Essays*, Boston: Beacon; (1961), *Pattern and Growth in Personality*, New York: Holt, Rinehart, Winston.

2. E. E. Whitehead and J. D. Whitehead (1984), *Seasons of Strength: New Visions of Adult Christian Maturing*, Garden City, NJ: Doubleday Image. See also D. J. Levinson (1978), The Anatomy of the Life Cycle, *Psychiatric Opinion* 15, 29–48; and *The Seasons of a Man's Life*, New York: Knopf. See also Gail Sheehy (1976), *Passages: Predictable Crises of Adult Life*, New York: Dutton

3. Victor E. Frankl (1962), *Man's Search for Meaning: An Introduction to Logotherapy*, Boston: Beacon; (1975), *The Unconscious God: Psychotherapy and Theology*, New York: Simon and Schuster.

4. Henri Nouwen and Walter Gaffney (1976), *Aging: The Fulfillment of Life*, Garden City: Image, 36.

5. Elizabeth Kubler-Ross (1969), *On Death and Dying*, New York: Macmillan.

6. B. J. Groeschel (1983), *Spiritual Passages: The Psychology of Spiritual Development "for Those who Seek,"* New York: Crossroad.

7. Hugh T. Kerr and John M. Mulder (1983), *Conversions: The Christian Experience*, Grand Rapids, MI: Eerdmans.

8. Wilfred C. Smith (1963), *The Meaning and End of Religion, A New Approach to the Religious Traditions of Mankind*, New York: Macmillan.

9. J. Harold Ellens (1988), The Psychodynamics of Christian Conversion, in *The Church and Pastoral Care*, L. Aden and J. H. Ellens, eds., Grand Rapids, MI: Baker.

CHAPTER 13

1. Carl R. Rogers (1980), *A Way of Being*, New York: Houghton Mifflin.

2. Joseph J. McMahon (1994), *Discovering the Spirit, Source of Personal Freedom*, New York: Rowman and Littlefield—Sheed and Ward.

3. Alister Hardy (1979), *The Spiritual Nature of Man*, Oxford: Clarendon. See also Hardy (1976), *The Biology of God: A Scientist's Study of Man the Religious Animal*, New York: Taplinger.

4. John Macquarrie (1972), *Paths in Spirituality*, New York: Harper and Row. Nicolas Berdyaev (1949), *The Divine and the Human*, London: Geoffrey Bles.

5. Rudolph Otto (1958), *The Idea of the Holy*, first published 1923, ninth printing 1966, New York: Oxford University Press—Galaxy Books.

6. Abraham Maslow (1970), *Religion, Values, and Peak Experiences*, New York: Penguin.

7. Philip Sheldrake (2007), *A Brief History of Spirituality*, Malden, MA: Blackwell.

8. Alister E. McGrath (1999), *Christian Spirituality*, Malden, MA: Blackwell.

9. Walter Brueggemann (2007), *Praying the Psalms, Engaging Scripture and the Life of the Spirit*, Eugene, OR: Wifp and Stock—Cascade Books.

10. Beverly Lanzetta (2007), *Emerging Heart, Global Spirituality and the Sacred*, Minneapolis: Fortress.

11. Ewert H. Cousins (1994), *Christ of the 21st Century*, New York: Continuum.

12. David R. Simpson, Jody L. Newman, and Dale R. Fuqua (2007, Spring), Spirituality and Personality: Accumulating Evidence, *Journal of Psychology and Christianity* 26, No. 1.

13. Walter Houston Clark, H. Newton Malony, James Daane, and Alan R. Tippett (1973), *Religious Experience,The First John G. Finch Symposium on Psychology and Religion*, Springfield, IL: Charles C. Thomas.

14. Donald Capps (1985), Pastoral Counseling for Middle Adults: A Levinsonian Perspective, in Robert J. Wicks, Richard D. Parsons, and Donald Capps, *Clinical Handbook of Pastoral Counseling*, New York: Paulist.

CHAPTER 14

1. Raymond A. Moody Jr. (1976), *Life After Life*, New York: Bantam. First published in 1975, 35 printings by 1981.

2. P.M.H. Atwater (1988), *Coming Back to Life: The After-Effects of the Near-Death Experience*, New York: Ballantine, xiii and 2.

3. Atwater, *Coming Back to Life*, 5.

4. Dannion Brinkley and Paul Perry (1994), *Saved by the Light*, New York: Random House.

5. Melvin Morse and Paul Perry (1996), *Transformed by the Light, The Powerful Effects of Near-Death Experiences on People's Lives*, New York: Parapsychology Press.

6. Melvin Morse and Paul Perry (1990), *Closer to the Light, Learning from the Near-Death Experiences of Children*, New York: Villard.

7. Michael Newton (2002), *Journey of Souls, Case Studies of Life between Lives*, St. Paul, MN: Llewellyn Publications.

8. Ken R. Vincent (1994), *Visions of God from the Near Death Experience*, Burdett (2002), New York: Larson Publications.

BIBLIOGRAPHY

Allport, Gordon W. (1937), *Personality: A Psychological Interpretation*, New York: Henry Holt.

Allport, Gordon W. (1950), *The Individual and His Religion: A Psychological Interpretation*, New York: Macmillan.

Allport, Gordon W. (1960), *Personality and Social Encounter: Selected Essays*, Boston: Beacon.

Allport, Gordon W. (1961), *Pattern and Growth in Personality*, New York: Holt, Rinehart, Winston.

Atwater, P. M. H. (1988), *Coming Back to Life: The After-Effects of the Near-Death Experience*, New York: Ballantine.

Berdyaev, Nicolas (1949), *The Divine and the Human*, London: Geoffrey Bles.

Brinkley, Dannion, and Paul Perry (1994), *Saved by the Light*, New York: Random House.

Bruce, F. F. (1990), *The Epistle to the Hebrews*, in *The New International Commentary on the New Testament*, Grand Rapids, MI: Eerdmans.

Brueggemann, Walter (2007), *Praying the Psalms, Engaging Scripture and the Life of the Spirit*, Eugene, OR: Wipf and Stock—Cascade Books.

Burkhardt, Frederick, and Fredson Bowers, eds. (1985), *The Works of William James, The Varieties of Religious Experience*, Cambridge, MA: Harvard.

Calvin, John (1963), *Calvin's New Testament Commentaries, A New Translation, Hebrews and I and II Peter*, D. W. Torrance and T. F. Torrance, eds., W. B. Johnston, trans., Grand Rapids, MI: Eerdmans.

Campbell, Joseph (1949), *The Hero with a Thousand Faces*, New York: Bollingen Foundation and Princeton University, reprinted by New York: MJF Books.

Campbell, Joseph (1959–1968), *The Masks of God*, 4 vols., New York: Viking.

Capps, Donald (1985), Pastoral Counseling for Middle Adults: A Levinsonian Perspective, in Robert J. Wicks, Richard D. Parsons, and Donald Capps, *Clinical
Handbook of Pastoral Counseling*, New York: Paulist.

Capps, Donald (2000), *Jesus: A Psychological Biography*, St. Louis, MO: Chalice.

Cayce, Hugh Lynn, ed. (1990), *Edgar Cayce, Modern Prophet*, New York: Gramercy.

Chopra, Deepak (2000), *How to Know God, The Soul's Journey into the Mystery of Mysteries*, New York: Harmony.

Clark, Walter Houston, H. Newton Malony, James Daane, and Alan R. Tippett
(1973), *Religious Experience, The First John G. Finch Symposium on Psychology and
Religion*, Springfield, IL: Charles C. Thomas.

Cousins, Ewert H. (1994), *Christ of the 21st Century*, New York: Continuum.

Delitzsch, Franz (1952), *Commentary on the Epistle to the Hebrews*, Volume I, Grand
Rapids, MI: Eerdmans.

Edwards, Betty (1989), *Drawing on the Right Side of the Brain*, Los Angeles: Jeremy
P. Tarcher.

Edwards, Jonathan (1746, 1959), *A Treatise Concerning Religious Affections*, Vol. 2 of
The Works of Jonathan Edwards, John E. Smith, ed., New Haven, CT: Yale.

Eliade, Mircea (1959), *Cosmos and History, The Myth of the Eternal Return*, New York:
Harper and Row.

Ellens, J. Harold (1988), The Psychodynamics of Christian Conversion, in *The Church
and Pastoral Care*, LeRoy Aden and J. Harold Ellens, eds., Grand Rapids, MI:
Baker.

Ellens, J. Harold (2006), *Sex in the Bible, A New Consideration*, Westport: Praeger.

Erikson, Erik H. (1959, 1980), *Identity and the Life Cycle*, New York: Norton.

Erikson, Erik H. (1963), *Childhood and Society*, 2nd ed., New York: Norton.

Erikson, Erik H. (1982), *The Life Cycle Completed: A Review*, New York: Norton.

Fowler, James W. (1976), Faith Development Theory and the Aims of Religious Socialization, in *Emerging Issues in Religious Education*, G. Durka and J. Smith, eds.,
New York: Paulist.

Fowler, James W. (1980), Moral Stages and the Development of Faith, in *Moral
Development, Moral Education, and Kohlberg: Basic Issues in Philosophy, Psychology, Religion, and Education*, B. Munsey, ed., Birmingham, AL: Religious Education Press.

Fowler, James W. (1981), *Stages of Faith: The Psychology of Human Development and the
Quest for Meaning*, San Francisco: Harper and Row,

Fowler, James W. (1984), *Becoming Adult, Becoming Christian: Adult Development and
Christian Faith*, San Francisco: Harper and Row.

Frankl, Victor E. (1962) *Man's Search for Meaning: An Introduction to Logotherapy*, Boston: Beacon.

Frankl, Victor E. (1975), *The Unconscious God: Psychotherapy and Theology*, New York:
Simon and Schuster.

Frazer, James George (1890, 1900, 1981), *The Golden Bough, A Study in Compara-
tive Religion*, originally published in two volumes in 1890 and again in 1900,
republished in one volume as *The Golden Bough, The Roots of Religion and Folklore*,
New York: Gramercy Books of Random House; again republished by Theodor H.
Gaster, ed., as *The New Golden Bough, A New Abridgement of the Classic Work*, New
York: Criterion Books.

Fuller, Robert C. (1988), *Religion and the Life Cycle*, Philadelphia: Fortress.

Groeschel, Bernard J. (1983), *Spiritual Passages: The Psychology of Spiritual Development "for Those Who Seek,"* New York: Crossroad.

Hardy, Alister (1976), *The Biology of God: A Scientist's Study of Man the Religious Animal*, New York: Taplinger.

Hardy, Alister (1979), *The Spiritual Nature of Man*, Oxford: Clarendon.

Henderson, Charles P., ed. (2003, Fall), Religion in this Way is Absolutely Indestructible, William James on the Gifford Lectures, *Cross Currents*, 464–5.

Horney, Karen (1937), *The Neurotic Personality of Our Time*, New York: Norton.

James, William (1956), *The Will To Believe*, New York: Dove.

James, William (1958), *The Varieties of Religious Experience*, New York: Morrow.

James, William (1958), *The Varieties of Religious Experience*, New York: The New American Library, Mentor.

Jaynes, Julian (1976), *The Origin of Consciousness in the Breakdown of the Bicameral Mind*, Boston: Houghton Mifflin.

Joy, D. M. (1983), *Moral Development Foundations: Judeo-Christian Alternatives to Piaget/Kohlberg*, Nashville, TN: Abingdon.

Kelsey, Morton T. (1974), *God, Dreams, and Revelation, A Christian Interpretation of Dreams*, Minneapolis: Augsburg.

Kerr, Hugh T., and John M. Mulder (1983), *Conversions: The Christian Experience*, Grand Rapids, MI: Eerdmans.

Kohlberg, Lawrence (1963), Development of Children's Orientation Toward a Moral Order, *Vita Humana* 6, 11–16.

Kohlberg, Lawrence (1973), Continuities in Childhood and Adult Moral Development Revisited, in *Lifespan Developmental Psychology: Personality and Socialization*, P. Baltes and K. Shaie, eds., New York: Academic Press.

Kohlberg, Lawrence (1974), Education, Moral Development and Faith, *Journal of Moral Education* 4 1, 5–16.

Kohlberg, Lawrence (1976), Moral Stages and Moralization, in *Moral Development and Behavior: Theory, Research, and Social Issues*, T. Likona, ed., New York: Holt, Rinehart, Winston.

Kubler-Ross, Elizabeth (1969), *On Death and Dying*, New York: Macmillan.

Lanzetta, Beverly (2007), *Emerging Heart, Global Spirituality and the Sacred*, Minneapolis, MN: Fortress.

Lasch, Christopher (1978), *The Culture of Narcissism, American Life in an Age of Diminishing Expectations*, New York: Norton.

Lasch, Christopher (1991), *The True and Only Heaven, Progress and Its Critics*, New York: Norton.

Leslie-Chaden, Charlene (1996), *A Compendium of the Teachings of Sathya Sai Baba*, Prasanthi Nilayam: Sai Towers Publishing.

Levinson, Daniel J. (1978), The Anatomy of the Life Cycle, *Psychiatric Opinion* 15, 29–48.

Levinson, Daniel J. (1978), *The Seasons of a Man's Life*, New York: Knopf.

Loder, James E. (1981), *The Transforming Moment*, New York: Harper.

Macquarrie, John (1972), *Paths in Spirituality*, New York: Harper and Row.

Madsen, Catherine (2003, Fall), What James Knew, *Cross Currents*, 329.

Maslow, Abraham (1970), *Religion, Values, and Peak Experiences*, New York: Penguin.

Massey, Morris (1972), *What You Are Is Where You Were When*, Video Tape Series on Life Cycle Development, Boulder: University of Colorado.

McGrath, Alister E. (1999), *Christian Spirituality*, Malden, MA: Blackwell.

McMahon, Joseph J. (1994), *Discovering the Spirit, Source of Personal Freedom*, New York: Rowman and Littlefield—Sheed and Ward.

Mertz, Barbara (1966), *Red Land, Black Land*, New York: Dell, Delta.

Moody, Raymond A., Jr. (1976), *Life After Life*, New York: Bantam.

Morse, Melvin, and Paul Perry (1990), *Closer to the Light, Learning from the Near-Death Experiences of Children*, New York: Villard.

Morse, Melvin, and Paul Perry (1996), *Transformed by the Light, The Powerful Effects of Near-Death Experiences on People's Lives*, New York: Parapsychology Press.

Newton, Michael (2002), *Journey of Souls, Case Studies of Life between Lives*, St. Paul: Llewellyn Publications.

Nouwen, Henri, and Walter Gaffney (1976), *Aging: The Fulfillment of Life*, Garden City: Image.

Odell, Margaret S. (1998), You Are What You Eat: Ezekiel and the Scroll, *Journal of Biblical Literature* 117, 229–48.

Otto, Rudolph (1958), *The Idea of the Holy*, first published 1923, ninth printing 1966, New York: Oxford University Press—Galaxy Books.

Piaget, Jean (1967), *Six Psychological Studies*, New York: Random House.

Piaget, Jean (1969), *The Psychology of the Child*, New York: Random House.

Piaget, Jean (1977), *The Development of Thought: Equilibration of Cognitive Structures*, A. Rosin, trans., New York: Viking.

Restak, Richard M. (1979), *The Brain, The Last Frontier*, New York: Warner.

Restak, Richard (1984), *The Brain*, New York: Bantam.

Restak, Richard (1991), *The Brain Has a Mind of Its Own, Insights from a Practicing Neurologist*, New York: Harmony.

Restak, Richard M. (1994), *The Modular Brain*, New York: Scribners.

Restak, Richard M. (1994), *Receptors*, New York: Bantam.

Rogers, Carl R. (1980), *A Way of Being*, New York: Houghton Mifflin.

Sheehy, Gail (1976), *Passages: Predictable Crises of Adult Life*, New York: Dutton.

Sheldrake, Philip (2007), *A Brief History of Spirituality*, Malden, MA: Blackwell.

Simpson, David R., Jody L. Newman, and Dale R. Fuqua (2007, Spring), Spirituality and Personality: Accumulating Evidence, *Journal of Psychology and Christianity* 26, No. 1.

Smart, Ninian (1969), *The Religious Experience of Mankind*, New York: Scribner.

Smith, Huston (1994), *The Illustrated World's Religions, A Guide to Our Wisdom Traditions*, San Francisco: HarperSanFrancisco.

Smith, Wilfred C. (1963), *The Meaning and End of Religion, A New Approach to the Religious Traditions of Mankind*, New York: Macmillan.

Springer, Sally P. and Georg Deutsch (1981, 1985), *Left Brain, Right Brain*, New York: Freeman.

Sweeney, Marvin S. (2001), *Ezekiel: Zadokite Priest and Visionary Prophet of the Exile*, *Occasional Papers* 41, Claremont: Institute for Antiquity and Christianity.

Tracy, David (1975), *Blessed Rage for Order: The New Pluralism in Theology*, New York: Seabury.

Van Leeuwen, Mary Stewart (1983), *The Sorcerer's Apprentice*, Grand Rapids, MI: Baker.

Van Leeuwen, Mary Stewart (1985), *The Person in Psychology, A Contemporary Christian Appraisal*, Grand Rapids, MI: Eerdmans.

Vincent, Ken R. (1994), *Visions of God from the Near Death Experience*, Burdett, New York: Larson Publications.

Westerhof, John (1976), *Will Our Children Have Faith?* New York: Seabury.

Whitehead, E. E., and J. D. Whitehead (1984), *Seasons of Strength: New Visions of Adult Christian Maturing*, Garden City: Doubleday Image.

INDEX

About the Author

J. HAROLD ELLENS is a Research Scholar at the University of Michigan Department of Near Eastern Studies, a retired Presbyterian theologian, an ordained minister, a retired U.S. Army Colonel, and a retired Professor of Philosophy, Theology, and Psychology. He served 15 years as Executive Director of the Christian Association for Psychological Studies and was Founding Editor and Editor-in-Chief of the *Journal of Psychology and Christianity*. He has authored, co-authored, or edited more than 75 books, including *The Destructive Power of Religion* (Praeger, 2004) and *Sex in the Bible* (Praeger, 2006).